BORDERLINE WELFARE

Tavistock Clinic Series
Margot Waddell (Series Editor)
Published and distributed by Karnac Books

Email: shop@karnacbooks.com; Internet: www.karnacbooks.com

BORDERLINE WELFARE

Feeling and Fear of Feeling in Modern Welfare

Andrew Cooper and Julian Lousada

KARNAC

LONDON   NEW YORK

First published in 2005 by
H. Karnac (Books) Ltd.
118 Finchley Road, London, NW3 5HT

British Library Cataloguing in Publication Data

A C.I.P. for this book is available from the British Library

  ISBN 978 1 85575 905 3

Edited, designed and produced by The Studio Publishing Services Ltd, Exeter EX4 8JN

Printed by the MPG Books Group in the UK

10 9 8 7 6 5 4 3 2 1

www.karnacbooks.com

CONTENTS

AUTHORS

ANDREW COOPER is Professor of Social Work at the Tavistock Clinic and the University of East London. He is a psychoanalytic psychotherapist and practices as a psychotherapist and clinical social worker in the Adolescent Department of the Tavistock Clinic. Over the last fifteen years he has undertaken several comparative research projects into child protection systems and practices in Europe.

JULIAN LOUSADA is a psychoanalytic psychotherapist and full member of the British Association of Psychotherapists. He is a Senior Clinical Lecturer in Social Work, and Clinical Director of the Adult Department at the Tavistock Clinic.

ACKNOWLEDGEMENTS

Thanks are due to many people in many ways for their contributions to the long gestation of this book. Our patients have been a vital source of inspiration, as have the individuals and staff groups of organizations to which we have consulted. Many students and trainees, especially those on the University of East London/ Tavistock Clinic Professional Doctorate in Social Work, have engaged with our thinking with creativity and tolerance.

We are indebted to all those who sustained and participated in the Psychoanalysis and the Public Sphere conferences through the late 1980s and 1990s. The intellectual vigour of those events gave us a bedrock of confidence to take the risks involved in using psychoanalysis as a tool for critical social engagement. Paul Hoggett and Lyn Froggett have led the way with their own psychoanalytically informed studies of welfare, and their work has been an important source of inspiration. We are grateful to David Armstrong, whose influence pervades the book. Thanks are also due to Sue Holland, Philip Spencer, Chris Jones, Tony Novac, and John Pitts, all of whom have provided stimulation and critical debate over a considerable period.

Nick Temple and Michael Rustin gave very helpful feedback on early drafts of the manuscript, and Margot Waddell has been a patient and encouraging editor throughout. Liz Webb has been a valuable and supportive colleague and co-teacher. Warm thanks are due to Jessica Evans who engaged minutely and enthusiastically with the final draft. Heather Price is also responsible for many improvements to the manuscript, and helped greatly to sustain the project with her encouragement. Finally, thanks to Joanna Rosenthall, and Esther Lousada for their forbearance.

Since it was founded in 1920, the Tavistock clinic has developed a wide range of therapeutic approaches to mental health that have been strongly influenced by psychoanalysis. It has also adopted systemic family therapy as a theoretical model and a clinical approach to family problems. The Clinic is the largest training institution in Britain for mental health, providing post-graduate and qualifying courses in social work, psychology, psychiatry, child, adolescent, and adult psychotherapy, as well as in nursing and primary care. It trains about 1,400 students each year in over 45 courses.

The Clinic's philosophy is aimed at promoting therapeutic methods in mental health. Its work is founded on the clinical expertise which is the basis of its consultancy work and research. This series aims to make available the clinical, theoretical, and research work that is most influential at the Tavistock Clinic. It sets out new approaches in the understanding and treatment of psychological disturbance in children, adolescents, and adults, both as individuals and in families.

This is an important and, in many respects, daring book. It addresses itself to some of the most urgent and challenging areas of contemporary social policy and professional identity. It bases its position and findings in the experience of working intimately, as psychoanalytic psychotherapists as well as social workers, teachers, and academics, with the basic reality of people's lives, both social and psychological. That is, the authors draw on both broad theoretically informed areas of mental health practice and public health and welfare provision, and on the detailed minutiae of actual experiences, whether drawn from the consulting room or from the broader teaching and consultative contexts with which they are also both involved.

They apply, as they say, "clinical sensitivity" to the study of a wide spectrum of social interactions and phenomena that relate to the ever changing nature of the welfare state in Britain, especially in relation to mental health provision. In so doing, the book revisits some of those now less familiar terms, ones of fundamental importance, those of "value", of "vocation", of "lived experience". The authors are concerned to explore and emphasize the links between contemporary welfare policy and the emotional factors that underpin and determine good decision-making; that is, the relationship between cognitive faculties and affective ones. In so doing, they tread a politically and professionally delicate path, subtly positioning themselves in a newly forged territory that takes into account both the context of late modernity and of more open-minded and integrative possibilities for which the authors are arguing and which they themselves exemplify.

Perhaps central to these is what the authors think of as the "state of mind" of society as reflected in its provision of care, variously for its citizens and for those experienced as "outsiders". It describes the hidden costs of the "service delivery" mentality and the sources of some of the social ills that are currently afflicting society. The brush strokes are both broad and fine and in so being introduce a new level of insight into what often seem like the overwhelmingly difficult problems of contemporary social existence.

CHAPTER ONE

Introduction: the psychoanalytic study of welfare

Part 1: Themes

Finding a position

At its core this book is an effort to understand and make sense of the authors' experience of the changing nature of the welfare state project in Britain. Our primary method is to explore what can be learned from our own experience and the experience of those with whom we work. The stimulus for the book has been our clinical experience as psychotherapists, our practice as social workers and mental health professionals, our teaching about these disciplines, our work as managers in the National Health Service (NHS), and the consultative work we undertake with public sector organizations. For the last twenty-five years we have worked variously as social workers in local authority social services departments, as psychotherapists and trainers in the NHS, and as teachers and trainers in the university sector. Our particular notion of "learning from experience" is a psychoanalytic one, but in this book we experiment with its application in ways that may seem unorthodox, and even unjustified.

This introductory chapter discusses in more depth the key principle to which we have tried to be faithful in this enterprise—the application of a clinical sensibility to the study of a particular range of social experiences and social phenomena. Our concern centres upon that what might be called the personal dimension of welfare. This is not to be equated with the personal social services, although the demise of this concept is indeed part of our preoccupation, but with something more like the "lived experience" of welfare state relationships. Because of our own professional experience, we do inevitably focus more attention on certain domains of welfare, such as mental health work, social care and so on; but equally we think that our analyses of the prevailing climate shaping the entire welfare project has a general application. Our project is therefore not to provide a critical overview of contemorary welfare, for this has been undertaken by others (e.g., Bochel & Bochel, 2003; Hughes, 1998), including those using psychoanalytic thinking (Froggett, 2002; Hoggett, 2000). Nor do we apply psychoanalytic concepts and theories to social life in any straightforward way. Instead our approach is to offer a particular way of thinking, and, thus, what we hope is a fresh form of intellectual practice.

In approaching this book from the perspective of learning from experience we do not wish to privilege this way of thinking unduly, but to suggest that it has a vital contribution to make to the understanding of modern welfare. In the attempt to use psychoanalysis as a part of political or social theorizing one should always ask, "What does it add?" The particular contribution to political thought that the psychoanalytic notion of learning from experience can make is part of our answer to this question. Bion's original formulation of this concept spoke of "emotional experiences that are directly related both to theories of knowledge and to clinical psycho-analysis, and that in the most practical manner" (Bion, 1962). He thus made it clear that learning from experience is a process that goes on in the minds of emotionally and intellectually alive persons. It is our view that neither personal nor social development runs smoothly, and that as a consequence learning from experience can be easily forsaken in the hope that a more rational or scientific approach will deliver us from the pain and frustration of our mistakes and limitations. Yet, in Bion's way of thinking, there can be no knowledge in the absence of a knower. Science and emotional experience go hand in hand.

Reason and emotion

Our view is that the rational and scientific are essential for a measured exploration of the changing nature of contemporary welfare policy and practice. However, integrated thinking and analysis cannot be achieved without a link between the rational and the emotional, and between the rational and the irrational. Linking disciplined thought with feeling is necessary not just for clinical practice but for any political or policy strategy that intends to engage individuals or groups on the basis of their intelligent lived experience. Our concern is that contemporary welfare policy has increasingly eschewed the emotional sources necessary for good, rational decision-making. This is reflected partly in what we argue is a much more muted and restricted climate of public debate about "values" in social life; and also partly in the dominance of rational–instrumental and outcome orientated methodologies in clinical and policy culture. The decline in validity of the idea of vocation as a generative source of commitment to undertake the kinds of tasks required by the welfare state may be taken as a further index of this trend.

To register concern about these matters is more than just to bemoan their loss. Rather, contemporary neuro-scientific research in particular encourages us to suggest that there is a good scientific basis for insisting on the *need* to maintain a vital, affective root to our political and policy endeavours. The whole thrust of recent neuro-scientific research findings points to the dependence of cognitive faculties on affective ones. People who manifest specific affective impairments are often severely hampered in their capacity to make ordinary rational decisions (Damasio, 2000). The brain of the infant and young child does not develop normally in the absence of properly attuned emotional care-taking, and early emotional trauma and neglect results in specific forms of organic developmental damage with implications for both later emotional and cognitive functioning (Perry, 2002). The brain is now understood to be a social organ, in the particular sense that attuned emotional relationships are essential to its healthy growth. These discoveries lend much needed support to the claims of psychoanalysis with respect to the importance of early emotional experience in shaping later psychological development. Bion himself was clear that the emotional experience, from which we may learn or not learn, is at root a bodily or somatic event, but he did not have available the research evidence to substantiate his theories in this respect.

Even these outline considerations open up a set of questions about the significance of the affective domain for the public sphere, of which in some ways this book is a tentative exploration. Is it meaningful, for example, to ask about the degree to which particular policy initiatives are rooted in a process of affectively informed and digested debate, rather than just technical reasoning? Would policy processes incorporating fuller, publicly observable, emotional engagement with the issues at stake result in more effective decisions and action? How do we distinguish the role of values, and the role of feeling, in such processes? Such questions are more implicit than explicit in much of our thinking in this book, but we do focus more specific attention on them in Chapters Six and Seven, when we consider some particular instances of highly emotionally charged recent policy formation in the field of child protection work.

Identities and identifications

In the light of such thoughts, the project of this book must be further situated in relation to the experience and biography of its authors. As already noted, we write in part as social workers and social work teachers, but also in an attempt to integrate our newer identities as psychoanalytic psychotherapists. Our work in both roles has always been carried out in public sector settings, and as psychotherapists also in private practice. This work has always involved a high degree of relatedness to the wider health and welfare context, and so the range of experience from which we seek to learn is, we believe, relevant not just to social work but to the broad inter-disciplinary project of modern mental health practice and public health and welfare provision. The management of our own, at times conflicted, professional identities has a contemporary feel in the context of multi-disciplinary work in health and social care. Making a professional home away from our social work home reflects our developing career interests, but also draws attention to a solution that was a response to the difficulties and frustrations we experienced in our previous roles. This was our particular route, but it echoes the professional instability that characterizes modern welfare, in which there is a constant reworking of professional boundaries—especially in the context of mental health work—together with a restless search for what skills belong where, and what in reality differentiates one professional from another.

In such circumstances, the temptation is to assert professional identity with reference either to history and tradition, or to abandon all reference to history in the belief that we can reinvent ourselves as professionals, as if such responses could give purchase on the unsettling flux of contemporary experience in the workplace. Here, there are echoes of much broader societal processes, in which a resort to tradition can function as a defence against the threat and exhaustion of perpetual innovation. As Anthony Giddens (1994) has persuasively argued, uncertainties associated with the experience of globalization are one potential source of the rise of fundamentalism. In our own discussions we have been drawn to mourn "the good old days" in which social work had a clearer sense of its professional role and direction. We have found ourselves thinking about a time when it seemed possible to consider social work's unique position amongst the caring professions, on the boundary between the social and the personal. We mourned the fact that many of those who inspired and taught us have slipped out of sight, as if their legacy has no relevance for a contemporary generation. We criticized both the professional organization and the academy of social work for not being robust enough in defence of the enterprise. And yet the experience of these discussions was not enlivening. Rather they produced a sense of helplessness and impotence, precisely because there was no active engagement with where we had come from in relation to where we now found ourselves, and more importantly, where we now wished to go.

Any attempt to examine modern welfare, or indeed any aspect of the contemporary social structure in what has been termed "late modernity", must negotiate a difficult path, between idealization of the new and concomitant denigration of the past on the one hand, and nostalgic identification with the past and possible resistance to innovation and change on the other. From a psychoanalytic perspective, these potential positions must be seen as detrimental to the sustained effort to remain open-minded and integrative, to be aware of both creative possibility and destructiveness. If, for example, narratives of loss prevail in the effort to assess current developments, then the complexity of social life, lived experience, and social organization is overlooked. This can mean that programmes within contemporary social policy, and their detailed implementation, can become positioned as simply instrumental of the workings of late modernity. Additionally, the customs and practices of the past may be construed in a way that forecloses upon their more benign purposes and potential value for the present.

Rights and relationships

We believe that in the whole range of welfare work, whether as psychotherapists, doctors, nurses, social workers, or teachers, we become exposed not just to the hope for change, but also the intense anxiety provoked by the prospect of change and the risk of the unexpected or unwanted development. In our experience, to do welfare work well is uncomfortable because it exposes the clinician to the feelings of the client, to the client's feelings about occupying that role, and to the tensions between the roles of provider and user. No amount of outcome-led practice can dilute the loving but also conflictual affective dynamic that underpins the user–provider relationship, a relationship that, from a psychoanalytic perspective, clearly resonates with the universal primitive experience of the infant's need for others to promote development and well-being. One of the central premises of this book is that reflection upon the experience of this working relationship with the user, the client. or the patient is a necessary precondition for good practice, and that no amount of protocols, targets, or outcomes can replace this necessity.

Reflecting upon what is happening in this relationship not only leads to a deepening of what can be known about the client, but also strengthens the sense of purpose and satisfaction in the practitioner. Implicit in outcome-led practice is the assumption that the outcome will bring relief or satisfaction. While relief or satisfaction is certainly one objective of welfare, the other is to provide continuity of care for those who do not attract obvious concern, or for those whose prognosis socially or physically is poor, or indeed for those where the only foreseeable outcome is imminent death. In an affluent consumerist society there is the illusion that we can have, and that we deserve to have, all that we desire; and that with the right consumerist stance by both provider and user it can be obtained. If this state of mind persists into the delivery of welfare, we argue that the results are shallow, driven by fashion, and avoid the complexity of ill health, distress, and injustice.

One inescapable characteristic of modern welfare is therefore the tendency to believe in "rights" as a solution to the complexities and ambiguities that the welfare relationship entails. We can act as if, being affluent consumers, we *should* be granted access to whatever we want, without the need to consider the cost to others; or the need for taxation to pay for it; or the fact that a whole range of outcomes cannot be achieved as a matter of entitlement. In our view, outcomes in welfare require work, and difficult, painful, conflictual, affective work at that. The danger lies in settling for a shallow set of objectives, avoiding the reality that hardship, inequity, and misfortune are part of life. As we shall argue, shallowness in welfare reduces the complexity of pathology and denies history and the injustices it has visited on us personally and socially. Instead of delivering freedom of choice and empowerment for the user, in fact public welfare conceived in this way can be seen as more restricted, insisting on outcome conformity for the user, and clinical fidelity to non-clinical principles for the clinician.

The social character of welfare

Both the authors of this book believe that social work and the other "social professions" have a role to play in contemporary welfare, yet we also see their distinctive aspiration of linking personal and social life being lost. This was probably always more of an aim than an achievement, but the aspiration drew attention to contested discourses about the existence of a relationship between "private troubles and public issues" (Wright Mills, 1959). A central theme of this book concerns the way that modern welfare seems content with a notion of service delivery split off from what we describe as the contemporary societal character, as if taking care of the one necessarily takes care of the other. Yet just as the infant benefits from, or is disabled by, the state of mind of their parents or carers so we believe the state of mind of society is reflected in the manner in which it provides care for its citizens on the one hand and for the stranger, the outsider, on the other. The quality of this provision is a reflection of societal well-being or the lack of it.

The notion of societal character is controversial. But concern and destructiveness, compassion and indifference, are not just individual human characteristics. Their manifestation in socio-economic, political, and ideological formations shapes our experience and possibilities as individuals, the condition of our organizations, and the attributes of our communities. Thus, any commentary on welfare must seek to discover what can be learned about the character of the contemporary period. While we accept that one cannot read off the nature of social processes from our understanding of how individual human beings function, yet societies, ideologies, and organizations are also human products. In exploring the relationship of "the least parts to the greatest whole" (Scheff, 1997) we may illuminate the character of both.

Throughout the book we work explicitly and implicitly with an idea of societal character that is dialectical. By dialectical we mean that there are complex relationships of cause and effect, and of meaning, operating between social structures, the typical patterns of social relationship that produce, reproduce, and also challenge these structures, and the prevailing ideas and beliefs (ideologies) that both sustain and flow from these. Drawing upon all these dimensions, our analysis of social experience aims to disclose some interconnections between them. This way of thinking draws inspiration from Raymond Williams' notion of "structures of feeling", which he elaborated in his writings about the societal contexts of literature and drama. This is how he tried to define this rather elusive concept:

> It is as firm and definite as "structure" suggests, yet it is based in the deepest and often least tangible elements of our experience. It is a way of responding to a particular world which in practice is not felt as one way among others—a conscious "way"—but is, in experience, the only way possible. Its means, its elements, are not propositions or techniques; they are embodied, related feelings. In the same sense, it is accessible to others—not by formal argument or by professional skills, on their own, but by direct experience . . . [Williams, 1993, p. 18]

This way of thinking is holistic in that it assumes that connections can be made between personal experience and the social world and that, to borrow another phrase, society is an "intelligible field of study" (Miller & Khaleelee, 1993) that may be accessed through enquiry into individual and local experience as much as through the collective and general. Although "structural" features of the welfare state, such as the prevalence of quasi-market relations, may have a powerful and general shaping influence on a broad range of more localized patterns of behaviour and experience, we do not assume that such structural factors are ultimately more "real" or more determinate in producing social character than are ideas and meanings or the ways in which people may actually relate. Certainly, there have been massive shifts in the structural conditions shaping contemporary welfare, but a study of these alone reveals next to nothing about the human experience of either providing or receiving welfare.

Others, such as those contributing to Hughes (1998), have also drawn on Raymond Williams' idea of structures of feeling, but our concept of how the interconnections between different dimensions of social life operate is specifically influenced by psychoanalytic practice and theory. Psychoanalysis discloses both the relative stability and recalcitrance to change of mental life, and the fluid, mutating, oscillating, and slippery nature of what we call "psychic structures". Like the stable patterns of social life we call structural, as clinicians we would note that the relatively stable patterns we call individual character, or patterns of enduring self-experience, are continually produced and reproduced by psychic activity. The experience of giving or receiving psychotherapy is in large part one of studying these processes, of the formation and reformation of psychic structures in oneself or others, and of coming to *know* them.

Structures of feeling: containment and compartmentalization

Thus, central to the book's analysis is the view that modern welfare is in a particular stage of struggle over our collective and individual capacities to sustain *knowledge* of the social, personal, and physical conditions of life that the welfare state was created to address. Learning from experience is at the heart of our method, because it enables a particular quality of knowledge, without which the quality of our interventions—our professional and social responses to suffering and disadvantage—will be shallower and more attenuated than they might be.

We would argue that government and the political classes have always been ambivalent, at best, about how far they wished to encourage deep-seated and widespread knowledge of social and personal ills. These matters have always posed a potential political and economic threat. But we would suggest that the original welfare state did bring into being a network of institutions and a professional class to shoulder the burden of engaging with Beveridge's "five giants" of idleness, ignorance, want, squalor, and disease (Beveridge, 1942). While this was a fundamentally humane and progressive project, it can also be argued that it allowed wider society to hive off its awareness of the worst of its social and personal ills. This knowledge could be seen as carried by a variety of increasingly specialized professional groups. In so far as this knowledge was "carried" successfully, and worked with, it could be described psychoanalytically as in part "contained". However, from the point of view of wider society, such knowledge could also be described as "compartmentalized", for legitimate defensive reasons. From time to time something disturbing or scandalous or socially fascinating escaped from one of these comparatively sequestered domains into the wider public arena. In response, the political process would be forced to engage, and to seek adjustments in our institutionalized response to public ills. But these intermittent eruptions of painful awareness were normally accommodated—rather as "acts of God", such as earthquakes, floods, or tornados can be assimilated—without too much social recrimination. However, this form of social settlement for the management of disturbing knowledge and events broke down, and in Chapters Six and Seven, in particular, we examine the consequences of this.

Knowledge of social and personal suffering is painful for society to bear. It is hard to know how to express this fundamental proposition without unduly individualizing the idea of society. But just as mental structures and organization contribute to the personally distinctive ways of managing experience and relationships, so we propose that different social structures and political arrangements make for different social patterns of feeling and relationship. Hiving off responsibility for the management of painful knowledge to designated agencies is actually quite a sophisticated and sensible strategy. This can be likened to the group setting aside a family quarrel or a professional dispute in order to get on with the work of the day. Ideally, at the appropriate time, the painful matter can be broached more widely once again. In fact, Bion (1961) suggested that "work groups", that is, groups who are able to address and tackle real tasks productively, may unknowingly create "specialized work groups" whose task is to manage the "split off" or compartmentalized difficult area. Hence, psychoanalytically, a degree of healthy splitting or disassociation from the experience of mental pain, a capacity for containment, is appropriate; but also, so is an ability to stay in touch.

Our argument in this book is that over a certain period one major socially sanctioned settlement for the management of our knowledge of social suffering and conflict, the original post-war welfare state, began to break down. A comprehensive empirical history of how this happened would be the subject of another book. Throughout, however, we attend to certain themes in the history of the breakdown of this settlement on the basis of our own experience. Our wider aim is to describe the consequences of this transformation and the social states of mind that have resulted; and thus to offer interpretations of the psycho-social conditions of welfare we now inhabit.

Structures of feeling: danger, risk, and control

The structures of feeling that we believe have now replaced the psychic settlement achieved during the initial decades of the post-war welfare state are the outcome of definite historical and political processes, and are still evolving. These processes have ushered in what we think of as a new social topography, a revised set of conditions in which we now work and transact our relationships with clients, patients, colleagues, policy makers, and our own organizations, communities, and families. They give rise to new characteristic patterns of social anxiety and defence, and new possibilities and constraints for the task of extending and deepening our humane engagement with suffering, disadvantage and injustice. At their core lie the complex, and much debated, continuities and discontinuities between the political project of the Thatcher–Major administrations, and the New Labour government that succeeded them. The former administrations decimated the strength and confidence of what Will Hutton (1996) refers to as the "intermediate institutions" of civil society—the network of professional associations, trade unions, local government initiativeism and so on—that formed a thickly textured context for public service development and welfare delivery. Into the political spaces that consequently opened up came public–private sector partnerships, organized by quasi-market mechanisms and regulated or "assured" by the new audit and inspection industries. These processes have gathered momentum under the subsequent two New Labour administrations. "Governance" now replaces government, service users replace patients and clients, and quality assurance systems replace professional self-regulation. Below, we comment briefly on the politically progressive dimensions of this project. But first we sketch out some aspects of the new structures of feeling that have arisen within these new arrangements.

We would like to suggest that daily working life in this new order is significantly organized by a giant "category mistake". We now inhabit a much more centralized, socially managed and directed practice and learning environment. A concern with the management and development of the *general* conditions necessary for supporting delivery of health and social services has become disastrously fused with the *particular* activities and contexts for that process of delivery and use of services. This fusion can be noted in many arenas: in the tension (or absence of recognized tension) between the requirements of evidence-based practice and the context of individual clinical experience and judgement; in the confusion and friction between national standards and competency-led training methodologies, and the particularized process of clinical or practice learning; in the way that systems of risk management obscure how individual and collective anxieties create climates of risk that become indistinguishable from risk itself; and so on.

Thus, we wish to argue that psychoanalytically it is helpful to ask a question concerning the extent to which any activity within the welfare sector can now be capable of being experienced as "ego driven" rather than "superego driven". Crucially, since we cannot live without a relation to the superego, it is also useful to ask what *kind* of superego relations pertain in any particular situation. When describing a social process such as the delivery of mental health services or primary school education as ego driven, we mean the extent to which it occurs under conditions of helpful, albeit relative, autonomy for those who undertake the activity in question. Of course, all such work is part of a social project or programme and usually publicly funded, so it cannot take place without explicit reference to social norms and aims, and in relation to what we call social policy. But social policy in modern welfare appears to us to play a complex and profoundly ambiguous role in generating the new structure of feeling that we are trying to describe.

As the discrete "containers" that characterized the structure of the original welfare state settlement have dissolved, and as evidence of the "dangerousness" they once contained has been splayed across the whole social field, we suggest that social policy now plays a far more prominent role in the management of the social anxieties that attend this more generalized awareness. Accordingly, in its irrational dimensions, contemporary policy culture seems to be as much preoccupied with a project of generalized control of dangerous forces and knowledge as with the provision of conditions via which social disadvantage and distress might be attended to. We explore the most prominent manifestation of this orientation to control in Chapter Three, but the succeeding two chapters are also case studies in the function that policy discourses have of simultaneously disclosing and foreclosing on real social engagement with acute social and personal difficulties. This double function of policy illustrates its defensive aspect, and represents what we mean by "borderline" states in society. The question becomes: how narrow or broad is the line of genuine emotional and social engagement facilitated by the defensive constructs of social policy in their relationship to practice realities?

Thus, we argue that the increased centralization of both policy generation and policy enforcement, allied with the weakening of the intermediate institutions of the welfare state noted above, have created social conditions for the delivery of ordinary welfare that seem to us analogous to living in the shadow of a permanently scrutinizing, punitive superego. A colleague describes it simply as "constantly being told what to do and how to do it". In her paper "Relating to the superego", Edna O'Shaughnessy (1999) delineates a range of possible registers of superego functioning. In discussing clinical practice, she proposes that

> a unitary conception of the superego may not encompass the varied phenomena met with in our patients: in some the superego, even when primitive and strict, is a guiding force, but in others an abnormal form of the superego is a destroyer of the self, its relations and its objects. [*ibid.*, p. 861]

In this respect, our basic structural schema for understanding the set of possible relationships between government and the machinery of policy, the workforce that provides welfare, and those in need of services, is as follows. We assume that, for professionals, the work of welfare is emotionally, intellectually, and practically challenging. We also assume that it entails engagement with free agents who bring complex needs, demands, ailments, predicaments, and experiences of suffering to service providers. It is in the nature of the work that it is arduous—for both provider and user.

A central argument of this book is that the nature of the work and the conditions needed to properly engage in it are the fulcrum determining what is now called "quality" of service provision. A degree of autonomy—which in part means protection from excessive external interference, control, scrutiny—is necessary if the complex transactions involved are to be genuinely possible, and if genuine quality is to be enabled. It is our contention that for a range of reasons the climate in which most welfare work is now undertaken is precariously balanced between a state of mind in which policy processes are experienced as "strict" but also as a "guiding force", and one in which they become "destroyers". Writing about one of her patients, O'Shaughnessy describes how she tried to speak understandingly of the patient's fear and disappointment in her as the analyst, but the patient replied "What I extract from what you say is—you're critical and pointing at me that I can't do it" (*ibid.*, p. 862).

After nearly two decades of neglect, when New Labour came to power in 1997, the British welfare state was arguably in fact "unable to do it" any more. The subsequent concerted push to raise standards, improve equity of service among regions and social classes, and integrate professional effort towards service user needs and demands, has been genuinely progressive in spirit and intent. In our estimation, its shadow side has entailed a degree of ruthlessness in attempting to *control* rather than *enable* the workforce in continuing with its arduous task within revised organizational conditions and changed priorities. Lacking mediation by a strong professional ego, the instruments of social policy have been felt to penetrate the very heart and soul of everyday practice and professional thought. It is as though the political class could only anticipate *resistance* to change, and in this state of mind broke contact and abandoned trust in their own good object of welfare—the workforce—rather than seeking to enter a more progressive alliance based on negotiation. This would have respected the inherent nature of the work of welfare and perhaps led to a very different climate of contemporary health and social care activity.

Borderline welfare

The processes outlined above lead to the emergence of the state of affairs we characterize as borderline welfare. This can be traced to several sources. First, we think it is related to a perceived failure of containment by the agencies of welfare of their painful tasks. As evidence of devastating cases of failure and professional corruption in social, health, and educational agencies has seemed to mount in the public domain, causing simultaneous social anguish and political unease, government moved in to "take control". In fact, there is little proven evidence that these crises were in themselves indices of new systemic performance difficulties. Rather, emotionally painful *knowledge* of the potentially impossible task of agencies of welfare, of their fallibility, and of their potential and actual infiltration by perverse and dangerous personnel, was increasingly put on public display. Second, this emotionally painful knowledge is knowledge about risk. This is risk in the sense of human failure that is held, in principle, to be avoidable or controllable, but which, when constructed as such, is also a potential source of acute political embarrassment and threat. Third, the trends indicated above intersected with the emergence of a new political administration dedicated to reviving the welfare state on revised structural principles and with new priorities. This required a massive degree of direct intervention and regulation. We suggest that these various transformations amount to a new collective state of mind in which the objects of welfare intervention evoke fear, whether this is seen in the form of perceived levels of mental illness, as represented by numbers of asylum seekers, as the problem of homelessness, or as children's educational under-achievement. Politically, such objects are potential sites of dangerousness and scandal, as much as they evoke compassion and the desire to ameliorate.

Herein lies one paradox of the state of affairs we address in this book. The modern welfare project is still quite young. Part of the optimism of its early flowering lay in the belief that by committing social resources to the amelioration of social difference, deficit, and disadvantage, inequalities and injustices would be gradually dispelled. Less clearly anticipated was the process through which engagement with sites of social distress and anger would be an agency for *disclosing* hitherto unexpected, suppressed—quite literally "unthought"—dimensions of suffering and conflict, often residing as much within the agencies providing welfare as within those receiving it. The situation is analogous to that of the psycho-therapy patient who embarks hopefully and willingly on a treat-ment, only to encounter a profound sense of anxiety and despair as the depth and apparently bottomless nature of their internal as well as external difficulties make themselves known, together with the potential and actual limitations of their therapist. Both situations confront our optimistic sides and our emotional resourcefulness with a choice, whether to persist in our engagement with this new painful knowledge or flee from it. That is the predicament of the borderline.

This predicament is simply not well articulated and examined as a shaping factor in the trajectory of modern welfare. We wish to note that delineating this particular emotional predicament for attention does not in any sense provide a complete explanation, or a more fundamental one, of the dilemmas of the contemporary welfare state. Many other forces act on governments and policy makers. But it is a predicament that is perhaps harder to bring into focus than many, and certainly less susceptible to demonstration according to "scientific" evidential criteria. We wish to show that it is this dimension of our social history and activity that psycho-analysis can illuminate in ways no other practice can.

Part 2: Principles

Introduction

Critical social analysis has always tried to reveal the individual psyche as shaped, constructed, or determined by social forces and processes. It has been less comfortable with methods of analysis that flow in the opposite direction, examining how social processes may be modelled on the amplification of dynamics most readily observed in the individual psyche. Equally, psychoanalytic theory and practice has always vigorously defended the autonomy of the psychic sphere, though with varying degrees of success. It has also sought to extend insights from clinical work to the social and public realms. Our approach in this book is informed by both traditions. Here, we want to outline the sources and principles that underpin its various levels of argument.

These principles suggest, but do not yet articulate, a methodology for the psychoanalytic study of society. For us, such a method is not primarily about the deployment of psychoanalytic concepts and theories, but about the application of a clinical sensibility to the study of social phenomena. We think the intellectual cogency of this venture needs to be justified, and we have broached this task in a separate chapter at the end of the book (see Chapter Ten). Some readers may feel that this is superfluous effort—that the proof of the pudding is in the eating, and no amount of appeal to the artfulness of the recipe makes for a more satisfying dinner. Our hope is that the approach we adopt represents a good beginning, but that once again disciplined attention to the rational dimensions of methodology will in time yield more refined ways of studying the inter-relationship of conscious and unconscious, rational and irrational forces in the production of social welfare.

Learning from experience

As outlined above, a first principle informing our work is that of "learning from experience". And as also noted, in psychoanalysis it was Wilfred Bion (1962) who developed this concept. While the scope of experience upon which we draw is probably much broader than he envisaged, we think our psychological and methodological stance is faithful to his work. Attention to one's immediate and continuing experience entails suspending judgement about what ought to be the case, or might have been the case, in favour simply of aiming to know what is the case. It is an observational stance, taken as the basis for an attitude of inquiry. From knowledge of what is, one can also infer what is not (what is omitted, obscured, forgotten, or neglected). From here one can consider what might be (recovered, remembered, and linked up with what is). The capacity to describe and name the qualities of psychic, interpersonal or social experience is foundational both to a psychoanalytic stance and to certain varieties of sociological inquiry. In attending to the nature of experience we focus particularly on its emotional dimensions and, at the same time, on the attributes of relatedness and belief that emotional experiences carry within them. For example, how do communications by this colleague, or patient, or organization, or government department impact upon us? What emotional response do they tend to elicit in us? In turn, how do such agents or agencies seem to respond affectively to our communications? What conceptions and possibilities for social and personal relationship are encouraged or discouraged by certain discourses of policy? And from this kind of reflective stance, what can we learn about the particular psycho-social character of our "lived" welfare environment; and especially, what forms of relationship we are being invited to engage in, and what forms not?

Surfaces and depths: tension, contradiction and growth

As clinicians we are accustomed to the fact that our patients, understood through our immediate experience of them, are not revealed as unified, coherent persons. From our own experience of being patients we are accustomed to the fact that we are not ourselves unified and coherent. We believe that the clinical psychoanalytic project is not about imposing coherence on fragmentation and disorder, but about facilitating growth, development, and integration in our personalities. This project is never complete, not least because we hold that conflict and tension between different trends in the personality is an irreducible fact of life. The clinical project of psychoanalysis is realized through increasing self-knowledge of the relatedness, or lack of relatedness of these disparate trends and of the endless struggle between them.

Thus, a second principle informing our approach in this book is a view of social processes and welfare regimes, as well as individuals, as organized by powerful emotionally charged forces that are replete with tensions, contradictions, and inconsistencies. Central among these various tensions is the disjunction between the "self-representations" of modern welfare and their representation in the experience of those who provide and receive welfare. So, the critical dimension of our own project is rooted in the effort to unmask surfaces and expose deeper layers of experience and meaning, while aiming to understand and illuminate the relationships between surface and depth. Occasionally, this entails explicit reference to unconscious forces and their part in shaping social processes; more often we are simply concerned to show, or reveal, how painful emotional realities are an unacknowledged, socially unsymbolized motor of development in modern welfare. This stance is related to Gordon Lawrence's (2000) distinction between the "politics of revelation" and the "politics of salvation" in the practice of organizational consultancy. Again, rooted in Bion's ideas about learning from experience, Lawrence's interest is in

> thoughts about experiences in the client enterprise, which are known, at some level (the unconscious), but have not yet been thought and voiced ... In my terms these are thoughts that come to be revealed—that is, they are products of the politics of revelation. [2000, p. 176]

In Chapter Six we extend this idea, and consider the possibility that social theory might also be conceived as a project of revelation, rather than explanation or active interpretation.

Psycho-social realism

We do not think that "depth phenomena" are more real than their "surface" counterparts, but we do hold that surfaces can obscure, and may be intentionally, as well as consciously and unconsciously designed to do so. A view of personal and social phenomena as multi-layered and thus susceptible to more than one account of their nature raises very contemporary questions about where, if anywhere, reality is to be found. Are all accounts of a phenomenon, from the many perspectives (or in Bion's (1984) term "vertices") via which it may be investigated and understood, equally valid, accurate, or truthful? Or are some accounts more truthful than others? If so, how does one discriminate between the more and less truthful or accurate? These are complex and profound philosophical debates, which we do not propose to enter upon beyond making our overall position as clear as we can.

This position might be described as psycho-social and realist, but not reductionist. The fact that the objects of our interest and analysis can be described, understood, interpreted, and explained in more than one way does not complicate this stance. Individual, group, organizational, and societal states of being, including their mythic and unconscious aspects, are real. They have socially constructed and historical properties that are central to their nature, but they are also patterned according to deep structural generative principles. In our view such psychological and social structures are best understood as relatively stable processes, more like the patterns or rules that organize a formal dance routine than the rigid framework of a building. Thus, no psychological or social structure completely determines the properties of what it generates, or is itself immutable in any universal or timeless sense.

The facts of life and the facts of welfare

Our psychoanalytic, realist position extends to arguing that there are certain core conditions, aspects of what it means to be human rather than animal, vegetable, or mineral, which delimit and define our human possibilities. These are sometimes called "the facts of life" in psychoanalytic discourse (Money-Kyrle, 1978). They include: our prolonged period of dependence on others in infancy and its consequences for later psychological development; the inevitability of death and our struggle with the knowledge of our mortality; the necessity of tolerating and managing our relationships with other people, and transcending our narcissism; the ubiquity of the struggle between loving and hating impulses in our relations with others and ourselves; the fact that the human mind and personality is the outcome of a developmental process which never ceases; the fact that anxiety is a necessary condition for being alive.

It is our view that in the face of painful realities social development cannot be taken for granted any more than can individual development. Social institutions, especially those of welfare, are in an active relationship with citizens, and it is in the quality of this relationship that the social health, or otherwise, of society can be discerned. Welfare represents a socially sanctioned system of concern. But the ethical foundations of concern can only be sustained at cost—economic cost to be sure, but also psychological, relational, and organizational cost. This is not to deny that welfare activity has inherent rewards, but as a complex socially organized system it demands sustained social and ethical nurture. It is possible to preserve an appearance of ethical duty and integrity in the face of degenerative anti-ethical pressure from within and without. But political inequalities, disjunctions between ideological rhetoric and daily lived experience, the ambivalent character of "modernization", are also facts that can be registered, assimilated, and understood, *known*—or not. We argue that the quality of welfare can only be sustained where these facts are known, via an approach to knowledge that includes social experience of the emotional aspects of relationship as a core dimension.

This book argues that in the past decade especially, the character of the welfare project in Britain has undergone profound transformations. In summary, the book is centrally concerned with the relational, emotional, and ethical conditions—the experiential facts of the situation—in which we now provide and consume welfare. We would maintain that there has been very little discussion of welfare matters from this standpoint. As we have outlined, we now live within new structures of feeling generated by these transformations. As professionals, we mostly become aware of the social impact and meaning of such structures of feeling only through a kind of persistent and inarticulate sense of complaint—complaint about perpetual change, policy and acronym fatigue, and about uncertain professional identities, structural conditions which engender an atmosphere of professional and moral exhaustion. While we take clear implicit and explicit positions about the evolution of social welfare in this book, we are mainly concerned to describe and illuminate the contemporary situation. It is hoped that our accounts will resonate, and will provoke debate, in the service of greater understanding. In this way, we also hope to encourage

others to experiment with new ways of apprehending and articulating their social experience, as part of the project of deepening our
collective capacity for the development of welfare in our times.

The structure of the book

In Chapter Two, "Borderline states of mind and society", we elaborate the concept of borderline states of mind in individuals and in
society that informs much of the analysis in the remainder of the
book. We illustrate this concept through a range of examples drawn
from clinical work, the tradition of group relations training, and
research into psychological life. At the end of the chapter we
also review a range of other psychoanalytically informed studies of
social processes that are close in spirit to those advanced in this book.

Chapter Three, "The state of mind we're in: sincerity, anxiety
and the audit society", offers a psychoanalytically informed analysis of the culture of audit, perhaps the most pervasive dimension of
the new structure of feeling shaping modern welfare policy and
practice. Through reference to clinical material, we attempt to illuminate the relationship between the emergence of a culture of
inspection and control in social affairs and the underlying anxieties
about dangerousness that elicit this form of defensive management;
but in addition, we point to the risks of corruption to moral and
professional integrity in a culture of excessive anxiety about the role
of agencies of scrutiny, inspection and evaluation.

In Chapter Four, "The psychic geography of racism: the state,
the clinician, and hatred of the stranger" we explore the ambiguities of contemporary practices and discourses of race, difference,
and diversity, and suggest that these may promote a retreat from
real social and emotional engagement with the damaging and toxic
phenomenon of racism, while appearing to do just the opposite.
Consumerist ideologies of the service user–professional relationship appear to promote a similar denial of authentically experienced real differences. The chapter thus proposes that policy
discourse and rhetoric may be serving a function of suppressing
knowledge of the complex feelings and dynamics of difference
through the construction of a pseudo universalism based on the
elimination of difference.

Chapter Five, "The broken link: polemic and pain in mental health work", examines the tensions in current policy and practice surrounding the value of the professional and clinical "mind". We suggest that it has proven very difficult to sustain a three-cornered relationship between on one side government, policy, and management, on another the patient or user, *and* third, the professional or clinician. The collapse in the direction of a dyadic partnership structure, excluding and immobilizing the authority of the professional, represents a variety of borderline functioning in which the inherent tensions of these triangular relationships are managed through splitting.

Chapter Six, "Surface tensions: the social containment of dangerous knowledge", offers an account of the emergence into public awareness of a particular instance of dangerous and anxiety provoking knowledge, namely of child sexual abuse. The chapter is concerned with philosophical themes surrounding the process of coming to know about previously unthinkable experiences. A clinical case study is introduced to illustrate the epistemological ambiguities that attend such emergent understanding, and these are compared to the confusion that accompanied the emergence into general social awareness of child sexual abuse during the Cleveland affair of 1987. Given the extreme difficulty that may attend knowing about matters that are nevertheless a part of everyday experience for many people, the chapter proposes the value of a concept of social theory concerned with revelation rather than premature explanation or interpretation. In this connection, public discourses about dangerous matters are compared to Bion's idea of the need for an "apparatus for thinking", if the unthinkable is to be assimilated into social awareness.

In Chapter Seven, "Surface and depth in the Victoria Climbié inquiry report: an enquiry into emotionally intelligent policy", we aim to read below the surface of a prominent public document that was the outcome of an inquiry into another eruption of extreme dangerousness in our society—the Victoria Climbié Inquiry Report. We suggest that events contributing to the tragedy of Victoria Climbié's death, as well as the inquiry report itself, exemplify a pattern in which individuals and groups but also discursive representations of social processes (official documents) may "turn a blind eye" with respect to painful realities. This defence, of both knowing and not knowing, is characteristic of borderline functioning. The chapter concludes with some preliminary thoughts about the idea of emotional intelligence, and its potential application in the realm of policy-making.

Chapter Eight, "The vanishing organization: organizational containment in a networked world", engages with questions about the changing nature of modern organizations, particularly their networked character, and the attendant psychological pressures of working within them. Weak or fluid organizational boundaries, and the requirement to function in partnership, expose us to a more primitive psychology that may resemble the acute anxieties about psychic survival underlying borderline type defences in individuals. The chapter delineates some key predicaments for the particular task orientation of welfare organizations arising from these trends.

Chapter Nine is the concluding chapter of the main body of the book. The title, "Complex dependencies and the dilemmas of welfare", is intended to evoke an engagement with the idea that struggles around dependency remain central within the emotional task of social welfare; but also that the contexts and perception of experiences of dependency have been rendered much more complex by changes in the patterning of contemporary social relations. The new structures of feeling shaping welfare experience may tend to obscure the obdurate facts of human dependency, partly by appeal to ideas of interdependence as a more desirable norm. Acute fear of dependence is one of the basic anxieties giving rise to borderline defences and states of mind, and contexts of real and imagined social complexity may exacerbate tendencies to develop such defensive solutions.

Chapter Ten, "Methodological reflections: clinical sensibility and the study of the social", aims to articulate the core philosophical and methodological principles informing the approach to knowledge found in this book. The account emphasizes the generation of psychoanalytic knowledge through practice, and the lived experience of relationships, rather than the application of intellectual frameworks to experience. The chapter examines how knowledge of unconscious forces at work in society may be accessed, and concludes by explicating some of the implicit principles in an established psychoanalytic method for making society an intelligible field of study.

CHAPTER TWO

Borderline states of mind and society

"During this period of work with the social services department, I sometimes felt my heart would break hearing of the
appalling experiences of some of the children, especially
when their hopes and expectations would be cruelly dashed,
and of the social workers themselves subjected to abuse and
criticism . . . The uncertainty I experienced about the perma-
nence of my post echoed the anxieties of many children who
lived in unbearable states of uncertainty about their future.
The deeper the emotional investment one makes, the more
intense the anxieties about it all coming to nothing . . ."

Louise Emanuel (2002)

What has happened to people?

What has happened to the idea of personal welfare? Or
to ask a slightly different, less polemical question:
what meaning do we give to the fact that no one any
longer sees fit to describe the function of welfare in "personal"
terms? The disappearance from official discourse of the "personal
social services", and its substitution with "user-led" services is a

significant marker of some dramatic changes in how the welfare
state is now conceived. Very few now dare speak, as Louise
Emanuel does above, of "heartbreak" in their work. Little reference
is made to intensity of feeling as lying at the heart of the work of
welfare. If people are no longer posited as the object of welfare in
Britain, it is nevertheless still people who provide and receive
services, manifest desires and needs, and offer ways of meeting
these, or in the contemporary jargon, enter into "partnerships" for
the same purpose. We believe the evacuation of the personal from
the heart of the welfare enterprise extends beyond questions of
discourse, language, or representation, and reaches to the very
centre of how we think, feel, behave, relate, and imagine ourselves
within the conditions established by modern social policy and
government.

If people, individually and collectively, with all their passions,
desires, hopes, disappointments, and resentments, no longer seem
to figure in the modern welfare imagination as they once did, then
what has happened? Our view is that at its inception the social
contract that founded the post-war welfare state provided a core
idea and a set of principles informing the aspirations of those working within it. At their best, professionals sought to establish
progressive conditions in which to conduct work in education,
social work, housing, or mental health. These conditions implied
engagement at a variety of complex levels with the real life situations
of those who depended upon others for help, or development, or
the realization of social justice. Again, at best, this progressivism
was also intended to enable the recipients of welfare to engage in
their turn, and this meant that the abstractions of the "social
contract" were largely assumed to be enacted through the medium
of relationships.

These relationships were not always comfortable, and could not
be so; in some sectors of the welfare state they were highly bureau-
cratized; but the aspiration was, and remains, rooted in recognition
of a reality—real desires, needs, conflicts, abuses, and antagonisms
demanding to be recognized and engaged with. But the public and
professional representations supporting these conditions changed.
A new variety of contract, enacted in quite different ways, began to
take shape. The fact that the original conditions transpired in some
respects to have been paternalistic, and on occasion, dramatically

fallible, disappointing, and corrupted—those entrusted with care and the provision of social justice proved in some instances to be perpetuating damage and inequality—is part, but only part, of the story of this transformation. Our belief is that a complicated conjunction of forces has created a state of affairs in which a substantial retreat from engagement by people with people has come to seem both legitimate and inevitable.

This creates a paradox. Day by day the welfare project continues to be about people, as it always has been and must be. Yet a parallel state of mind has been created and maintained through the adoption of a position that denies, ignores, and repudiates this experience. The welfare project is now largely enacted in the puzzling, contradictory, and uncomfortable space bounded by these two realities. This is the place of the welfare borderline.

In this chapter we elaborate further upon the concept of borderline states of mind that we introduced in the opening chapter, and we go on to discuss how the concept will be applied in the reminder of the book. First we describe some core features of the concept of borderline functioning as derived from psychoanalytic theory and practice. Second, we introduce a number of short vignettes that illustrate aspects of borderline states in clinical and organizational contexts. These lead, third, to a proposition concerning the importance of secure boundaries in welfare systems. We illustrate how these can delimit a safe enough internal world for the delivery and management of welfare activity. Finally, we discuss some previous attempts to relate psychoanalytic theory to the understanding of social life, and link these to a review of sociological perspectives that resonate with the idea of borderline welfare.

What is the borderline?

In using the concept of borderline states to illuminate the condition of contemporary welfare we are not intending to proffer a diagnosis or build an explanatory model. Rather, we hope to elaborate a "generative metaphor" (Schon, 1979) for an aspect of social life, in order to disclose something of the subjective experience of this system of relationships.

In her paper about abnormal superego relationships, Edna O'Shaughnessy (1999) describes her work with a patient who showed great difficulty in seeking and maintaining meaningful communication with other people, including his analyst: "Feeling unlikeable, agitated, anxious, he was without links in himself and between himself and others . . . I was often without any emotional link to him and could do no more than make descriptive commentaries" (1999, p. 863).

The patient failed to attend a session before a Bank Holiday when his analyst would not be working on the following Monday, but left a phone message, ". . . his voice cold, his manner casually dismissive" (ibid., p. 866). In the subsequent session, following some detailed work on his absence and an associated dream, a new perspective emerged:

> Mr B. replied aloofly and unpleasantly that he could actually have come to that session when he rang—he had no temperature. And indeed I felt this was true for most of the current session: he could have worked with me, but he was choosing not to. [ibid., p. 867]

Later the author comments, "We see here the full adversity of Mr B's psychic predicament. He has only a doubtfully good object with whom he identifies intermittently; his instinctual conflict between making or breaking contact remains undecided" (ibid., p. 868).

We introduce this brief clinical example because it describes as well as any the fundamental predicament informing borderline states of mind. Sustained "contact" with painful, despairing, hating, conflicted emotional states of mind, in the self or in others, is hard to bear. Psychoanalytic theory and research shows us that as individuals we are confronted with this emotional predicament from the earliest moments of life. Bion's (1962) theory of containment describes the relationship-based processes between infant and caretaker that either enhance a capacity for toleration of painful and frightening emotional states, or inhibit and distort them. The rich literature on borderline states of mind and pathology are all efforts to describe the complex forms of mental functioning—systems of defence against unbearable mental pain—that are seen to have taken root when conditions promoting such capacities are absent or have failed. O'Shaughnessy's reference to her patient's "instinctual conflict between making or breaking contact" hints at something we take very seriously: the idea that this conflict is inherent in every one of us and is never fully mastered. While clinical psychoanalysis concentrates our attention on extreme and disabling states of mind, in so doing it also discloses fundamental features of mental life that are universal and everyday.

Thus, we propose that the generic idea of borderline states of mind has a broad application, which can illuminate much larger arenas of affective life than that of the individual. The test of this proposition is the substance of the remainder of this book. For now, we want to further delineate some aspects of the clinical presentations that are the source of our thinking when we use the idea of borderline states.

The literature on borderline states of mind is extensive. Rather than reference the following account in minute detail, we refer the reader to a number of key texts that offer incisive accounts of the processes described. These are Bateman (1991), Bion (1962, 1967), Britton (1998), O'Shaughnessy (1999), Rey (1988, 1994) and Steiner (1993).

Containment and failures of containment

Freud observed that the "ego is first and foremost a bodily ego; it is not merely a surface entity, but is itself the projection of a surface" (Freud, 1923b). Developmentally, the mind first of all grows out of bodily, or somatic, experience and our earliest sources of satisfaction and frustration are found in our experience of a relationship with one or more primary caretakers. "Experience" at this stage must be primarily sensation based. Until there is a capacity to think *about*, rather than just *have* such experiences, it is difficult to say that the infant has a mind. On this view of development, the gradual emergence of something like adult mental capacities is dependent in turn upon capacities located within the mother or primary caretaker to give meaning and coherence to the powerful raw material of infantile experience.

Bion gave the name "beta elements" to the raw material of mental experience, and the name "alpha function" to the capacity the caretaker brings to bear upon her infant's communication to her of these raw elements. Through a process of taking in and containing the emotionally charged elements of raw experience (the contained), thinking about and finding meaning in them (a process he termed "reverie"), Bion believed that the basis for mental capacity becomes established for the infant. This is if all goes well in the relationship and the processes just described. However, if the infant's distressing and painful experiences are not accepted and given meaning, then she may experience a kind of double dose of frustration and pain, which Bion called "nameless dread". Without the capacity to symbolize and make sense of such elements of experience, the mind, or some part of it, may find difficulty in developing and maturing. Failures of containment may thus leave the dependent child struggling with a burden of painful and senseless emotional experience. Some means of managing this must be found.

Projection and splitting

From the start of life there is pain, frustration, and rage and they are felt to be threatening to the capacity to survive and endure. Melanie Klein and the tradition of psychoanalytic thinkers who succeeded her emphasize the psychological necessity of the earliest and most powerful defensive responses to this situation, projection and splitting. The infant, and later the child and the adult under at least some circumstances, copes with this sense of threat by ejecting or propelling the sense of rage, frustration, danger, and threat into someone, or something, else. This step has the consequence of alleviating the immediate threat to well-being, but at the potential cost of "losing" a part of the mind or the self now it is located in someone else. The self may now, for example be felt to be restored and "good" while the figure projected into becomes potentially dangerous and threatening in turn. A split has developed. This process may take place at two levels—in the internal world or phantasy structure of the infant mind, but also at the level of real intersubjective interaction with other people.

In its most powerful manifestation, the defence of splitting may establish a nearly permanent structure of relationship in which the person or figure who has been projected into assumes (identifies with) those aspects of the self of which the other has rid themselves. In turn, the person who has projected the unwanted part of themselves experiences the recipient of their projection as concretely assuming (identified with) these hating, frustrating, or otherwise threatening aspects. This is projective identification. For the person who persists in later life in deploying such defences against psychic pain and frustration, the consequence may be an acute loss of ability to truly differentiate between themselves and other people. This is one manifestation of what has come to be known as borderline functioning.

Confusions of self and object

Thus, confusions of self and object are prominent in the person who has lost whole parts of him or herself in others. Rey (1994), in particular, delineates how personal intimacy becomes fraught with danger as a result. The individual attempts intimacy through phantasized occupancy of another's mind or body (rather than through relating to them as a separate person); but this induces terrible fears of engulfment or entrapment that may be experienced as claustrophobic anxiety. Retreating from this situation to one of isolation may be the attempted solution, but in turn this arouses acute anxieties of abandonment and isolation, or agoraphobic fears. The outcome of this perpetually oscillating psychic dilemma may be that the person functions within a very restricted emotional range, surviving "on the edge" in many senses.

The abnormal superego

Psychotherapy with patients afflicted by borderline anxieties often reveals the presence of a particularly harsh and cruel superego. The atmosphere generated within therapy, and presumably for the patient in many aspects of his or her relationships is evoked well in the quotations above from O'Shaughnessy's (1999) paper about superego relations. Writing of one of her patients she comments that both therapist and patient found themselves operating on ". . . a narrow line of confrontation, condemnation and denudation where neither . . . is able to 'do it'" (1999, p. 863). This image evokes one used by Britton (1998, p. 42) when he describes a treatment situation in which "Patient and analyst were to move along a single line and meet at a single point. There was to be no lateral movement". For Britton, this state of affairs is associated with difficulties in establishing a "third position" in the mind, from which a subject may observe themselves and others, and thus acquire a sense of mental space.

Psychic retreats and "turning a blind eye"

Bion clearly differentiated between processes in which some basic respect for external and internal reality is maintained, and those in which reality, and the sensory organs through which we relate to and apprehend external reality are themselves attacked. If the latter takes place, then psychotic mental functioning is likely to be the result. Borderline mental states, on the other hand, occupy a boundary position, in which a relationship to ordinary inner and outer reality is maintained but very precariously. Steiner (1993) developed a particularly fruitful account of these states of mind, and gave theoretical depth to the everyday concept of "turning a blind eye" to painful realities, so that they are simultaneously "known and not known". This notion is especially valuable for us in this book, since we are centrally concerned to elucidate the conditions that help or hinder us in our social capacity to tolerate knowledge of disturbing and painful realities. Steiner also evolved a concept of "psychic retreats", positons taken up in the mind in which, once again there is no radical rupture with inner and outer reality, but rather a suspension or disengagement from real engagement.

Summary

The term "borderline" therefore describes a state of mind in which there is a core problem of identity. This arises mainly from processes in which mental pain is managed by expulsion or projection rather than through toleration and containment as a necessary part of learning. In borderline states a person constantly moves between an inflated or denigrated judgement of their objects and themselves, never securely finding a good-enough relationship from which realistic differentiation between self and other is possible. Acute anxieties about psychic survival are managed by projecting aspects of the self into an object that is then felt to be entrapping or suffocating. This gives rise in turn to frantic efforts to evade contact or intimacy, resulting in equally acute fears of isolation or abandonment. These are processes occurring in the internal world, but also with respect to other people in the external world who become ensnared in the powerful projective identifications that are the main mechanism of defence. This is the clinical situation that the therapist encounters in the transference and countertransference.

Thus, the identity of a borderline patient is under constant threat as a result of the confusion between self and other, consequent upon massive projection into others. Typically, there is an oscillation between agoraphobic anxieties where feelings of catastrophic isolation accompany any experience of separation, and claustrophobic anxieties associated with the fear of becoming fused or merged. The attempt to solve this predicament often results in a way of living, and a failure of identity development, characterized by being neither fully one thing nor another—a kind of "threshold" existence. As Henri Rey (1988) expressed it, "a group of persons [exists] who have achieved a kind of stability of personality organization in which they live a most limited and abnormal emotional life which is neither neurotic nor psychotic but a sort of frontier state". (1988, p. 203).

For these patients there is a constant oscillation of mood and affect with the result that something akin to procrastination is the only defence against going mad. These patients frequently become stuck in a grievance that cannot be given up because this would entail facing a sense of guilt. This is guilt associated with what they have done to their inner and outer objects of sustenance and affection—how they have failed or let them down. Therapy frequently uncovers a persecutory superego from which there is "escape", either in manic activity, or by occupying the place of persecutor through identification with the superego. The harsh and unremitting relation of the superego to the ego, and vice versa, allows for no psychic autonomy or freedom of mental space. As O'Shaughnessy found with one of her patients, the relationship to the therapist and to all other people may be conducted along ". . . a narrow line of confrontation, condemnation and denudation where neither of us is 'able to do it' i.e. no psychic work, let alone working through, can take place" (1999, p. 863).

In borderline states there is not the radical rupture with psychic reality that is involved in psychotic states. Relationships can *appear* to be conducted on fairly normal lines, but efforts at increased intimacy fail and emotional contact remains at best "thin". Because there is no real mental space or emotional capaciousness through which a deeper or more complex engagement can be achieved, people and relationships may have a two dimensional, "as-if" or false quality about them.

Applications of the borderline in social and welfare settings

The rabbits in the headlights

Two psychologists sit facing a crescent of ten professionals. The crescent of ten is the staff of a Group Relations Conference (Miller, 1993), a five-day experiential event that creates a temporary institution for the purpose of learning about the dynamics of organizational relationships, dynamics that typically include those between management and the workforce, as well as among small groups. The two psychologists are trainees at the Conference but are also fully qualified and experienced professionals. The ten staff are led by the Conference Director, who sits near the middle of the crescent. They have become constituted as "management" for this particular phase of the event. The two psychologists are members of one of a number of small, self-selected groups who have become positioned, *de facto*, as "the workforce". They are initially charged with finding an appropriate name for their small working group. For their part, the management team undertake all their work in public, deliberating and engaging with representatives of workforce groups as they approach "management": puzzling, arguing, and above all thinking together about the processes of which they are a part in order to understand them.

Prior to the encounter between the two psychologists and "management", there has been a long period during which management has sat alone waiting for contact with the smaller groups. A number of group representatives have subsequently approached them, either as observers or delegates. These are two of the roles available to the membership of the Conference at this point. Such roles offer only restricted opportunity for engagement, decision-making, and action. A third role is that of "plenipotentiary". This role confers full autonomy on a group member in their engagement with management. Yet, up until this point, none of the workforce groups who have made themselves known to management has sent a plenipotentiary or indeed found a name for their group. Almost without exception, delegates entering the room have brought with them one or more "observers". Just as they lack a name, it seems these groups have also lacked any purpose within the terms set by the task of the exercise—to learn about relationships and dynamics within a managed environment. They are searching for their identities, and, lacking a substantive identity, cannot name themselves.

Management has publicly puzzled and worried over this phenomenon of the absence of identity and names. It suggests that groups are having difficulty "taking up their authority" for the task. At the moment this is about all that management can learn of the "state of the system" comprising the various groups. When delegates have engaged with management, to date they have usually brought questions—asking for clarification of the task (which is available to all in writing), or asking how they can be of help to management (as though nothing can develop without an instruction or the granting of permission). Sometimes the questions seem to disguise what is in effect a complaint, usually to the effect that management has not provided clear enough statements of purpose or task.

But now, as they enter the room, the two psychologists tell the staff team that their group does have a name. It is the "Rabbits in the Headlights" group. Rather than ask questions or seek permission, the pair begin to discuss their particular group experience. They reflect that their state of mind has indeed been like rabbits caught in headlights—petrified, terrified, unable even to fight or flee. In identifying and naming their emotional experience, they have begun to free themselves from its paralysing effects. The possibility that the group might just think for itself, and then share its thoughts with management (and other groups) in pursuit of a common project of learning and development has, in this particular group, hitherto been obliterated by a terrified state of mind. The group experienced management as cruel, persecuting, and dismissive. Now, the two members say that they propose to visit other groups to share their own experience and discover what sorts of struggles these other groups may have been engaged in. They suggest they would like to return and discuss their findings with management. The Director says that he finds this an interesting project. At this point, when contact has been made, dialogue and engagement can begin.

In this experiment in group relations, one can see that without an actively thoughtful conference membership, willing to accept authority for its own experience and action, and also prepared to *relate* to management, so that they in turn can relate to the membership on the basis of shared experience, the live functioning of the whole system is in jeopardy.

For most of the duration of the processes described above it seemed to us that the prevailing state of mind of this small workforce group, perfectly captured by the name, "Rabbits in the Headlights", could plausibly be described as prevalent throughout the whole temporary institution as it existed during this phase of the Conference. Such a state of mind is borderline in character. For the membership, there is contact with the reality of the total system of which they are a part, but of a very thin and intermittent kind. At first, any capacity to reflect on group emotional experience seems absent among the membership; infrequent contacts with management are conducted on a variously suspicious, fearful, compliant, and complaining basis and there is no contact with other groups. No reality-based sense of identity can therefore take shape. For management, the experience is one of being variously "in the dark", isolated, accused, and tantalized. Under pressure from these states of mind, at some junctures, it did seem that management began to identify with, and enact, the role of a persecutory superego. For a considerable time, in this example, relationships between membership and management were conducted along the ". . . narrow line of confrontation, condemnation and denudation where neither . . . is able to 'do it'" (O'Shaughnessy, 1999, p. 863) that we cited above. Hence the whole system was temporarily ". . . lost in the domain of a terrifying superego. This terrifying superego is the reverse of an internal object that modifies anxiety—it magnifies anxiety" (*ibid.*, p. 865).

Recovery began to happen as one of the membership groups assembled the basis for ego-related functioning, represented in a capacity to think about experience, and to negotiate and mediate with management on the basis of some sense of authority and self-possession. When this state of mind emerges, it does not expel or repudiate the superego, but renders it ". . . normal, and manageable, by contrast with the "abnormal" superego which watches the ego from a "higher place", but . . . is dissociated from ego functions like attention, enquiry, remembering, understanding" (*ibid.*, p. 868).

Borderline states of mind are never wholly fixed, inevitable, static conditions in individuals, or in groups. As illustrated above through their emergence in the conference, they are an aspect of the continual, dynamic oscillations of our complex mental life. Probably none of the participants in the conference described above would merit anything like a diagnosis of borderline personality disorder, yet the evidence is that all of them, including the staff group, could be drawn towards a mode of functioning that deserves this name. Group relations conferences are artifices, constructed for the purpose of learning. But they constitute a powerful form of evidence for the proposition that unconscious forces are at work in the social sphere, producing, among other things, systems of defensive organization that are best understood by reference to our knowledge of borderline phenomena.

The colonized professional mind

So far, our clinical points of reference in exploring the idea of borderline functioning have been drawn from the two-person situation of psychoanalytic treatment. Even the complex intergroup experience discussed above relied largely on an examination of "management" relationships with "workforce" members. But in the social arena of the welfare state, the structuring of intergroup relations is usually much more intricate, and thus more psychologically and systemically challenging to understand and to work within. In the vignette below, we take a different perspective on the kinds of relationships discussed in the "rabbits in the headlights" example, introducing a third element. Our focus is the relationship between professionals, service users *and* the policy culture they also inhabit.

In a residential conference, members from five mental health trusts had been brought together for three days to work on the theme of "partnerships". About twenty people attended from each organization—chief executives, senior and middle managers, frontline practitioners (psychiatrists, nurses, social workers, occupational therapists), administrators, and several service users linked to each trust. The total membership numbered about a hundred and twenty. The work of this conference was mostly exercise and theme-based, but with considerable space for individuals to initiate workshops and discussions in a more spontaneous register. The event was not designed to explore intergroup dynamics, or to promote any particular view of how mental health work should be conducted. Its purpose was to work straightforwardly at what it declared—partnerships among the "stakeholders" in the mental health system. In this way the proceedings enacted a core principle of modern public sector organizational life—transparency of aims and processes. Of course subsidiary agendas emerged, such as rivalry between the different trusts. At one workshop, initiated by a team leader from an urban-based trust to discuss "what works well" in her organization, a subtle process of bragging for the benefit of the members and users from a rural south-western trust seemed to overtake the process. But occurrences like this are expectable, and everyday.

By the end of the conference we found ourselves rather depressed, even though there had been much energy, enthusiasm, enjoyment, and creativity in the work done. It felt churlish to admit to these negative feelings. When we reflected, it seemed possible that this underlying state of mind was connected to the seeming absence, in the minds of the participants and their transactions with one another, of any live and lively sense of users as real persons, and themselves as practitioners who drew on their own subjective resources in order to engage with the predicaments and sufferings of the users. In one session, individual trust groups compiled a case study or profile of a potential service user for one of the other trust groups to work on. To us, the profile that emerged of a service user seemed one-dimensional, as though he or she had been assembled from an off-the-peg repertoire of "issues", "problems", "events" and "diagnoses". When the group was handed a case profile produced by another group, it had the same quality. The discussion of how to respond to the case was conducted almost entirely in terms of service relationships, service functions, and the parcelling out of aspects of care among the system. Most strikingly, the vocabulary in which these profiles were assembled and analysed seemed to derive from *a procedural and policy language rather than a practice language or clinical language.*

It was as though the personhood of both the practitioners and the users had become equated with the organizational system and the policy discourses that shape it. The practitioner mind, the state of mind of the patient or user, and the policy mind seemed to be fused, almost indistinguishably, into a single entity. Although the task of the conference was to explore partnerships and not working relationships with service users, there was little intimation that the latter might be in any way shaping thinking about the former. Considered in one light, this focus on the partnership system is absolutely congruent with the requirements of modern organizational functioning in welfare. As we explore more fully in Chapter Eight, it is now the organizational network, not the stand-alone organizational unit, that is the locus of operational concern.

In the light of this, it was of note that at various plenary sessions we attended, mental health service users themselves spoke with what we experienced as real emotional conviction and thoughtfulness about themselves, their relationships with professionals, their ideas for service improvement and so on. At times, there were expressions of genuine gratitude towards professionals who had "stuck with them" through difficult and painful episodes in their lives. Equally, criticisms were voiced, although not in a hostile spirit. The emotional relatedness between professionals and users was being voiced, but it was the latter who seemed to carry all the life in the relationship. The former were pervaded by a sense of deadness. The evidence against this, and for the emotional aliveness of professionals, was only available through the accounts offered by service users of a history of emotional resilience and care by professional staff. It seemed not to be present in the here and now.

We suggest that this state of affairs can be understood in terms of a dynamic of projection and identification among various elements of a total system. A more conventional and alternative, clinically-grounded analysis might suggest that professional staff are left holding an experience of "deadness" that may belong in some part to service users, who in turn are left to be the repositories of emotional "liveliness", including contact with mental pain. However, this more conventional analysis ignores the contribution that seems to be made by *policy* and the demands of the policy culture within the total system. Here we assume that policy is an active participant, lived out in the minds of the actors in the room. In psychoanalytic terms it assumes the role of a psychic object, particularly freighted with significance and potency by its presumed origins in government. The active role played by policy seems to be contradictory. On the one hand it impels everyone towards partnership. On the other it seems to underpin a deadened and fragmentary state of mind in professionals, who cannot enter into live here-and-now relationships with service users and their painful experiences. Professionals seem to have introjected a certain message from the policy discourses, at the expense of being able to engage in potentially helpful forms of emotional contact with users. The professional staff body has difficulty in having a mind of its own that is also rooted in its *relatedness* to others—both service users and government. At least one dimension of partnership is missing from the scene.

We propose that this state of affairs reflects prevalent difficulties in the social arena of handling relationships where three or more participants are involved. A broad underlying thrust of government policy over the last decade has been to incorporate and empower the voice of service users in clinical and policy processes. At the same time, professionals have often experienced the policy culture as mistrustful and critical of their desire and need for relative professional autonomy. The progressive aspiration to counter institutionalized professional paternalism and self-promotion, and to match this with increased confidence and participation on the part of users, has been enacted through a dynamic of splitting.

We came away from this experience thinking about Winnicott's (1965) idea of the False Self and the True Self, and in particular the role of the mother or caretaker in instigating these states of being. In the passages cited below, Winnicott explores the conditions under which a capacity for genuine creativity in the baby's (and later the adult's) relationship to the world is facilitated or submerged by the early emotional caretaking environment. Crucially, he links a sense of the mother's confirmation of the infant's nascent personal autonomy with the capacity to symbolize self-experience, thus enabling the infant to *create* (as distinct from just use or borrow) a language for experience:

> The good enough mother meets the omnipotence of the infant and
> to some extent makes sense of it. She does this repeatedly. A True

Self begins to have life . . . The mother who is not good enough is not able to implement the infant's omnipotence, and so she repeatedly fails to meet the infant's gesture; instead she substitutes her own gesture which is to be given sense by the compliance of the infant. [Winnicott, 1965 p. 145]

The True Self has a spontaneity, and this has been joined up with the world's events. The infant can now begin to enjoy the *illusion* of omnipotent creating and controlling, and then can gradually come to recognize the illusory element, the fact of playing and imagining. Here is the basis for the symbol which at first is *both* the infant's spontaneity or hallucination, *and also* the external object created and ultimately cathected. [*ibid.*, p. 146]

The False Self lives in what we think of as a state of colonization by the needs and desires of the person upon whom the baby is (or was) completely dependent. It has taken the needs and demands of the other into the self, and, in Winnicott's words, "substituted" the other's idiom for its own spontaneous potentiality.

Health and welfare organizations mediate between the domain of practice and the domain of policy. They are both the principal conduit through which policy is implemented and the crucial sites of potential influence upon policy and its formation. They perform these functions to the extent that they can act as arenas wherein knowledge of lived experience at the front line of welfare can be formulated *as it arises from experience.* But for this to be effective and meaningful, an organization's membership and leadership must be capable of independence of thought and action—capable of taking authority for the transformation of practice experience into policy relevant knowledge on terms that remain reasonably faithful to that experience. This is analogous to the capacity for symbolization in the individual, something that in Winnicott's view can only develop under good enough environmental conditions. We would argue that there should be a clear point of demarcation between the arenas of practice and policy, in order that a genuine dialogue—or even contest—of ideas that are rooted in experience can take place at the boundary, or in the intermediate third area between the two.

Herein lies the analogy between Winnicott's concept of good mental health and the quality of relationships pertaining among policy makers, professionals, and users. The individual becomes capable of genuine autonomy or growth and development when she or he can confidently negotiate the intermediate area between inner and outer world, self and other, and thereby effect a *contribution* to the outside world that makes a difference, or mark, with its roots in authentic self-experience. This is impossible if the self (or the organization and its membership) are in effect already occupied and controlled by the language, assumptions and ethics of the "other". This was the state of affairs we felt we had encountered in the course of the "partnership" conference described above.

In contrast to the two examples given above, our third illustration of the potential for "borderline functioning" in contemporary welfare practice comes from discussion of individual practitioners describing particular pieces of work with clients.

Stranded

During a radio interview a school mentor described her support of an adolescent boy who had been repeatedly excluded from school. The boy, also interviewed, described how one of his siblings was in prison. He also spoke about how difficult and complicated he found his family and school life. They both attested to the strength of emotional contact between them, the one enjoying her work and the other being excluded far less regularly. After a few months and at precisely the time the boy joined another school, the mentor had said with conviction, "We must draw this work to an end because we do not want to expose him to dependency."

Touchingly, the mentor concluded her interview by saying, "Only time will tell how I will manage my feelings of having to finish my work with this boy." Perhaps her anticipated feelings reflected a thought that she might be engaged in a retreat from her young charge, not an ending. The pervasive conviction that dependency is by definition prejudicial to the social and emotional well-being of those we support in practice (Hoggett, 2000) creates the very conditions in which systems of care are driven by anxieties aroused by closeness and the associated feelings of love and hate. It was distressing to hear the young boy concurring in the interview, poignantly adding, "I hope I shall be all right".

Neither the boy nor the mentor could be described diagnostically as borderline. But in the flight from dependency something borderline is established in the system of which they are both a part. Anthony Bateman (1991), writing about borderline personality disorder, says

> . . . such a state of mind leads borderline patients to make fleeting contact with themselves and others, only to find that such an experience is so unbearably anxiety-arousing as to require a massive retreat . . . Clinically, such an internal state of affairs may be represented by a borderline patient who begins a relationship with someone only to find that contact arouses such powerful feelings of dependency and need that retreat becomes necessary to ensure feelings of survival. [Bateman, 1991, pp. 342–343]

By commenting in this way, we do not intend any criticism of the mentor, but hope to draw attention to how a conviction about "dependency" can create a valency in systems of care that reproduces two of the basic characteristics of borderline states of mind: fear of closeness, and an oscillation between seeking intimacy and then retreating from it.

Indeed, one of us recalls supervising a social worker several years ago who was leaving his post and ending five years of work with a schizophrenic man. At the last meeting, the client asked if he would visit from time to time. On being told that this would not be possible, he said "Will you send a postcard, or write then?" The social worker agreed, but reported in supervision that this had felt like a "capitulation". In discussion it emerged that the worker had been gripped by a conviction that he must "maintain boundaries" and that to continue any kind of relationship with the client might compromise his successor in their efforts to establish a new professional relationship. The supervisor encountered this colleague again recently. In discussing past experiences, the social worker mentioned that he had never written to his client and was left with a residue of guilt.

Borderline states of mind mobilize primitive thought processes of an extreme either/or kind. They have the quality that Melanie Klein (1946) described as "paranoid–schizoid" thinking, in which circumstances and people are conceived of as entirely good or bad. The scope for negotiation, freedom of thought and considered risk-taking becomes narrow to the point of disappearance. This situation is illustrated by a woman who came for therapy suffering particularly with these kinds of difficulties. Not long before her rather premature decision to terminate her therapy, she came to a session having taken the underground train. The train had come to a halt for some minutes at a station *en route* to where she was due to see her therapist. Another train going in the same direction arrived at the adjacent platform, so she got off her train and started to cross the platform, but then became anxious that the one she had left might now depart first. She became frozen, standing on the platform unable to decide which train to take. To her therapist, this image encapsulated how she often felt as though she was forced to live within a rather narrow emotional range, for fear of the consequences of deeper emotional engagement within existing relationships that were in fact available to her. This particular episode was no doubt closely associated with anxiety and disappointment linked to the impending separation from her therapist.

Underlying the thought processes that organize these rigid and potentially paralysing states of mind there are usually intolerable fears about separation, the terror of loss, and fear and denial of the anger that any separation may arouse. The paradox of this situation is that an opportunity to express rage and fear and still witness the loved person's survival can release all concerned from the grip of the borderline condition. The ability to freely hate the abandoning object is a precondition for being able to experience true separateness from it, and then mourn its loss. Through this, a real capacity for psychic autonomy can be developed, in which dependency on others is not opposed by the terror of engulfment or abandonment by them.

Our final example is not an illustration from the world of psychotherapy, group relations or welfare practice. Instead, we draw on research into the more ordinary, less specialized world of the mother–infant relationship.

The world of the infant and the world of welfare

In the decades after the founding of the modern welfare state in Britain, most professionals were schooled in a point of view that, though paternalistic in many respects, still emphasized the autonomy and self-determination of the client, the best interests of the patient, the specific needs of the tenant, and so on. Notwithstanding the very real problems of professional self-interest and protection-ism, health and welfare services were always to be there *for* the patient, the user. An ethos of public service informed the founding principles of the welfare state. But there was another, less well recognized feature of how welfare was implicitly conceived. We are thinking of a different connotation of the concept of "using" ser-vices. This is one in which the recipient is active in the sense that they bring to the service transaction a manifold range of hopes, conflicts, anxieties, material and perhaps psychological deficits and demands, and then establish a living engagement with welfare services in a manner that is shaped by these states of mind. The user makes a direct and unmediated *impact* upon the doctor, nurse, social worker, or housing officer because this is what they seek and need to do. Welfare work can then take place in the arena created by this impact, and by the nature of the practitioner's response to it.

In his research into different patterns of emotional and commu-nicative response observed in the relationships between several mothers and their developing infants, Stephen Briggs (1996) des-cribes how some mothers demonstrate a "concave" pattern in which they seem to shape themselves around the emotional and physical needs of their baby, allowing him or her to communicate states of mind and body in a full and rounded way. Others, how-ever, seem to meet their infant's neediness and distress with a more mechanical, routinized, or emotionally "flat" response. Still others are observed to actively organize their responses more on the basis of their own needs, routines, and emotional states. Briggs suggests they effectively push these needs into the baby, making for a pattern he names "convex". In the first concave pattern, the moth-ers are not emotionally or mentally passive, but their activity is stimulated and led by that of their child.

As a template for one image of welfare, this is a suggestive metaphor. What quality and depth of emotional and practical engagement is created in the welfare relationship, and who origi-nates its terms? If welfare provision is conceived of as being there to be *used* in the sense described above, because people have complex and often inchoate predicaments that need an arena in which they can be thought about, and then worked through, this in turn requires service providers to be available to engage in such transactions. Such work is demanding. Providers and professionals have to be protected from too much unhelpful intrusion and inter-ference. Above all they have to *believe* that they are trusted, so that they *feel* trusted to do their jobs.

We might think that the space or arena in which such transac-tions occur constitutes a kind of protected space, an "internal world" of welfare activity, just as the relationship between infant and mother creates the conditions in which the internal world of the growing child is formed. In welfare this is, or should be, a place where sensitive, private, complex, ambiguous, and perhaps shame-ful matters are negotiated, thought about, and acted upon. Obvi-ously this should be in a way that relates to the "external world" of policy, procedure, service organization, and so on, but it should not be dominated or intruded upon by this world more than is absolutely necessary. It is possible to think about the conception and implementation of welfare in this way, from the most mundane and local of transactions through to how we understand the ulti-mate aims of grand policy reforms and transformations of struc-ture. Looked at this way, the object of welfare is to make available resources (education, mental health services, fostering, well woman clinics, housing stock, and so on) with which people can engage in a manner that enables them to effect transformation in their circum-stances, because the impact of their needs and demands is taken in, recognized, metabolized and respected.

The external and internal worlds of welfare

We have shown how, in psychoanalytic theory, borderline states of mind are largely conceptualized as a matter of intrapsychic dynam-ics. They are underpinned by a set of defensive processes found in individuals who are managing particular kinds of intolerable anxi-ety. We have subsequently alluded to examples that show how, inevitably, this state of affairs is never confined to just the inner world. We continually emphasize the idea of relatedness not simply because our main theme concerns welfare—an aspect of social life that cannot be discussed without attention to the nature of rela-tionships. More importantly, as we have tried to show, intrapsychic worlds play a crucial part in shaping qualities of "relatedness" between people. Additionally, social systems take on a life of their own that is partly a product of the intrapsychic and interpsychic potential of the people who constitute the system. However, once the system has assumed a dynamic pattern of its own, it then shapes the psychic possibilities for individuals and smaller groups within its boundaries. Because we do not theorize cultural and social phenomena such as language, ideology, and discourse as belonging to an entirely separate realm from that of individual and small group psychic life, we also think of these dimensions of social life as psychic objects. They form part of the continual weft and warp of the construction and deconstruction of social processes.

There are many ways of conceptualizing the different arenas or sites of activity in the welfare state: organizational units such as schools or hospitals, multi-agency networks, local communities, professional associations, research centres, and centres of political power such as local authorities. None of these, from the smallest to the greatest, functions in isolation. Each is a system touching upon many other systems, in relations of reciprocal if not symmetrical influence. But arguably, to function effectively and creatively, each system must have a boundary, a "skin" that is both sensitive to the pressure of external influence and strong enough to protect the internal relationships and life of the system. Without this, we propose that one of the central features of the borderline state of mind is more difficult to defend against. This is the fear of loss of a separate and secure identity. As we have noted, in borderline functioning, the fear attendant upon potential psychological separateness is managed by projecting aspects of the self into another person. This happens intrapsychically, but also interpersonally. It can give rise to extreme difficulty in knowing the difference between "self" and "other". One of the main—and paradoxical—sources of the characteristic borderline terror of loss of identity, or of abandonment, is found here in this lack of psychic differentiation.

In Chapter Eight of this book we look at some of the contemporary social changes that are affecting organizational life. We argue that these mean it is now much harder to know how to maintain organizational identity. This is a hugely significant challenge, not only for modern welfare, but perhaps also in our contemporary personal relationships as well. For the moment, we want simply to note that central to our overall analysis are questions about how our welfare systems maintain the capacity for an *internal life*, and the conditions to support it. Such a life is both autonomous and appropriately related to the life of other systems. When we refer to the "internal world of welfare" we are therefore referring to this specific internal life or inner world, and its relationship with external realities. The capacity to sustain modes of functioning that are flexible and creative, rather than rigid, fearful, or borderline, resides in the quality of this relationship between the inner world of welfare and the external realities governing it.

In contemporary organizational life, the moves towards networked relations, working in partnerships, integrating policy initiatives across different professional fields and maintaining "joined-up working" can reflect genuinely progressive developmental aspirations. But they also constitute massive challenges to our ability to simply go on functioning as practitioners and managers. These contemporary organizational changes were alluded to in the Introduction to the book through our concept of two "structures of feeling" organizing the conceptualization, experience and forms of relating characteristic of modern welfare. We suggested that the first of these structures, described as a "contained and compartmentalized" post-war settlement, was characterized by the hiving off of social and personal ills and the enclosure of these within the professionalized world of welfare. The second, more contemporary, structure of feeling was described as being characterized by centralized governance, accompanied by loss of faith in traditional professional practice and also by the initiation of public–private partnerships, organized by quasi market mechanisms. We do not intend these categories of two structures of feeling to be taken as absolutes, but as a way of framing an underlying trend that raises important questions about how to sustain the inner life of professional practice.

In the remainder of this chapter, we review the work of a number of other authors who have used psychoanalytic thought in the effort to illuminate aspects of contemporary welfare practice and policy. We then discuss authors who introduce social theory that explains the origins of the broader social trends that make sense of the phenomenon we are calling borderline welfare. The review is deliberately selective. It focuses on work that we hope will resonate with the themes developed so far in the book, and will inform and enrich readers' engagement with later chapters.

States of weakness

Because self-esteem is fragile, injury to our self-esteem or narcissism can breed its own particular forms of virulence. This creates a further variety of the borderline state that is more sinister. In his paper, "Primitive mind of state", David Bell (1997) maps the close parallel between certain "structures of feeling" found in people who violently repudiate their weakness and vulnerability, and the ideologies informing the "marketization" of welfare from the late 1980s. Bell notes how earlier theorists, such as Wilhelm Reich, tried to expose the latent roots of organized fascism in all of us:

> Reich explored how, through identification with a tyrannical (Nazi) figure, masses of the oppressed population were supported in their wish to project their own hated vulnerability elsewhere. The Nazi propaganda machine provided objects for this projection, namely Jews, gypsies, homosexuals and blacks. [Bell, 1997 p. 49]

Bell links his clinical experience of this more virulent form of the borderline state to his perception of the ideological and material transformations that the NHS was undergoing from the late 1980s. He continues:

> . . . in the course of working with patients suffering from profound narcissistic disturbances . . . I gradually became aware of the workings of what I can best describe as a sort of *internal* propaganda machine that held the patient in its thrall. It was as though any ordinary wish for help and understanding was quickly attacked and suppressed—admitting dependency was tantamount to a crime. These patients use words such as "whingeing", "spineless", "wimps", to describe people in their lives who were expressing any need . . . The more I listened the more I became aware that the language used bore striking resemblances to the language of ultra-Right propaganda attacks on welfare-ism. [*ibid.*, p. 50]

Bell is delineating a territory of absolutes, of primitive categories of good and bad, right and wrong, of blame, punishment, and scapegoating. This is a psychic world in which there is no emotional and moral complexity and hence no depth. In this state of mind, or "mind of state", the real and painful tensions which ordinary welfare policy and practice might expect to have to engage with can be disavowed. People can be constructed in one-dimensional terms; for example, as either demanding, irresponsible, and feckless, or as autonomous, self-sufficient, and strong.

Jessica Evans (2003) presents one study of some of the processes by which, in the name of "welfare", government and policy makers may contribute to conditions in which extreme, borderline states of mind are mobilized. She looks at the eruption of a local vigilante movement—that of the residents of the Paulsgrove estate in Portsmouth, who were campaigning for "Sarah's law". Following the death of eight-year-old Sarah Payne, who had been abducted and killed, and closely modelled upon the US campaign for "Megan's law", this short-lived protest movement sought to establish the rights of parents in local communities to have access to information about the location and identities of listed sex offenders. Evans argues that a rhetoric of "purified" communities can become established when there is a policy context in which government seeks to locate responsibility for crime prevention with local communities, while retaining responsibility for the monitoring and punishment of offenders.

In her paper, Evans reveals the complex interactions occurring between the vulnerable, anxious, but also powerfully projective states of mind of those leading the vigilante movement: the representation of paedophiles and their treatment found in the mass media, and the ideological conditions established by governmental crime policy. These interactions produced what she calls a "quasi-psychotic episode" within a particular community, an episode that occurred in the name of "welfare" (the welfare, supposedly, of the children in that community). Evans draws attention to the psychic circumstances surrounding the protest:

> But what are communities supposed to *do with* knowledge that is presented to them in the spirit of the co-production of community safety? . . . Those taking a psychoanalytic approach will be bound to point out that this question cannot be satisfactorily answered without paying attention . . . to what community members *feel about* this knowledge. [2003, p. 181]

The example of the Paulsgrove estate protesters provides a good illustration of a central idea we are advancing: that welfare is always organized and produced through definite if complex and ambivalent structures of feeling. The borderline is a domain governed by the intense need to *simplify* these structures, and to eliminate uncertainty.

Michael Rustin (2001) draws on very similar material to that in the example above when he writes about child psychotherapists[1] working in the public sector who have identified borderline patterns of behaviour in social service institutions caring for children. The psychotherapists found practices in which ". . . they encountered a surprising but symptomatic mindlessness":

> It is not that the social services department or caseworkers concerned were callous or indifferent—this was not the case. It was the diffuse awareness of the pain being suffered by these children and families, and the difficulties of processing it in the mind, that gave rise to these structures of defence. Just as psychoanalytic psychotherapists have to be able to introject very distressed and painful states of mind in their patients before they are able to help them recognise and reflect on them, so in institutions, acknowledging the extent of mental pain and anxiety, and bearing some of its costs, are a precondition for bringing about more responsive practices. [Rustin, 2001, p. 131]

Rustin introduces these observations in the context of a broader analysis of the possible links between borderline states of mind and social or political processes. These include, at their extreme, a

> . . . gangster or Nazi solution to the pressures of extreme anxiety. All weakness and evil is expelled into stigmatised objects, while the self narcissistically identifies with an omnipotent and idealized object, whose essence is violent and cruel. [*ibid.*, p. 129]

This is strong stuff, but we would suggest, *pace* the writing of David Bell, that the intolerance of suffering, weakness, dependency, and failure in our own selves may be the outcome of a deep sense of injury sustained to our self-esteem. In the welfare sector, this may be severe and ongoing injury to a sense of a professional "caring" ethic. We are suggesting that just as people may turn on their own internal sense of weakness or vulnerability and repudiate it, it may be possible for professionals to deny their clients' needs, and to turn upon their own associated sense of pain and fear, when they have experienced their own efforts to help being severely attacked and repudiated.

Structures of feeling and paradigms of policy

The concept of the borderline is specific to psychoanalytic psychotherapy—it is first and foremost a clinical concept. Can it intersect with more conventional ways of thinking about social policy and political processes?

Psychoanalysis is *par excellence* a "depth psychology". This is because of the philosophical assumptions it makes about the deep structures underpinning psychic and social reality, and because of its clinical aim of helping people engage with their emotional, cognitive, and moral depths. Borderline mental functioning is characterized by a retreat from engagement with mental pain in favour of a life lived in the emotional shallows. One does not have to search far in the contemporary sociological canon to find analyses of social trends that resonate powerfully with this aspect of the borderline state of mind.

A variety of social theorists have remarked upon the trend in modern social and cultural life away from "depth"—or more accurately, from recognition of the distinction between surface and depth. Different thinkers attribute different meanings and causes to this trend, and also valorize it differentially. But there is an important convergence in the work of writers as disparate as Frederic Jameson (1991), Deborah Harvey (1990), Francois Lyotard (1984) and Jacques Baudrillard (1988). They all describe the emergence in the later decades of the twentieth century of forms and conceptualizations of social life that announce the dissolution of any necessary connection between surface and depth, representation and reality, language and the world, identity and biography, history and future. Such forms and conceptualizations in turn contribute to the way life is concretely lived and experienced. In Jameson's and Harvey's work this trend is largely represented as philosophically mistaken and politically regressive. For Lyotard and Baudrillard, these trends are partially celebrated, as a form of emancipation from the constraining frameworks of "modernist" thought and social practice.

The modernist project, which includes psychoanalysis, is concerned with interrogating surfaces and appearances through the power of reason, and hence debunking received ideas and fixed ways of seeing. This applies to modernist projects in the realms of the psychological, the social, the scientific and the cultural. In this sense psychoanalysis has always been associated with emancipatory aims and with a commitment to the possibility of truth or at least a nearer approach to realms of truth.

But the deep structures that are the objects of modernist enquiry—whether in the physical world, the psyche, or society—may also constitute limitations for human possibility. If this is so, then "anything goes" may not be a defensible stance either morally or practically. Modernism may have involved, as Michael Rustin (2001) observes, "its own austerity and dogmatism". However, writers such as Jameson and Lyotard divide on the question of whether this justifies an outright abandonment of any recognition of such limits, philosophically, or politically, or morally. The central question for these social theorists concerns how far the liberating possibilities of human knowledge can be extended without loss of contact with a knowable "reality". In our own methodological discussion in Chapter Ten, we articulate a philosophical position that remains committed to the presence in psychic and social life of both surfaces and depths. We suggest, with Bion (1976), that psychoanalysis provides us with unique and distinctive tools for accessing certain kinds of reality, namely unconscious processes. But equally we are cautious about claiming that these layers, or domains, have an absolute or privileged role in shaping the nature of the complex social totalities that are our object of investigation in this book.

Frederic Jameson's (1991) account of the postmodern sensibility sees it as produced in association with the globalization of capitalism, a distinctive phase in the development of world socioeconomic relations. The postmodern sensibility serves the ends of this development. This view is important for the argument of the present book, because when called upon to ultimately explain contemporary trends in welfare state development, we refer to the penetration of the welfare sector by the demands and logic of modern capitalism (and this is further discussed in Chapter Three). As we note in Chapter One, psychoanalytic ideas can be used to illuminate the weakening of the boundaries of an original social welfare container, formed by the conditions of establishment of the post 1945 welfare state. Thus, at various junctures we suggest that the post-war welfare state was established in large part as a social defence *against* the incursions and vagaries of the market.

In the contemporary social climate, there are specific characteristics of the postmodern sensibility that are generated by late capitalism. Waters (1994) neatly summarizes these:

> The postmodern culture which focuses the mind on the centrality of global space, and dislocates individuals from the realities of their own situations, has four characteristics:
>
> It is "depthless" (i.e. "what you see is what you get"). Cultural products have no intensity and no emotion behind them because they are decentred from the people who produce them. They are merely consumable images.
>
> It is ahistorical and immediate. It provides no reference back to previous human suffering and struggle. Transitions can be "mixed and matched" in pastiche rather than drawn upon or resisted.
>
> It is timeless. It focuses on the organization of cultural meaning in space. The time-relationship of these fragments is not signified externally but has to be reconstituted internally by the individual actor.
>
> It conceives of the world as a technological entity rather than as a natural one, as a computer network rather than an ecological balance. [Waters, 1994, p. 207]

Depthless and emotionless, ahistorical and non-developmental, timeless and technocratic. This is a stark vision, notwithstanding any liberatory potential that might be implied. There is a congruence between Jameson's formulation of the qualitative shift in social and cultural relations under "late capitalism", together with Waters' characterization of the "postmodern" social and cultural response it gives rise to, and some of the characteristics of contemporary welfare policy discourse and practice we have nominated as borderline. Yet it is important to recognize that there were oppressive and delimiting features of the earlier modernist project, features that postmodernism is, in one guise, an attempt to surmount. Thus, in this context of considerable complexity, borderline states of mind may even be understood in part as a sensible retreat. They occur in the face of potentially overwhelming emotional and psychic risk and uncertainty. This is a retreat from the exigencies of *thinking*, in the face of near-unbearable complexity, mystery and doubt about the status of the present and the future.

One argument of this book is that the project of social welfare has become more complex over the last thirty years. This is in part because of the dissolution of the old certainties that founded and sustained the original welfare state. While these certainties provided a container within which welfare activity and thought could be safely conducted, they also functioned as a constraining framework. They perpetuated silences, exclusions, and marginalizations with respect to certain social groups and certain states of mind or behaviours troubling to the status quo. If our contemporary sense is simply that a secure container has been breached by the invaders of market diversity and managerialism, we risk ignoring the host of other challenges to the "safe" universalist assumptions of the founding contract for welfare as it arose in the mid twentieth century. The rise of new social movements, of an organized and vital politics of diversity, the explosion of awareness of widespread child sexual abuse—these and more cannot be lamented as the unfortunate consequence of an attack upon universal public sector welfare in the Thatcher–Major years. In themselves, such social changes constitute a widening and deepening of the challenge to the old order of welfare. This is a challenge largely independent of trends in the political economy of welfare enacted since 1979, although it may be historically entangled with them.

Lyn Froggett's work (2002) is the most ambitious attempt to give real substance to the congruence between psychoanalytic frameworks of theory and the development of welfare policy in Britain. She identifies four "ideal-type" models, or "positions", of welfare. All of these have been implemented and valorized in some measure since the origin of the British welfare state. They are: "old" (or paternalistic and statist) welfare; "no" (or privatised, competitive, market-governed) welfare; "mixed" (or consumerist, contractual, stakeholder) welfare; and finally, an emergent or aspirant state, "beyond welfare". Froggett takes as her project the understanding of the ". . . social relations, cultural meanings and institutional structures" of these different forms of welfare, ". . . from the perspective of mental states 'or positions'" (*ibid.*, p. 24). For her, there are characteristic associations between these different welfare models and particular relationships of attachment and separation. She discusses these, using Kleinian terms, as "paranoid–schizoid" and "depressive" patterns of functioning. Any of the welfare "positions" can constitute conditions for the encouragement and elaboration of particular characteristic states of mind. Each of the positions is in turn supported or nourished by these states of mind. The characteristics of any position shape processes at all levels—the private and intrapsychic, the interpersonal, the organizational, and the socio-political. In line with our own position, Froggett consistently tries to evade any suggestion that these welfare forms "reduce to" or are finally explained by a psychodynamic deep structure: ". . . it is difficult to see why one or other level of social analysis should be underprivileged in the consideration of systems which penetrate areas of life as intimate as birth, death, suffering and care" (*ibid.*, p. 18).

Her work, and the present book, raise important questions about how we can develop an adequate philosophical and methodological strategy for studying welfare in its psycho-social complexity; a strategy that mediates between the idealization of surfaces and relativist assumptions, while eschewing the dogma of explanatory frameworks that assign ultimate priority to deep structures, or depths.

Conclusion

In summary, we propose there is an *inherent* tension between depth and surface, or depth and shallowness, in all manifestations of welfare at all its levels. Psychoanalytic thinking is especially well placed to illuminate such connections. As local and historically specific forms of welfare delivery intersect with this tension differentially, they support or discourage the capacity to maintain depth engagements. Additionally, there are global socio-economic trends acting on nation states and their populations. These may evoke social anxieties to which thin cultural responses in welfare activity are an understandable response; equally they may encourage and enable more thickly-textured varieties of engagement. The present book is devoted therefore, to illuminating a particular state of affairs, a structure of feeling that has arisen under definite, and surely temporary, conditions. In so far that we wish the book to be received as an intervention, rather than just a commentary, we hope it may assist a process of developmental struggle in the overall welfare project.

Note

1. The title and the broad concept for the present book originated while one of the authors was listening to Janet Philps, one of the child psychotherapists referred to, presenting her research into borderline states in the professional and family systems surrounding children looked after in temporary placements outside their families of origin. We are grateful to her for her inspiration. (See Philps, 2003.)

CHAPTER THREE

The state of mind we're in: sincerity, anxiety, and the audit society

Introduction

In Chapter One we proposed that relationships within the welfare state, and between the welfare state and other sectors of society, are conducted within a new "structure of feeling" that has replaced the climate of assumptions, values and practices that organized the post-war consensus about social welfare in Britain. The advent of the "audit society" is perhaps the most powerful and pervasive manifestation of this transformation. "Audit" is an instrument for acquiring a certain kind of knowledge and, as we have suggested, it is how society chooses to relate to the evidence for unwelcome and disturbing aspects of social life that underpins the quality of welfare engagements and relationships it promotes. The instruments through which knowledge is gathered and assessed directly affect the depth and scope of what comes to be known, and the minds of those doing the knowing. This chapter explores how our characteristic states of mind have been subject to a process of social transformation that shapes our possibilities for depth knowledge in modern welfare.

There is only good news

The collective states of mind associated with the "audit explosion" (Power, 1994) have taken hold of our society with extraordinary rapidity, and are embodied in extensive and very expensive public institutions and practices, which have themselves been introduced without public debate or analysis, or even very much public awareness (Rustin, 2004). Michael Power captures something vital about the meaning of these developments when he says,

> It is undoubtedly a sign of the times that an accountant with financial auditing experience might have something to say about the field of psychotherapy. Accountants may require therapy and psychotherapists probably need good tax advice, but the fields themselves have, until relatively recently, had little to do with each other. [1999, p. 23]

But this intersection of unfamiliar practices is not limited to psychotherapy. Peter Preston has referred more colourfully to how we now

> live in a relentlessly superintended world, a quangoed regime of commissioners, inspectors, and regulators doing the things that governments themselves aren't so keen on. That has always been the British way, perhaps, but it has come to seem the only way since the Thatcher and Major privatisations, all of them accompanied by new offices of invigilation with academic luminaries or ex-civil servants in charge. [Preston, 2000]

The introduction of clinical governance in the NHS, the role of the Quality Assurance Agency for Higher Education (QAAHE) in the university sector, and of the Office for Standards in Education (OFSTED) in the lives of everyone who is a parent or child, mean that almost no one is unaffected by the culture of which Peter Preston writes. In one respect these institutions are evidence of a dedicated effort at ethical and political renewal in the public realm. Setting and maintaining standards, and improving quality and equity of service delivery in publicly funded institutions, are their overt primary tasks. But, as with the other cultures of policy we examine in this book, beyond the rational and surface presentation of the audit phenomenon there are complex and experientially disturbing forces at work. In particular, we suggest that the audit society is characterized by a "structure of illusion", which serves to manage the relationship between the complex, thickly textured nature of everyday welfare activity and the imperatives of policy and political processes. This structure of illusion might be likened to a compromise formation, an over-determined system of meanings and behaviours that, like psychological symptoms, serve to maintain a precarious equilibrium of competing and conflicting forces at work in the mind—or in the social arena.

We propose that this structure of illusion is the product of a number of interlocking forces and developments at work in modern social life. First, we note the escalation of social and political anxiety about the dangers, or risks, inherent to the welfare task and the political consequences of accountability for such risks. Second, we note the retreat by government from the exercise of traditional means of governing in large areas of the welfare state, and their replacement by systems of regulation, inspection, monitoring, and audit—the characteristic practice of what is now known as governance. Third, in a context of under-funded services and increasing demand, an imperative arises to push responsibility for quality and governance downwards in order to locate accountability for "failure" outside the sphere of government. But, fourth, because the consequences of alleged (or actual) failure are believed to be so catastrophic for both government and service providers, a complex dance ensues between the two parties designed to produce illusions of success. Under these circumstances there can arise a pressure to produce only good news, and a loss of contact with the complex, messy, uncertain nature of welfare realities. A central danger of this state of affairs is that propaganda and crude forms of ideological management of reality make their appearance as substitutes for sober engagement with uncomfortable truths.

In summary, the story unfolds as follows. The retreat by government in the 1980s and 1990s from direct responsibility for a wide range of social provision led to the emergence of forms of discipline, ordering, and surveillance that have a noticeably irrational character. The retreat by traditional government was associated on the one hand with policies designed to facilitate a more "mixed economy" of care, but also with the apparent failure of traditional forms of professional regulation and self-regulation. Serious mistakes, oversights, failures of accountability, and cover-ups were revealed, and our trust in traditional forms of social trust was shattered. Where would the next disaster appear? Who would be to blame, or at any rate blamed? Could society stand the prospect of so much guilt, failure, and knowledge of fallibility circulating in its midst? Our contention is that a widespread culture of control sprang into being to deal with this predicament. We address this less as a political concern and more as a moral and philosophical one, because it appears that important principles of truth, meaning, and authenticity are in danger of being sacrificed in order to reassure the critical "superintendents" that we are in fact "doing it right" and won't make the same mistakes again. We try to illuminate this collective state of mind in various ways, which include making use of clinical material from psychotherapeutic work.

We hope our discussion will reveal that this state of mind is not just about being *subjected* to something unpleasant in this new inspectorial order. We are all to one degree or another implicated in the collective state of mind we want to discuss; at the political level we are implicated in its emergence by virtue of our activity or passivity as citizens. Our thesis is slightly different from Peter Preston's, since we hold that less that government has merely hived off an unwelcome aspect of its task to the audit and regulation industry, but rather that the latter has actually *replaced* government in those social spaces that, since the advent of privatization and marketization, government itself has abandoned. Thus, the question posed so starkly by these developments is; can we do without government? And therefore, what exactly *is* government, as distinct from bureaucracy, regulation, law, or social order? The first welfare settlement, of which we spoke in our introduction to this book, was sustained by its own characteristic structures of illusion. Here, we try to explicate the character of their successors.

Government, surveillance, and anxiety: two vignettes

We want to embark on our analysis by presenting two seemingly unrelated fragments of experience. What links them is the idea of a pervasive, scrutinizing faculty of mind that can be observed at work both within individuals and within social arrangements. The question explored in this chapter concerns the different qualities of overall mental and social functioning that may be generated by different characteristic forms of such scrutiny.

The panopticon

For a time we undertook a regular consultation with the Staff Development Team of a Home Counties Social Services Department. This is a large county, and we met in two different locations. One of them was a Social Services Training Centre situated in a semi-rural location at the edge of a large town. Before we first went there we were told that it had been an asylum, but it was only after several visits that we realized that this charming redbrick building was built on the nineteenth-century "panopticon" principle, with three small wings radiating out from what would once have been a central observation tower, from which a warder or superintendent could in principle observe all inmates of the asylum with a single sweeping gaze. This is the classic nineteenth-century design for prisons and asylums, originated by Jeremy Bentham and much discussed by the French philosopher Michel Foucault (1977) as the defining symbol of modernity's desire for an omnipotent capacity for surveillance. Foucault links the development of the panopticon to the forms of social discipline that arose in the nineteenth century to manage the effects of plague. The imperative to isolate, register, control, and order the movement and condition of sick individuals within the general population is contrasted by him with the social response to leprosy in which a division between the sick and the well is effected by a process of exclusion, confinement or exile.

> If it is true that the leper gave rise to rituals of exclusion, (which to a certain extent provided the model for and general form of the great Confinement) then the plague gave rise to disciplinary projects. Rather than the massive, binary division between one set of people and another, it called for multiple separations, individualising distributions, an organization in depth of surveillance and control, an intensification and a ramification of power . . . The exile of the leper and the arrest of the plague do not bring with them the same political dream. The first is that of a pure community, the second that of a disciplined society. [Foucault, 1977, p. 198]

Foucault is not always explicit about this, but here he is recognizably describing two different forms of defence against anxieties about contamination, contagion, and destruction. His analysis is as applicable at the level of social fantasy and the construction of social defences against anxiety about collective psychic experience as it is to the understanding of disease control.

The watcher and the watched

Our second vignette concerns the psychotherapy patient discussed in more depth later in the chapter. In the early weeks of the therapist's work with this man, the former would arrive at his consulting room a few minutes in advance of the beginning of his sessions, and would notice the patient sitting and waiting in his car. Often he was positioned so that he was facing away from the entrance used by the therapist, but equally so that he could, the therapist believed, observe this entry using his wing mirror. It did not take long for a powerful fantasy to take root in the therapist that the patient was observing him carefully while seeming not to do so. Moreover, now that he had observed the patient (as he thought) observing him while seeming not to, the question arose in his mind of whether the patient might wonder whether his therapist had observed him observing the therapist. Through this thought process the therapist gained some insight into how maddened this patient might feel at some level, and how maddening he might become, if he was not able to make some use of the experience just described. The therapist's experience, and by inference the patient's, is of having lost any solid ground on which to stand in relation to questions of knowledge: how we know what we know, who knows what about whom, and how? Why should we trust what we believe to be knowledge, and so on. It is a situation of profound epistemological anxiety. During his treatment, the therapist came to believe that this arose from a crisis of authority in the patient, an internal state of affairs in which he ceaselessly undermined his relationship to the good internal parental objects that were capable of authorizing a capacity for truthfulness.

We believe the same kind of epistemological anxieties are generated within our superintended welfare and health culture, and we want to explore whether these are also related to a crisis of authority. In the patient, in the welfare culture we are investigating, and in Foucault's disciplinary regime, we find a need for unending watchfulness or vigilance. The question in all cases is; what requires this degree of extreme, anxious, and continual observation?

Vacating social space

Part of the answer is suggested by the following experience. When one of us presented an earlier version of these thoughts to a psychotherapeutic society, a therapist who consults regularly to a special hospital for mentally ill offenders related how the government had just given this institution £25 million to build a second security wall round the existing one. The only problem with this was that nobody had ever escaped from this hospital; the first wall has never been breached. Most people inside don't even want to escape, he commented, or at least if they do it is into some part of their own mind, not the external world. The story suggests that we may be afflicted by social anxieties that if we are not intensely watchful, *then something very dangerous will escape and do terrible damage.* How has this state of mind arisen?

We live in an age of small government, in which responsibility for welfare now rests with a range of public, independent, and private organizations whose structural ties to wider society, state, and democratic and political processes, is weak by comparison with the network of strong "intermediate institutions" based in the workplace—trade unions, local government, community and professional organizations—that mediated relations between the state and civil society until they were swept away by the Thatcher revolution (Hutton, 1996). Political authority, and the system of values and relationships upon which political authority rests, no longer works to organize this domain in the way it once did. In education, social care, health, it has been replaced by the vast and complex system of regulation, inspection, performance management, and audit, which has bred the new quasi-profession of auditors, regulators, and inspectors to administer and manage it. These social spaces and the institutions that occupy them—schools, hospitals, universities, residential homes, and so on—have been largely freed from traditional forms of political accountability and loyalty.

This was a conscious and deliberate political project on the part of the Conservative administration that first came to power in 1979. But we suggest it also had unintended consequences. It exposed society to deep anxieties about how these social spaces should be governed, and what kinds of events and processes might happen within them, anxieties (and realities) that needed a new form of governance. As traditional forms of political and cultural authority were vanquished, an unpredictable state of affairs was revealed in which undisciplined spontaneous activity might flourish outside the boundaries of earlier forms of social regulation, whether for good or ill. The fear that it might be more for ill than good gave rise to the culture of anxious regulation.

In the mixed economy of welfare, where government once willed the means to provide for needs, now it tends to prescribe the ends while others are increasingly left to supply the means, and of course these people must be watched, regulated; and, as with all instrumentally orientated practices, the logic governing the attainment of these ends is the logic of rules. In short, where government was, now regulation, inspection, performance management, audit, and quality assurance is found in its place. The retreat by the state from its traditional role in directly funding and delivering welfare has created a new set of social conditions and possibilities. These simultaneously constitute a *threat to government* and a site of potential *creativity in welfare*. It is this necessary relationship between the potential for disaster and failure and the potential for creativity that has gone unnoticed; of how fear of disaster and failure has led to a culture that threatens creativity and, as we shall argue, of authenticity in the relations between practice and policy.

Professional judgement, the exercise of discriminating powers of decision-making by trained staff, *was* one important means by which *self*-regulation traditionally occurred in the spaces of the welfare state, but this was thrown into question in the 1980s as the logic of increased demands for public accountability joined forces with the neo-liberal assault on vested social interests, including professional interests, that might obstruct the expansion of market forces into the welfare arena. The exercise of autonomous professional judgement is closely tied to the management of risk and the management of the professional anxiety that attends risk. Thus, there is a complex interplay between a politically led movement to govern risk or risk behaviour in the professions, and the capacity of professionals and professions to withstand the consequences of public exposure for failure—normally failure adequately to assess or manage risks. It is now clear that professional social work and its well documented decade of public humiliation for child protection failures in the 1980s was just the first target in a continuing war aimed at bringing all professions to heel through decisive intervention at the point of their maximum vulnerability in the aftermath of tragedy or "failure". Hence, following the Bristol children's heart surgery scandal of 1998, the introduction of clinical governance in the NHS, which has placed the medical and para-medical professions under the same kind of inspectorial regimes as those provided for teachers, social workers, and other "soft" professions.

An important series of transformations, which together constitute a radical change of character in health and welfare, is the outcome of this process. Professional self-discipline or self-regulation has been significantly re-cast in the form of externally authorized social surveillance; professional self-examination and an ethos of learning from experience transmuted into one of "transparent" public audit of practices and the systems shaping practice; professional development through creative struggle within a dialectic of ideas, understanding, and practice experience, refashioned in the direction of evidence-based practice. During a case-based group discussion for a comparative research project that examined child protection practices in different European countries, an English child protection social worker said, "But what do we have to go on in our work, without the child protection procedures?" (Hetherington, Cooper, Smith, & Wilford, 1997) This young man, not very long qualified, was completely sincere in his perplexity. The logic of proceduralism had, in his case, become identical with professional meaning and values. The methodologies and intellectual habits that constitute proceduralism, inspection, regulation, and all the technologies of new public management are notable for the manner in which they first refer us to *external rather than internal criteria* for assessing and evaluating our work, while also taking up occupancy of these internal spaces, so that *externality becomes the principle by which internal life is lived and reproduced.* This is the "colonized" professional state of mind we previously evoked in Chapter One.

Trust in trust

We do not suggest that this state of affairs is by any means total, or monolithic. But, as old structures of feeling dissolve and new ones take shape, so do unfamiliar constraints and possibilities appear. The central problem with which our contemporary social formations are now struggling is that of trust. In part, our trust in traditional forms of social trust and authority has been justifiably thrown into question. The revelation of widespread and systematic abuse in children's homes, of corruption at the heart of government, of doctors and nurses sometimes being murderers, means we cannot turn a blind eye to these matters; the institutions that were established in earlier times to safeguard standards have failed us to some degree. We no longer feel able to put faith in these institutions as the vehicle for standards and the transmission of quality through the generations. We puzzle about which way to turn. We cannot revert to traditional assumptions about social trust, but the direction in which we find ourselves travelling also seems fraught with danger. This seems to me a central problem of our times—how to reconstruct trust in social and political authority under circumstances in which it has failed us, but in which we continue to need it.

Before considering possible responses to this predicament, we want to deepen our exploration of the predicament itself. In approaching this through the analysis of clinical material we are working by analogy, proposing that the problem of how to manage the threat of social disorder and yet preserve the potential for creativity in social life, has a striking parallel in the internal and external predicaments with which the man described below presented.

The man who didn't dream

The inability to tolerate empty space limits the amount of space available. [Bion, 1992)]

One morning, the therapist sits waiting for the patient to begin speaking. Today, he is silent for longer than usual. For months now, on each morning he sees this man, during the silence which normally marks the start of the session the therapist finds himself agitated and troubled by thoughts about demands arising from his work—phone messages not yet answered, tasks not properly completed, internal voices reproaching him for tardiness in all sorts of matters. These anxieties relate to actual circumstances in his working life, but after much reflection over many weeks he has also concluded that he is especially prone to the experience of being invaded by these worries while sitting with this patient. He begins to think that the man is unconsciously using the silence, the space, to rid himself of states of anxiety of a similar kind by propelling them into the therapist.

The state of mind is mildly unpleasant for the therapist, and it is usually a relief when the patient finally begins to talk. But this morning the silence continues for fifteen minutes or more. It is hard to focus attention on the patient in this silence, but from time to time he succeeds in putting aside his worried state and concentrating attention on the situation there in the room. Later in the session, he speaks to the patient about what seems to be his continuing tendency to try to evade, or rid himself of, certain kinds of thoughts and memories, particularly those which might cause him anxiety, guilt, or worry. The therapist suggests that it is only when he is capable of tolerating the feelings associated with such thoughts that he will be able to *think the thoughts at all* and thus take proper possession of his own mind. One week later, the patient reports only the second dream he has remembered in the course of three years of three times weekly therapy.

The therapist feels fairly sure that the two experiences are linked; the patient, by subjecting him to a more prolonged and disturbing experience of that part of his mind which he manages through evacuating the troubled and troubling thoughts it contains, and enabling him to formulate in words an understanding of how he has been using the mind of his therapist as a kind of dustbin for unwanted contents, has recovered some ability to think in the special and important way that remembered dreams allow. The assumption is that the therapist's own uncharacteristic state of mind (excessive guilt, anxiety, worry, and the distraction arising from these) is the consequence of the patient projecting his equivalent thoughts and feelings into him as a way of ridding himself of uncomfortable experiences. This works to alleviate his anxiety, but at the cost of him losing part of his mind.

The dream dreamed by the patient is about the possibility of dreaming, and of creativity. He was on his way to an exhibition in which many of his artist friends would be showing their pictures, but it was unclear to him whether or not his own paintings would be included in the exhibition also. The patient's actual work, or craft, is that of picture restoration, rather than picture-making. But in this dream the possibility that he might make pictures of his own in his mind, or at least remember the pictures he makes, is emerging. Hitherto, the therapist had often experienced the content of the man's spoken material in sessions as itself dream-like; rich in metaphor and symbolic resonance, and in need of the same kind of decoding as a dream, even though its narrative structure reflects everyday events (Steiner, 1980). It was as though the patient required the actual presence of another person, specifically his therapist, in order to be able to dream. Some weeks after the exchange described above the man related how he visited a furniture and household superstore in connection with the refurbishment of part of his house. Normally, he said, he cannot carry a visual image of a room or physical space in his mind, but on this occasion he had found he could, and his wife had communicated to him her surprise at this.

The capacity to think thoughts and the capacity to dream are dependent on the availability of a mental space in which these activities occur. But mental space, like any other form of space can be empty as well as filled; and psychic or emotional emptiness is, for all of us, hard to bear. But the cost of the incapacity to bear empty space within ourselves is huge—the sacrifice of mind itself. Loss creates emptiness, or to put it another way, loss is always experienced in some way as emptiness—what was present is now absent; thus the contemplation of an absence, an empty space, will remind us of loss. Equally frustration, the experience of unfulfilled want, of not being in control of the means to fulfil our desires, also includes an experience of emptiness. The experience of "nothing there" may, accompanied by frustration and rage, quickly and easily transmute into something bad and dangerous that *is* there and must be eliminated because its presence is painful, accusatory, persecuting. Wilfred Bion referred to the capacity for tolerating such experiences of internal mental pain as an aspect of the "non-psychotic" personality in us, and the incapacity as part of the "psychotic" personality. Thus,

> This non-psychotic personality must be capable of (a) frustration, and hence awareness of temporality (b) guilt and depression, and hence an ability to contemplate causality (since contemplating causes involves the possibility of having to contemplate one's own responsibility for certain events in the chain of causes) . . . One result is that the verbal reporting of a dream is only possible when

enough work has been done for the patient to be able to tolerate temporality and causality, i.e. frustration and guilt-depression. [Bion, 1992, p. 1]

If the ability to dream is an index of creativity, then it seems creativity presupposes the capacity to bear loss, and the anxious feelings and thoughts that may attend loss (was it *my* fault?); as children we surely need help to surmount the fear, which attends loss, that "things may never come right", anxiety about what damage we may have done. As many psychoanalytic thinkers, but particularly Melanie Klein, have recognized, the content of childhood play is significantly concerned with the impulse to "put things right" or repair the damage done in fantasy to loved people, toys, or other figures.

Viewed like this, creativity is a meeting point between destructive impulses and reparative ones. The damaged but loved figure is restored and "made good" by the same agent. But the wish to authentically repair the damage done to a loved figure entails the capacity to feel *for* the injured person, and to bear the connection between the injury done and one's own destructive impulses, actions, or thoughts. Genuine creativity is thus possible only if the truth or reality of destructiveness is first of all faced. But what if, instead, we are aided and abetted in our desire to *evade* painful questions concerning our own destructive impulses and actions? What if the accusatory voices that attend loss or minor everyday acts of destruction are simply too difficult to bear and have persisted unrelentingly, unmodified or unmodifiable, by parental forgiveness? What happens when an *appropriate* sense of guilt is not affirmed, but brushed under the carpet, perhaps with the collusion of others who also do not want to contemplate the anxious thoughts that guilt brings? What kind of internal and external world is brought into being under these circumstances. What kind of person or, we want to ask, what quality of *social* arrangements?

One answer is that trends towards fraudulence may be encouraged into being. Here we glimpse one of the most important questions about the endlessly superintended, inspected, regulated world we now inhabit. Is the "quality enhancement" supposedly produced by our systems and cycles of audit, genuine or fake quality? Are those responsible for the professional practices under inspection encouraged towards an authentic concern for their improvement or a placatory one, in which *seeming* to be engaged in high quality work in order to achieve good outcomes in audit exercises becomes fatally confused with good work itself as evaluated by some internal standard? The fact that we find the possibility of such confusion to be endemic in the modern welfare state should not be taken as an argument against the necessity of standards and methodologies for assisting the development and improvement of our practices. On the contrary, our concern is that because of the epistemological, methodological, and moral confusion at the heart of these systems of governance in health and welfare practice, these systems may be contributing much to a deterioration of standards, while sustaining an illusion that they are achieving the opposite. If this is accurate, it is a serious state of affairs, akin to a corruption of the moral standards at the heart of public life. How does this arise?

A tax inspector calls

> ... being observed is generally more problematic for most of us than observing. Being observed, especially if we are being observed in a crisis situation, may evoke the feeling of dread that what we are doing is wrong and will be exposed to the world to be critically judged by others. [Healy, 1998]

The psychotherapy patient described above first sought help at a point in his life when his business and marriage were both threatened with collapse. For some years, beginning with a period of recession, he had avoided paying bills, taxes, and other demands, not through any conscious, planned, or deliberate strategy to defraud, but by "turning a blind eye" to the ordinary realities of running a small business. Tax demands and invoices would simply be shelved, or stuffed to the back of the drawer, "out of sight out of mind". For a long period, it proved possible to muddle through in this way, even to the extent of concealing the situation from his family. Until one morning he woke to find the bailiffs knocking at the door.

When he began individual psychotherapy, he at first treated his therapist and the consulting room with an extreme degree of respect and caution, typified by precise punctuality and concern not to damage or dirty the furniture. His therapist thought that the patient feared an explosive, furious response in him should the patient make the tiniest "mistake". This gave rise to excessive anxiety for the patient, and a need to try and placate the therapist as a potentially punitive therapist figure. As the man talked about his fear of encounters with bank managers, tax inspectors, landlords, and other figures of authority, it became clearer that while this extremely harsh, authoritarian, inspectorial figure was a product of the patient's own fantasy, "he" nevertheless inflicted enormous anxiety upon the rest of the patient's psyche. It was this anxiety that mostly led to his excessive vigilance with respect for his therapist, for he feared that he also was under permanent and deadly scrutiny from the therapist.

Internally and externally his way of dealing with this predicament had been to attempt quietly to bribe and corrupt such figures, to "buy them off" in the hope of evading their attentions, demands, and punishment. This emerged in admissions that, on the one hand, over the years he had engaged friends to be his solicitors rather than accepting the need for a degree of "professional distance" in such a relationship; on the other hand he had played the part of the over-indulgent parent with various bankrupt and delinquent clients. This was the relationship that mirrored his own father's relationship to him. A seemingly benign and scrupulous professional, his father had indulged him in money matters as a child rather than oblige him to face financial realities and arrive at a proper *emotionally truthful appreciation of the value of things*. This had the effect of leading the son to believe that basic anxieties associated with autonomous functioning, with the need to *work, think, and negotiate uncertainty* in pursuit of desired goals could be avoided. Desired ends (or outcomes), including developing into a viable adult, could be attained without developmental struggle and pain, in effect by taking short cuts, cutting corners, or, at the extreme, cheating.

Anyone who has experienced the particular anxiety, and the high stakes, associated with a major professional audit or quality inspection knows that they encourage, or at least encourage the contemplation of, forms of cheating. Laying "paper trails" and writing "retrospective" minutes and policy documents are examples.

Thus, they come perilously close to a form of cheating in themselves. People who have been encouraged to believe that it is possible to take a "short path" to adulthood, success, authenticity, often report dreams about examination anxiety and cheating (Chasseguet-Smirgel, 1985). Certainly, major audit or quality assessment exercises are as much an exercise in representation as reality, in theatre rather than "life". This is linked to what one health service academic calls the "virtual politics of the NHS",

> a parallel world where belief in the difficult reality of change in a particular policy arena is suspended and all becomes possible. In virtual politics it is the immediate symbolism of the policy illusions which are of paramount importance, rather than the practicality of the content . . . It is not a new idea, but an interesting development of an old one where politics is regarded as literally a creative art. [Salter, 1998, p. 1091]

In this sense, audits function like traditional examinations, wherein a year or sometimes two years of accumulated learning is tested in the space of a few hours, and they stimulate the same kinds of primitive anxieties as do school examinations.

Shortly before a review of this kind, one of us dreamed about a member of the visiting assessment team, who many years before had been a supervisor in the course of a professional training. The dream was that she was performing badly in the inspection, apparently "drying up" and forgetting her lines in one of the crucial meetings of the review. Of course, projection occurs in dreams, and the root anxiety was that we would be found wanting by *her* in this exercise, not the other way round! Yet the dream might also pose the more profound question about who is failing whom, and in what sense, in this audit culture. In effect, the anxious question is whether the *political* parents are failing us by subjecting the workforce to forms of monitoring and testing that as much detract from as enhance authentic social, emotional, and educational development?

Authenticity, or truthfulness, are the key concepts here. As the man described above made significant progress in therapy, it emerged that in his work of restoring paintings there was a deeply rooted code of ethics that he had forged for himself almost without knowing it. At first it appeared as if the minute and detailed work he undertook with the damaged paintings brought to him was restricted to a form of obsessional activity, which "consists of a compulsive repetition of actions of the undoing kind without a real creative element, designed to placate, often in a magical way" (Hinshelwood, 1989, p. 413). What is being "undone" is the pulverising destruction resulting from the attack on reality itself— anything that constitutes evidence of difference, and hence "otherness", including the difference between the generations and the sexes. The psychic debris that results from this destruction is either hoarded (and this man's attics and garages as well as the compartments of his mind were stuffed to bursting) or expelled wholesale (as when he fills the therapist up with worry, anxiety, and fears of accusation), or both. But either way, it must be controlled and subjected to unceasing vigilance or surveillance, because it is dangerous, containing as it does the guilt-ridden evidence of destructive activity. Obsessional activity, even when in the service of "repair", is about control of danger rather than creativity. Genuine creativity is to be feared, since it provides evidence of difference, otherness, of our own real dependence upon others, of others' *separateness from us*, and their capacity to join together in productive and creative intercourse. Part of the fear of empty space is the fear of what creative activity might produce there, and of how, since other people are necessarily part of the creative process, we are potentially excluded by them.

Often, the man's clients brought him paintings that confronted him with difficult ethical and practical questions about the line between restoration and forgery. Not infrequently these clients seemed half to hope that he would collude with them in their wish to possess, through forgery, a different or more nearly perfect painting than the one they actually had, and half that he would stand firm as a guardian of ethical standards, leaving them disappointed but morally intact. On one occasion, a woman brought a pair of paintings, one of which the restorer assessed to be an original, the other a later copy or pastiche created in order to make a pair for the first. Both pieces were dark and dirty, but a light shone into the first revealed depth to the work, whereas in the second the painted figures were revealed as sketchy and insubstantial. If both paintings were cleaned the discrepancy in quality between them would be clear, and the only solution to almost completely re-paint the later copy.

Shallowness and depth, authenticity and fakery, are here encountered by the patient as irreducible properties of the outer world, residing in external objects, and confronting the man with a stubborn question about his relationship to reality—is it to be respected and dealt with in its own terms, or ignored and manipulated according to his, or someone else's, wishes? It was part of his passage to recovery and comparative health that he *discovered* that at root he had made a choice in favour of respect for reality, and that this was in part a truly ethical choice.

Sincerity, ideology and the welfare project

The audit society faces us all with a similar choice. Do we believe that the principles and methodologies of the inspectorial regimes of welfare yield up authentic measures of quality, or counterfeit ones, or perhaps something of each? Of course, the question cannot be answered with an absolute affirmative or negative. All knowledge is selective, theory laden, context dependent, and so on. But while all knowledge is "slippery" (psychoanalysis is just one of the methods of inquiry that reveals this) knowledge can still be distinguished from dogma, speculation, misrepresentation, and lies. Some of the distinguishing criteria concern the relationship between inquiry and *evidence*; others relate to what may be counted *as* evidence, while yet others are organized around the social and psychological conditions under which the knower comes to know. Thus, an acknowledged truth inculcated into someone under duress has a doubtful status as truth or knowledge. Equally, propaganda may sometimes contain aspects of the truth, but remain propaganda because of the coercive or deceptive relationships entailed in its propagation. As Paul Hoggett has suggested in his extended discussion of similar matters, the project may be akin to what the Marxist thinker Antonio Gramsci had in mind when he spoke of "pessimism of the intellect, optimism of the will", that is "to know the cold, hard facts of the situation and yet sustain a creative orientation towards life" (Hoggett, 2000, p. 139).

The idea that as individuals we can contain a compromised or even corrupted relationship to knowledge of our own states of minds, distinct from just a frightened or evasive one, links the insights of psychoanalysis to political theories of ideology. Our explorations in this book of various ways in which policy discourses both disclose and conceal, construct and delimit, the possibilities of welfare engagements in response to core social anxieties, can be recast as a kind of psychoanalytic exploration of contemporary welfare ideology.

Concepts of ideology have developed beyond the earliest formulations of Marx and Engels (1970) that saw "false consciousness" as a layer of systematically propagated illusion covering over the truth, rather like a blanket of snow that, once melted, reveals the underlying terrain of reality. If cynicism about the meaningfulness of the judgements produced by the audit systems of our superintended welfare state is an index of their problematic character, we are all, to one degree or another, also implicated in its production. We are its knowing, rather than unsuspecting, victims. In our view, then, this is not something from which we can conveniently excuse ourselves by holding that "they" are perpetrating it upon "us". Rather, we seem to be engaged in a reciprocal dance in which, although one partner may be leading (which is to say has more power), nevertheless we voluntarily, even if reluctantly, follow. It is in the elucidation of this kind of reciprocity in the production of social processes that psychoanalysis has something to offer, since it proposes a relational view of intrapsychic development and functioning in which latent capacities or dispositions for almost any state of mind and its attendant behaviours may be present in most ordinary mortals

In his long essay "Sincerity" (1994), the psychoanalyst Donald Meltzer writes of two aspects of sincerity: being able to know what one means and being able to mean what one says. Some people have great difficulty in saying what they mean, although they may know, or have a largely intact capacity to know, what they mean. Some patients in psychotherapy are more or less silent for many months, or even years—but one cannot thereby assume that they do not know what they would mean to say if only they could say it. In the clinical episodes recounted above, it seems the patient is in the opposite position at the outset of his treatment. He does not know what he means, or how to come to know what he means. Happily, he is able to trust the therapist sufficiently to discover, and give him a living experience of, the fact of *not knowing what it is that he really means*. Who is watching whom for what reason, whether truth or lies are the currency of communication, who is fooling whom with what degree of awareness or malice aforethought, are all revealed as profoundly in question. Perhaps we can intuit that these states of mind were attended by a distinct sense of concern, anxiety, and shame for this man. It is a transitional state for him, in which he discovers over time that he can say what he means, and that what he presently means is that he is unsure whether he means what he says. The consequence is that he becomes aware that he has simultaneously fooled himself, and made a fool of others. Writing of such states, Donald Meltzer observes:

> He notices that he is, in fact, unable-to-mean-what-one-says. It is not insincerity, incompleteness of honesty, but unsincerity, dishonesty, that has resulted. He is not deceiving his audience but taking advantage of their trust, inferior subtlety, or ignorance of facts or language. [1994, p. 232]

The patient described above deceived people, misled them, and told them falsehoods, but he did not lie. But such a distinction, in Meltzer's formulation between unsincerity, or a deficit of sincerity, and insincerity, or knowing dissimulation, places us in the position where in the domain of public affairs we must consider what stance we take in relation to those who appear genuinely not to know that they are misleading us. More significantly, we need to take a clear-sighted stance with respect to the possibility that a public cultures might be founded on such collective unknowing self-deception.

In his book *The Sublime Object of Ideology*, Slavoj Zizek says:

> The most elementary definition of ideology is probably the well known phrase from Marx's *Capital: Sie wissen das nicht, aber sie tun es'*—"*they do not know it, but they are doing it*". The very concept of ideology implies a kind of basic constitutive *naivité*: the mis-recognition of its own presuppositions . . . a divergence between so-called social reality and our distorted representation, our false consciousness of it. That is why a such a "naive consciousness" can be submitted to a critical ideological procedure . . . to a point at which it can recognise its own effective conditions, the social reality that it is distorting, and through this very act dissolve itself. [1989, p. 28]

Here we can see the congruence between the psychoanalytic project and the project of ideological critique clearly delineated. Both are concerned with the identification and, perhaps, dissolution of false, mystifying, or distorting self-conceptions. The one is about personal self-knowledge and the other about social self-knowledge. We are accustomed to interrogating and criticizing inadequate and misleading political or policy formulations about social reality in terms of knowing or wilful misrepresentation. Our thesis in this book is that such misrepresentations are also to be understood as the product of our social need to secure a tolerable accommodation between the anxieties inherent in social life and our wish to face and respond to these. Such accommodations are the product of a dynamic process of struggle and change in society. Different periods produce different characteristic solutions to the struggle, which in turn are best *understood* before embarking upon a project of critique and change. The fact that we see such settlements as partly rooted in the play of unconscious force within society, does not mean that they should not be subject to evaluation. We seek to understand patients in psychotherapy, and to encourage self-understanding, not, we would argue, as an end in itself, but as a necessary condition for the prospect of change. So it is with the relationship of social theorizing to social change. This notion that we must distinguish carefully between discourses of explanation and interpretation on the one hand, and discourses of judgement, responsibility, and blame on the other, is examined further in Chapter Seven, where we take the Victoria Climbié Inquiry report as a case study.

Governing welfare and the relationship to truth

As the treatment progressed and the patient struggled with the final stages of straightening out his affairs with the Inland Revenue, he spoke once more of finding that he had failed to make some necessary arrangements with the Inspector; he had quickly rescued the situation, but now reproached himself for what he saw as something fundamentally dishonest in him. He now recalled that many years ago he had run his business from a small cottage in the country; he had a client who was a shady dealer, virtually a crook, who would come and confide in him; also at this time he had employed a friend of his to be his accountant, thus "muddling up professional and social relationships". The therapist said to him that he thought one part of his mind was constantly seducing another, inspectorial part not to notice what is really going on, so that a situation of internal bribery and corruption develops in him. In the transference the therapist sometimes experienced counterparts to this in the form of unspoken pressure to reassure the patient that he was progressing well, or in other words that he is pleasing to his therapist, or, in the idiom of this chapter, to agree that there is only good news.

Finally, there arrived a moment when some transformation occurred in relation to his core state of mind. The experience described at the outset of the paper, of having no way of knowing who knew what about whom, in relation to who might or might not be observing whom, directly, or through the use of mirrors, suggests a state of mind in which there no solid contact with psychic reality. The situation involves a kind of infinite regress of epistemological possibility. It turned out that the patient felt rather tyrannized by his landlord, to whom he had actually been in debt because of his chronic mishandling of his affairs; but now he had taken hold of this situation and succeeded finally in clearing his debts. Then, one day, he described the following scene. He was outside loading something into his car when across the road he suddenly noticed a man waving wildly at him, advancing upon him. It was his landlord, shouting and fulminating at his failure to pay some component of an agreement that had been drawn up between them. The patient said "He was terribly agitated, and I don't think I've ever done anything like this before in my life, but I got hold of him by the arm and I said 'Look, I have paid you every penny I owe you. There is nothing more to pay at the moment, we have paid you every penny which was agreed'. And you know the amazing thing was he calmed down, just like that." The therapist said to the patient, "You knew where you stood," and he said, "Yes, and what's more I knew that I knew where I stood." We can see how the infinite regress has gone into reverse, as though it now has a plus sign rather than a minus sign attached to it. It is as though metaphorically the patient and therapist can finally clasp hands and really feel that each other exists.

The capacity to know the truth rather than indulge in evasion and cover-up, entails risking *publicly*, *intersubjectively*, nailing one's colours to the mast—so that in principle the other may say "Yes I concur", or "No, I don't". It is as though at this moment the patient was confident that he could go to the polls, or contest the matter in court, and believe he might win. Our social arrangements for the conduct of debate about the nature and quality of the welfare state must be funded on similar principles, that both facilitate a sense of responsibility for failure or under-achievement so that the truth about it can be known and faced, while avoiding arrangements that threaten to persecute, blame, scapegoat, and punish, so that *truth is driven underground*. Only under these conditions will we preserve a capacity to *develop* a system of humane welfare, rather than drive ourselves to "deliver" one that fulfils the controlling fantasies of the audit society, while cynically evading true engagement with suffering, deprivation, and loss.

This would be politics and policy founded in "telling it like it is", not telling how it should be, or how we would rather it were not. Good news in other words, is only really good if it has an internal relation to bad news. Truly good news is surely the transformation of something difficult, deficient, unsatisfactory, unjust, into something better; and this means first squarely facing the unsatisfactory state of affairs we wish to transform. A genuine capacity to face bad news is a form of good news. Genuine hope, rather than the cynicism that emanates from despair about the possibility of such transformation, is surely rooted in a confidence in our own ability, and that of our leaders, to master difficulties, not misrepresent them.

The quality of quality

When in society, and specifically the welfare state, we set up one kind of agency to inspect, monitor, and assess another, the nature of the relationship between the two functions is important for the well-being of the first and the integrity of the whole. Does the first respect the second, or is it inclined to bully, control, and manipulate in the service of its own ends rather than those of the first activity? Is the psycho-social space created by the relationship between the welfare service or provision and the audit or inspectorial function brought to bear upon it a space that promotes creative thinking about problems and their solutions, or one that promotes placatory, propitiatory activity more in the service of avoiding criticism than discovering truth? Because, of course, not all assessment, inspection, audit, and monitoring is destructive. All confrontation of unwelcome truths about ourselves is painful and likely to be evaded, but that is a different matter. Herein lies the difference between "normal and abnormal" superego functions (O'Shaughnessy, 1999) in the social arena, and between borderline states of mind and more ego-orientated ones.

This is a terribly important distinction. Because in all aspects of welfare there is much to think about that we would rather not think about, perhaps this is the central social and moral preoccupation of this book. There is much that escapes our understanding, much that needs improvement, and much corruption and dangerous practice. We often bemoan the gulf between policy and practice, between the deep, particularizing, emotional engagement and practice wisdom of the individual operative and the simplified, reductive sweep of the policy perspective. Yet no form of *social* welfare, as distinct from simply the exercise of individual compassion, can avoid questions of collective organization and planning, and a confrontation with obstinate realities about limited resources, and inadequate or substandard services. The capacity to think creatively within a space bounded by limits, constraints, competing resource demands, and a host of unwelcome realities, is part of both personal and social maturity. To function thoughtfully in this difficult area is to exit from the borderline.

As Kevin Healy has written in a very creative paper about clinical audit,

> Clinical audit is an ongoing process of enquiring and thinking within existing structures . . . Superego type audit activity is characterised by a dread or terror in those being audited of being found out, being criticised and being harshly judged . . . In contrast, a clinical audit process that is ego-driven stems from curiosity, a wish to learn about one's working practices and a desire to perform better. [1998, pp. 54–55]

CHAPTER FOUR

The psychic geography of racism: the state, the clinician, and hatred of the stranger

A loss of innocence

The very fact of a welfare state poses profound questions about the foundations of moral and civic relations among strangers. It is the relationship between individual need and the entitlement to use the resources of unknown others to meet such need that is at the heart of both the antagonism and the hope that welfare represents. Consistent moral behaviour is impossible in the absence of some minimum agreement, within any given society, about the necessary preconditions for the development and welfare of its citizens.

The need for a socially organized system of welfare arises because the individual needs others to provide for him or herself. Here we are thinking not just of public health, social welfare, or education services, but also of the fact that ordinary psychological health and well-being depends on the capacity of individuals and social systems to mobilize nourishing interpersonal relationships. Paradoxically, given these axioms, two themes seem to haunt contemporary welfare. First, the question of how to provide efficient and comprehensive services without courting accusations of creating dependency; and second, a fundamental preoccupation about with whom we share mutual obligations. It is the second question that is the main focus of this chapter.

We see a puzzling contradiction between the contemporary preoccupation with access to services and the valorization of diversity and difference, on the one hand, and a deep ambivalence about providing care for certain classes of stranger, on the other. Welfare exists to provide care and services to the stranger. The preoccupation with diversity and difference is not, we suggest, straightforwardly magnanimous, but a reaction formation to the knowledge that the stranger provokes hostility more readily than they do compassion.

The contemporary preoccupation with identity, culture, and nationalism, draws attention to the need for clear boundaries in the context of a global world in which mass social mobility and the weakening of nation states creates a situation where more and more of our lives are spent among strangers, with whom we must learn to share, on the one hand, and negotiate the assumptions and values that support sharing, on the other. We suggest that this is an enterprise that provokes ambivalence or, at worst, hatred.

In this context, we wish to draw attention to how extensively the project of the welfare state has become denigrated. The welfare state is not just criticized for a failure to provide good enough services, but for acting as a "nanny" and working against the citizen's interests. The difference between the nanny and the carer is that one is a stranger, while the other is a member of one's own. As Polly Toynbee (2004) wrote:

> The nanny state is a good state. A nanny is what every well-off family hires if it can afford it. So why do the nanny-employing Tories use the word as an insult? In the Commons and in their press they bray like a bunch of prep-school bullies calling anyone cissy if they do what nanny says . . . Yesterday Labour sounded apologetic like bullies' victims, anxious not to be called nanny's boys . . .

The uncovering of widespread sexual abuse in "places of safety" (something of the social turbulence created by this discovery is explored in Chapter Six) and the gradual exposure of institutional racism at the heart of the establishment have provoked massive changes in both attitude and practice. It is ironic that it should be the discovery of such perversion that has provoked such change. Both represent the humiliation of the powerless by the more powerful; both produce a degree of social and psychological damage that is hard to quantify; both are predicated on a perversion of thinking, and, most uncomfortably of all, both, albeit in a forbidden, managed, or disavowed way, are familiar to us all. No society, no system, no individual, cares to be confronted with their own perversion and so, perhaps, much of the venom that is projected on to professionals where these issues are concerned may be due to their incapacity to protect the citizen from this exposure. In so far as the welfare project has been responsible for encouraging such exposure, it must also bear the consequences of the ambivalence of society's resulting loss of innocence.

The believed-in family

In spite of knowing what it is that is needed to nourish life for the stranger—food, shelter, love, security—these communalities make little headway against the appeals of nationalism, racial and social indifference. A preoccupation with those deemed different provides knowledge of who we are; that is to say, we know who we are because we are not the other. The extent to which a system of welfare is inclusive depends on how, or whether, the other is held in mind as an object of obligation. Concern for, and a sustained obligation towards, the stranger is in dynamic relationship with an idealization of the familiar, which by definition has the valency to exclude. The important point to stress is that the "mental" management of the stranger is a dynamic that preoccupies the individual, the social system, and its professional agents. Whether the mentality is driven by anxiety, persecution, envy, and fear, or concern, guilt, and reparation, depends not just upon internal psychic processes but on the quality of containment, leadership, and justice provided by a third object, the state. The conduct and containing function of the State and its agencies can fuel anxiety leading to the wish to exclude, or to a sense of reparation, and thus to the motivation for concern and inclusion. But this is no easy discourse. Sustaining a sense of obligation towards the stranger is at best precarious, a volatile state of mind, which, when exposed to anxiety and fear, is predisposed to forgo obligation and duty towards others in favour of protecting the familiar. The quality of the welfare rests upon the nature of the shared belief that reciprocity between and obligation towards others is the basis of social concern and citizenship. The dilution of this sense of "belief" weakens the authorization of State in its role of managing services aimed at meeting this obligation.

Upon the quality of relationship between citizen and state depends the depth or shallowness of social concern. Racism is a consequence of a loss of confidence in what we might describe as the "believed-in family", symbolically represented by this relationship. The large minority of citizens who no longer vote give some evidence for this loss of faith, of a de-authorization of the agency of concern. In the process of de-authorization two things of great importance are lost or damaged. First, our confidence in the parental objects associated with the State to contain difference is diminished; and second, there is a loss of capacity for and interest in the discovery of common need. There is a triangular relationship between the citizen, which extends to the mental representation of family and community, the State, and the stranger who, critically, is also a citizen. So, it is precisely in those circumstances where the stranger is stripped of their citizenship that racism becomes most malignant. Thus, the contemporary preoccupation with ethnic and cultural identity is, we would argue, a reaction formation to the increasing sense of alienation and detachment from the experience of the believed-in family; the loss of the idea of a civic family identified with communities, shared values, and goals undermines the developmental hope for, or a sense of, vision that transcends the familial and ethnic boundary.

Otherness

The loss of the believed-in family, the state, produces an experience of a loss of containment with the result that social concern for the stranger is at risk of losing out to the psychic valency to reject the other in favour of "brotherhood". This process is reinforced by the reality of economic globalism, and the consequent impact on the capacity of the national state to take up anything that resembles leadership. This is the canvas upon which the contemporary manifestation of the hatred of difference gets enacted. It seems as if on this canvas the civic family is either represented in a narcissistic manner as no longer being needed, or in such a way as to say, "I have mine and it is not available to you". All the more so if the stranger turns out to be mentally disturbed, traumatized, an asylum seeker, black, or not to share our mother tongue. However, being the other is not simply an experience attributed to the migrant, the asylum seeker, or the black.

The fundamental dynamic of welfare relationships, whether as user, patient, or client, is the experience of being the other. In such relationships, as well as being a citizen the individual is, for a shorter or longer period of time, the other in need of help from a stranger. Being a user, a patient, a recipient, is a role taken up reluctantly, a role that is predicated on the failure of physical, or psychic health and/or on the failure of familial, social, or economic containers. As with any other role, what determines the experience is a negotiation between subjective feelings towards, and about, the role, and how the role is perceived, thought about, and responded to by others. Being the other means having to come to terms with being different, whether momentarily or permanently. Furthermore, the experience of being dependent on others for care provokes primitive feelings towards those perceived to be enjoying good health. The potential for the projection of blame, envy, grievance, and anger is great. Not only are these feelings visited on those that are providing care but crucially are projected outwards on to "foreign objects" envied for their health and attacked because of the fantasy that their health has been achieved by a theft of the resources that would have made us, the patient, better. "Welfare" is therefore the site where ambivalent attitudes towards the stranger are articulated, fought out, and, in good times, contained.

No policy initiative today is undertaken, and no training validated, without a demonstrable commitment to working with diversity. Respect for difference, whether religious, ethnic, cultural, racial, or sexual, is "signed up to" in all manner of ways. The very choice of terms such as "difference", "diversity" or "cultural sensitivity" seem so overworked as to be in danger of obscuring the very issues they were invoked to understand and respond to. There is nothing remarkable about difference as such. What is remarkable is the intensity of feelings that are generated by the encounter with difference; on the one hand, the fear that something precious will exist in more abundance in the stranger, on the other, the phantasy that the stranger will steal what is precious puts the very future at risk. There is something inescapable about the fact that under conditions of threat, anxiety, and fear the intuitive wish is to be with, or helped by, someone like oneself and not by a stranger. Under these same conditions concern for the stranger, who themselves might be in need of help, is far from secure. To use difference, or diversity, as if they occupied an understood, civilized, and agreed moral high ground is to ignore the continual oscillation between these states of mind.

The ambush

Over a considerable period of time a psychotherapy patient recalled the following events. He was seven, and he and his mother were leaving their GP's consulting room As he passed through the waiting room he inadvertently trod on a woman's foot. "Can't you look where you are going, you stupid little nigger!" she snarled. His mother quickly bundled him out. He knew he wanted his mother to stand up for him and in some way hit back. The patient went on to describe how he had grown up knowing about incidents like this. He knew how to recognize the racist thug; he could see them coming, and in his family he had learnt in countless ways to be watchful and on guard. This he knew. As Adam Philips says:

> Thereafter, one fights a rearguard action to keep other elements of oneself in focus, and it is hard to get though the day without the shoulder coming into play. I don't mean the "chip on the shoulder" I mean the "glance over the shoulder". Once somebody has mounted a stealth attack on a part of who you are, you had better be wary for you know it's coming again. [Philips, 2004, pp. 4–6]

Some days later, he was once more with his mother when the same woman spotted them and came running over. "Oh, I am so glad to see you, I wanted to apologise for my outburst—I just went out of my mind." The woman looked relieved, pleased, and expectant of forgiveness. Far from being reassured by this second encounter, the patient found himself feeling more tentative and anxious as if now he could never be adequately prepared for what might happen next. The hateful outburst was in some sense more insidious because it cohabited with guilt, but not in such a way as to inhibit the outburst. The racist thug would attack you in the street, he thought, fully conscious of his hatred even if not knowing why; while the woman's outburst of "hatred" was more like an ambush. To make matters worse he had come to understand that *both* he and this woman had been the subject of an ambush—she from within, and himself from without. At any moment and with only limited provocation the individual or group can self-evidently go out of its mind. The capacity to preserve a mind capable of striving for a co-existence with the other is replaced with a mind that protects itself by annihilating or attacking and denigrating the other. What this woman came to represent for the patient is how precariously balanced is the sense of equilibrium towards the stranger and how pernicious are the consequences when the balance is lost.

What this patient explored was not just a single racist state of mind but how the geography of racism as a psychological phenomenon involves a number of distinct states of mind, some of which are clearly more toxic than others but all of which are related. It is their constancy, variety, and interaction that makes racism so complex and so hard to dislodge. The toxicity of racism lies not only in its enactment but extends to the considerable difficulty that is encountered when it is discussed or theorized. While no psychological theory can fully explain, nor of itself determine, the political response to racism, it can provide some insight into the processes that make the repetition of racist attitudes so effortless on the one hand and the need, in the outside world of politics, to keep in mind the inside world of experience on the other.

The psychic geography of racism

There are many significant discourses about the material conditions that promote racism, which space does not allow us to review here.

Rather, we wish to draw attention to the powerful psychological processes at work that are fundamental to the reproduction of racism and ethnic nationalism. While these manifestations of hatred are not identical, they are none the less in large part members of one "family" whose project is to attack the developmental objectives that seek to integrate and preserve the stranger and in their place erect boundaries whose purpose is to exclude. Phil Cohen (1993) sets out the terrain most succinctly:

> It seems that whenever the preservation of home, or traditional values, are used as the basis for the oppression of the immigrant, the stranger, or to provide a rationale for racial harassment and ethnic cleansing, or to claim superior entitlement for the "indigenous" to scarce domestic resources, what is being articulated is a myth of origin which evokes a structure of feeling and fantasy belonging to quite another scene. Racist discourses appear to be obsessed with the enumeration of external and visible differences, and with the mapping out of a moral system of justification based upon them. But what these differences are in fact made to signify is a set of internal and invisible features, which belong to what the body—and the body politic—is imagined to contain in its function as a primordial home. To be born as a human subject, one is not only forcibly evicted from our first home in our mother's body, we also have to make a home away from home in language, and in the whole symbolic order of culture that belongs to another. [1993, p. 5]

Cohen goes on to describe how, in order to acculturate to the world of its parents, the infant has to give up his own subjective world, and in the process of discovering and managing his or her dependency on others must give up omnipotence. The infant has, in effect, and with some difficulty, to give up a narcissistic world that is dominated by "thoughts" such as, "I am the sole occupant of the world"; "I was 'here first'"; "This is where the world began, and my desires and needs have priority"; "I am at one with myself". It is a space of belonging populated by idealized figures, which "I" in turn omnipotently invest with goodness and authority. It is a world "I" long to return to, an uncontaminated place of origin, where there is no complexity of history and no room for division or inequality. It is the residue of these feelings and phantasies, together with the rage that is associated with the painful and bewildering experience of being obliged to find an accommodation with and dependency on the stranger, that provides the geographical terrain on which racism is predisposed to thrive. It seems that under threat there is a marked tendency to turn against the stranger. For the fascist the tendency is a way of life unmediated by guilt and therefore hard to contain. When the fascist is able to subvert justice and recruit the citizen, it is then that the full dangerousness and cruelty of racism becomes evident.

The phobic racist

Returning once more to the patient, he described growing up knowing about the dangerousness associated with what might be described politically as fascists, or in more psychological terms as the phobic racist. The phobic racist describes someone who habitually deals with situations that are likely to cause anxiety and conflict by avoiding them and by refusing to be parted from an ideal environment, or what is symbolically represented by a protecting parent. The phobic racist deploys a way of thinking that is as apparently simple as it is dangerous. Michael Rustin (1991) cites a passage from Jean-Paul Sartre (1948):

> I noted earlier that anti-Semitism is a passion. Everybody understands that emotions of hate or anger are involved. But ordinarily, hate and anger have a provocation. I hate someone who has made me suffer, someone who condemns or insults me. We have just seen that anti-Semitic passion could not have such a character. It precedes the facts that are supposed to call it forth; it seeks them out to nourish itself upon them; it must even interpret them in a special way so that they may become truly offensive ... The anti-Semite has chosen hate because hate is a faith. At the outset he has chosen to devalue words and reasons how entirely at ease he feels as a result. How futile and frivolous discussion of the rights of Jews appear to him. He has placed himself on other ground from the beginning. If out of courtesy he consents for a moment to defend his point of view, he lends himself but does not give himself. He tries simply to project his intuitive certainty onto the plane of discourse.

What this passage does so beautifully is to draw attention to how the phobic racist thinks. Hate is a faith; it precedes facts; it must interpret facts offensively. What Sartre is describing is a state of mind in which thinking about difference is not just intolerable but life threatening. Hatred and violence against the other is the only stance for self-preservation.

The oscillation between hatred and concern

From a psychoanalytic point of view this state of mind has its origin in the infantile perception of the difference between subject (the self) and object (the other), at a time when the infantile state of mind is dominated by the irrational and is out of touch with anything but itself. Waddell (1998) describes this primitive paranoid–schizoid state of mind as one which

> Encompasses both the nature of the predominant anxiety, that is the fear of persecution, and the nature of the defence against such fears. This last is the "schizoid" or split functioning in which both people and events are experienced in very extreme terms, either unrealistically wonderful (good) or as unrealistically terrible (bad) This state of mind is characterised by an exclusive concern with one's own interests. [1998, p. 6]

What is described here is the absence of curiosity about the object, an anxiety and aggression directed towards their difference and what is unknown about them. It is the fear associated with the unknown object that provokes a wish to attack, as if the object was fundamentally prejudicial to the well-being of the self. This emotional state of hatred towards the other is devoid of guilt, and consequently there is no investment in the other's survival because they have been psychologically stripped of any nourishing or developmental qualities. In their place is aggression and persecution. Psychologically, the other is frightening because they have had projected on to them all the aggressive feelings belonging to the self. The relationship that follows is therefore dominated by a "part-object" configuration. We are here describing the initial stage of a complex developmental process whereby the infant must learn to convert raw emotional experience into something that has meaning, associated with an object that in turn develops in the infant the capacity to be a thinker with a mind. Hinshelwood writes:

> The combination of registering an experience with, and the special quality of, meaningfulness creates an object of thought and this is represented in the mind. To simple recognition is added meaning, and this combination produces what I call a "representation". In the immaterial world of the mind a representation is a felt experience, a thing that feels tangible, and manipulable. Representation is not just a passive process. It indicates that something has been "minded" (i.e. means something to me). [Hinshelwood, 2003, p. 184]

In the subsequent developmental position, the more "depressive" ambivalent attitude towards the other emerges. A relationship with the other where curiosity and concern protect the object from aggressive wishes and what is different about them can be explored and thought about. For example, the role of the monster in countless children's stories has the therapeutic function of enabling the child to objectify and hence gain control over sadistic feelings. However, in those circumstances where the monster cannot serve this function it becomes the device for projecting these feelings on to real others and thence becomes available for capture and further elaboration by the racist imagination. Yet the "depressive" position does not completely replace the paranoid–schizoid. Rather, both represent states of mind that are throughout life capable of deployment. As Waddell (1998) notes:

> In Klein's work there is a sense of a life-long fluctuation between a predominantly selfish and self-serving attitude to the world and an attitude of generosity and concern, albeit one which is always inflected by a concern for the self. [1998, p. 7]

What the patient described above discovered in the woman at the doctor's surgery was how thin-skinned she was when in pain. Without thinking, her response was not to remonstrate with him about his carelessness but rather to attack him for his blackness, as if the two were necessarily associated. What he could never come to terms with was the silence of the other patients, both black and white, in the waiting room. What then was the relatedness between the bystanders, the angry outburst, and the act of reparation? None of the bystanders is uninvolved, but all are seemingly caught in identification with the supposed "victim". What is evident here is collusion and fear manifesting itself as indifference.

A further question raised here is the gap between the act and the apology for the act. How long and how much violence is tolerable before a reparative state of mind is re-convened? On the international stage we can see this process at work in the protracted indecision about intervention to stop genocide in Cambodia, Rwanda, or Srebrenica. When is enough violence enough? It is as if the woman dazzled the other patients, the bystanders, who for a period were immobilized and perhaps even excited by her aggression. This is what Norman Geras (1998) explores in his book *The Contract of Mutual Indifference*.

The splitting off of aggression

The preoccupation with difference and the meaning attributed to this idea was explored by a patient who sent her therapist a Christmas card depicting a kitten snuggled up to a piglet with a message within saying, "Don't they make a lovely couple". In the innocent charm depicted by this image was reflected one aspect of her perception of the therapeutic relationship; but the card also conveyed an anxiety that something could go wrong, or perhaps was already not quite right, a fear that perhaps some differences were insurmountable with the consequence that conception would never lead to a legitimate birth.

In the treatment it became clear that the choice of card, albeit an unconscious one, conveyed something of considerable symbolic importance. The temptation was to understand the card's communication solely in terms of the complex relation between black and white, as manifested between therapist and patient; indeed, the patient initially took it up in this way, but what was more painfully discovered was the process whereby her own internal struggle to make sense of her violent and disrupted childhood made use of racism as a metaphor for abuse and violence of all kinds. One the one hand there was the experience of being a racialized subject, but on the other the projection on to racism as a vehicle to "explain" other sites of pain. Racism provided a partial explanation, but in the context of her therapy also felt depersonalized, and partial in the sense that it obscured very complex familial and social relationships. For example, she had experienced sustained physical cruelty from her family. However, she preserved them as loved through a massive projection on to the anonymous but ever present racist. Distinguishing between this psychic process in the mind, and the need in reality to be prepared for an anonymous attack, act of denigration, or ambush, was difficult.

The card seemed to convey a wish for reconciliation, or retreat to a place in which there is a renunciation of aggression. For the kitten and the pig there could be no possibility of a fight, or even a lovers' "tiff", without one being mortally damaged, and the other persecuted by their own destructiveness. The absence of a capacity for aggression towards a loved object means that it can never be wholly known. Likewise an idea, or an injustice, that cannot be robustly knocked around becomes disappointing, fixed, and decaying. For this patient there could be a part-object relationship with the therapist but not the sort of relationship that could survive regression to the primitive states of mind that intimacy provokes. Instead, the card conveyed a longing for an intimate relationship where love was permanently split off from aggression and anxiety.

A similar fear of aggression seems to pervade many of the debates and policy formulations that inform anti-discriminatory and anti-racist practice. These discussions frequently seem dominated by certainty, right or wrong stances, as if to censor the aggression of debate. To censor aggression is to censor exploration and the possibility of making the mistakes that inevitably accompany discovery. When this "fact" is driven out of the mind, what is left is either the manic "loving" solution conveyed by the card or a rigid assignment of the roles that may be taken up in debate, typically those of victim or perpetrator. What gets avoided and becomes so hard to explore is not just the psychic damage that can become associated with being the racialized subject, but the universal quality of distrust and hatred that becomes associated with the stranger. This is not to say that everybody is equally guilty of acts of terror or racism, but to acknowledge that the capacity to be a terrorist or racist is within us all. Anxiety and aggression accompany the experience of the new, the unknown, which is both primitive and demanding and cannot be managed by "bureaucratic" solutions. Too frequently, what gets exported from the discourse of difference is personal familiarity with the very central characteristic of the racist: a compelling wish to preserve something of oneself at the expense of the other.

The emptiness of the "significant other"

For example, at an experiential conference designed to explore the impact of diversity and difference on organizational life, the associate director in her introduction made reference to her "significant other". But, we may ask, significant in what respect? What is the nature of the object conjured up by the idea of a significant other? Seemingly, an object that can have no gender, or sexuality; an object associated with no ideas or ethnicity, indeed an object that is purposely completely anonymous, and yet immensely significant. This introduction, in the context of working with diversity and difference, drew attention to an issue that is to be preserved out of reach, with no possibility of contributing to or being influenced by the thinking and experience of the conference. What this significant other represented was how an important part of the self was to be kept out of view, a self that is free to express itself at home and away from the demands of the difference and diversity of the conference. In addition, the reference seemed to point to an anxiety associated with a range of "privileging" differences, her marriage, her class, her whiteness. This evoked awareness of both her guilty feelings and the satisfactions she enjoyed, satisfactions possibly not enjoyed by others. In the context of the conference it seemed as if envy and the affect it might stimulate was a toxic issue. The significant other came to represent a sort of fact of life: the conundrum that on the one hand in public there was undoubtedly a sincere wish to work with diversity, but at "home" what is mine is private, protected, and celebrated with one's own kind.

For the conference staff, what was established from the outset was a kind of intellectual and emotional deal. The agreement seemed concerned to create a modus operandi that would protect the conference's work, and especially the staff, from their own differences. The "deal" was to split off some of the individual emotional content of working with difference from the conference task. This implies no criticism, but rather draws attention to the fact that a civilized society always has the task of containing the primitive character of the individual's internal world, but has to undertake this task in the knowledge that these aspects of the individual can, under certain conditions, break out and demand satisfaction. Thus the structure of feeling established in this working conference gave rise to some central questions that we address in Chapter One. How do we manage the social task of both addressing toxicity and damage in a contained or safe enough manner without thereby sequestering it, or pushing it so far out of mind that we come to turn a blind eye to its reality?

Freud (1927c) writes: "Thus civilisation has to be defended against the individual, and its regulations, institutions and commands are directed towards this task" (p. 143). And in a much quoted passage, he elaborates

The fateful question for the human species seems to me to be whether and to what extent their cultural development will succeed in mastering the disturbance of the communal life by the human instinct of aggression and self-destruction. [Freud, 1930a, p. 145]

To summarize, then, in order to achieve its task the conference had to agree on what could be, and implicitly what could not be, explored. Difference could be explored in terms of history, culture, and nationalism, all of which were experienced as less problematic than what was known to be located in the figure of the significant other. The task for both the staff and membership was to build a boundary round their thinking. The toxic nature of many working conferences on racism, anti-racism, working with difference, and culturally sensitive practice, are legendary. The hostility that such events so frequently produce is undoubtedly informed by a residue of the pain and anger associated with the lived experience of being a racialized subject, but also with the knowledge that the wish to exclude and the irrational hatred towards those who seek inclusion are not exclusive characteristics of the racist, but are known and deployed by all.

In such processes there is the wish to surgically remove the cancer of racism. In the event there is very little evidence that this wish has any chance at all of success, and it is the anxiety at the point of discovering this that produces an enactment of hatred, vengeance, and despair. Moreover, the wish for surgery draws attention to a hope and belief that change, social and psychological, will be achieved by a restorative and reparative intervention, via the agencies of social justice, which are so significantly represented by anti-discriminatory and equal opportunity policies.

Failure of justice

One of the most damaging aspects of being a racialized subject is the failure of justice to protect and to take responsibility for retribution. For those of us who rely on "justice" it is hard to understand what living without it must feel like. Returning once more to the patient and the incident in the surgery, one of the issues was how to explain the absence of a response from the doctor. The General Practitioner, who had always shown interest and concern in the patient, failed to protect him. For the patient it was as if this symbolic agent of justice, whom he became convinced had heard the outburst, chose to look the other way.

No discussion of racism can advance far without trying to explore the conditions in which the state, the container for the citizen and of the idea of citizenship, with its agencies of concern and justice, becomes unreliable, corrupted, or collapsed. The state's function is not simply to be a provider of services but to maintain a symbolic function representing concern for the other. It is in those circumstances where the quality and psychic health of the state—its relationship with the citizen and its authorization by the citizen—becomes weakened that cruelty, nationalism, and an aggressive enactment towards the stranger step in.

A black man, Rodney King, is brutally assaulted by several policemen in a garage forecourt in Los Angeles. The unprovoked attack is recorded on video for all to see and yet a jury of the perpetrators' peers acquits them. For the jury it was as if a special mental process had to take place in which thinking about the evidence was replaced by identification with the act of aggression. The verdict could only have been possible if the jury had "lost" its thinking mind, and was in the collective grip of a more primitive relation to the stranger. The point here is that racism depends upon a capacity for precisely such a psychic mobilization. In these circumstances a commitment to justice seemed less of an imperative than a loyalty to "their own kind". What was mobilized was an indifference to the truth, and the capacity for thinking upon which it depends. The verdict could only have been reached in the psychic context of denying Rodney King the status of being a subject. No indictment was forthcoming because in effect he did not exist.

The perversion of thinking that underpinned this verdict draws attention to a further aspect of racist thinking: the fact that the verdict was only possible by a suspension of the capacity to experience guilt or remorse. For the patient discussed above, the woman's apology was taken as sincere but he never for one moment thought that under similar circumstances she would act any differently.

What ties the perpetrator and the victim together in an endless and deadly interchange is precisely the failure of justice. Put another way, the absence of a container capable of containing and detoxifying hatred leaves the phobic racist in a guilt-free world in which there is no agency able to manage his hatred, envy, and the fear of annihilation. For the victim the failure of justice can leave him dominated by the wish for revenge, which in turn becomes corrosive.

Never should we underestimate the consequences of the failure of justice, because it leads to the conversion of the wish for retribution into the wish for revenge. In those circumstances where the system of justice fails to secure adequate retribution on behalf of the victim, it is not just the self but the internal objects represented by the parents, family, community, or nation that are the recipients of damage. By justice, we mean not just the legal or governmental system but also an internal system of justice (symbolically represented by the good-enough mother) that is capable of containing and detoxifying the hateful wishes associated with the wish for revenge. Where this container is psychically or socially absent, the individual or social system is left in what Bion (1993) describes as a state of "nameless dread".

In the absence of a container, revenge seems a compelling vehicle for the restoration of the stolen, lost, or damaged dignity associated with the good internal objects. The depletion of these objects are experienced, and responded to, in a very primitive manner.

Justice's failure to give satisfaction allows other motives to become attached to the initially just cause. Old hatreds, based on narcissistic wounds, greed, jealousy, oedipal rivalries, and especially primitive destructiveness rooted in envy, take over and give revenge its insatiable nature. . . . When the death instinct comes to dominate revenge is not satisfied until the object and with it the self is totally destroyed. [Steiner, 1993, p. 85]

Dilemmas for the clinician

For the clinician, the thinking required to understand the meaning attributed to difference involves the capacity to resist the intoxication of self-righteousness and grievance on the one hand, or recourse to "political correctness" on the other. Political correctness depends upon a reduction of complexity and has the consequence of freezing thinking. The tendency is then to search for someone who has infringed the rules, and this person becomes a site of projection for "crimes" that belong elsewhere. The problem of political correctness is that its concept of the management of change is rigid, and obscures the guilt that is the foundation for the reparation upon which change depends. Guilt involves recognition of both the aggressive wish towards object *and* the wish that the object should survive. Both are kept in mind. Political correctness freezes the former in the service of supposedly strengthening the latter, but in the process produces a sort of rigidity that disallows any more permeable attitude to change. This is a dilemma well known to the adolescent. How, on the one hand, to be completely dissociated from the parental way of thinking, while on the other to retain them as loving objects; how to sustain a critical posture without having to lose one's loving attachment to the parents?

Throughout this chapter we have attempted to describe the soil upon which the behaviour that manifests itself as racism is nourished. We do not suggest that this is the only soil in which racism flourishes. But it is the one in which we, as clinicians or practitioners, get our hands dirty, because it is the place we occupy in trying to be of use to our patients. For the mental health clinician, thinking about racism means trying to understand something that is complex, not black or white, good or bad. It means, if we are to make any contribution to an anti-racist discourse, let alone help our patients, that we must develop a practice that can engage with what is different, but also engage and elaborate what might be thought of as basic to our common humanity. This is not an easy task, and the problem of finding a way of thinking in this toxic domain is well put by Wideman:

> Common ground. How can we seek it, understand it without slipping into talk about race? And once race enters the discussion doesn't a net settle over our heads, capturing nothing but destroying what passes through its deadly weave? Chaos looms because race can mean everything or nothing. A denial of diversity, a claim of profound, unalterable difference between kinds of human beings. An empty word, a word bristling with the power of religious dogma and faith. . . . a word hovering like a toxic cloud, obscuring discourse at all levels. [1995, p. 12]

The clinical task is made more difficult when difference is closely associated with persecution and oppression, whether racial, ethnic, religious, or sexual. The difficulty for the clinician is to stay in role in an attempt to understand how the patient's lived experience has impacted upon them, so that they have presented as being in need of our help. It is very difficult in the highly charged and political context in which "working with difference" is presented for the mental health clinician to be confident about their primary task, which must be to mobilize the patient's knowledge of both their "healthy" and their "damaged" social and psychic capacities so that relationships and the vicissitudes of daily life can be engaged with.

For the mental health clinician it is not enough to identify with the project of emancipation, important as this is. The task must be to discover how lived experience, both persecuting and nourishing, has become internalized, and with what impact, upon the patient's current social and psychic functioning. The pressure is frequently against this process of discovery of what is inside the patient; the powerful invitation is to side with the patient in a grievance against an absent bad object or system, and in so doing join them in a collusion with a belief that their problems are located elsewhere, in someone else, and that psychic relief can be achieved only if the bad object is made to pay. The attraction of this collusion is that the discomfort of engaging with the pain and disturbance of the patient is transformed into another project associated with social change and justice. In practice this is seldom an act of liberation. Rather, it renders the patient and the clinician alike impotent because the work is identified as located elsewhere, outside the immediacy of the clinical encounter. This means that the clinician is spared the discomfort of becoming, in the transference, associated with the bad persecuting object.

For example, a clinician felt very identified with a young woman of colour whose history of migration, and family and social struggle were much like her own. Initially, the patient and therapist made progress, but it became clear in supervision that the work was stuck. It was extremely painful for the clinician to consider any evidence in her patient's material that suggested that her identification with and "understanding" of her patient's experience was not considered helpful by her patient. Indeed, the clinician's "understanding" seemed to have the defensive aim of protecting herself from the patient's denigration and contempt. There was therefore little opportunity to work through the patient's feelings of rage towards the "system" precisely because the clinician's stance removed the system from *immediate* view.

It was only when the clinician could loosen the grip of her identification that the patient could more safely explore, and in the session be angry. In enabling this shift the clinician had, in the transference, to experience being hated; not by a stranger, but by "one of her own", and by any stretch of the imagination this is a difficult experience.

The contribution to change made by the mental health clinician is never simple; there are opportunities and resistances in the social environment as well as opportunities and resistances within the patient. The management of both is necessary if lasting change is to be secure. It is the dialectic between what is outside and what is inside the mind that makes up the complex terrain of mental health work. This point was well understood by a young Bat Mitzvah girl who, in her address, described the Jews' flight from Egypt and concluded that "it was easier to get the Jews out of Egypt than it was to get Egypt out of the Jews" (Lousada, 2001).

Conclusion

For the clinician, the anodyne term "working with difference" does little but obscure the mental pain that has been, and continues to be, the inevitable consequence of being a racialized subject; that is, being oppressed, humiliated, denied rightful opportunity, or even murdered on the basis of being an ethnic stranger.

Additionally, adherence to working with difference or diversity is in danger of sanitizing the primitive and destructive way of thinking associated with racism by substituting a preoccupation with difference. The integrity of the clinical role is dependent upon the clinician being willing to look at mental wounds and not turn away from what is seen there. Patients would not be patients or clients be clients if they had completely survived the pain of their experience. Wounds are not pleasant to look at, and less pleasant to endure, but looking at them is a precondition for "working them through" and for change. For the clinician, the wounds of racism can be especially hard to endure because of anxiety about being implicated in their making; or because of the persecuting fear that intervention will be felt to make things worse, with the unbearable accusations of racism that might follow.

"Working with difference" is not a radical slogan. In our view it serves an ambiguous and unhelpfully defensive role in the context of modern welfare services by eliminating, rather than helping us face, the reality of what is done to people because of *fear and hatred of difference*. We cannot reverse this disposition in human relationships through a strategy of just positively connoting "differences". Bion's celebrated dictum with respect to psychoanalytic work serves to remind us that when we evacuate our awareness of fear from the heart of our clinical engagements, we abdicate the possibility of change: "In every consulting room there ought to be two frightened people: the patient and the psycho-analyst. If they are not one wonders why they are bothering to find out what everyone knows" (Bion, 1990, p. 5).

CHAPTER FIVE

The broken link: polemic and pain in mental health work

Introduction: policy rhetoric and practice reality

I n this chapter we explore how the lack of controversy accompanying Care in the Community policies for the mentally ill has produced an environment in which the complexity associated with mental distress has become overshadowed by a policy and practice consensus that has considerable difficulty in accommodating thoughtfulness about the pain associated with mental distress. In this way of seeing things, it is common sense that care should be in the community, and not in institutions, that intervention should be informed by outcomes, that partnerships are preferable to standalone systems, and that users know, if not best, then at least as much as the clinician, and that "dependency" is corrosive. While there is strength in all of these propositions, there is a folksy quality about them, which makes their interrogation all the more difficult. The problem is that by definition mental distress defies common sense. It is a repudiation of what is common and what is sensible, and brings with it a complexity that requires engagement and understanding, not rhetoric. Jacoby (1977, p. 25) pithily draws our attention to the danger when he writes: "Common sense is the half truths of a deceitful society".

New policy that invokes common sense in its support draws attention to the absence of new ideas. New ideas, by definition, provoke and require debate and controversy. In the arena of modern mental health work, we find in their place a persuasive rhetoric that exhorts but does little to guide the clinician who comes face to face with mental disturbance. In our experience as consultants and trainers, we are frequently confronted by front-line mental health workers unused to debate and therefore predisposed to disavow both the complexity and difficulty of their task. The difficulty that faces contemporary practice is the need to protect the value of reflective practice against the implicitly superior claims of the scientific, associated with evidence and competence based practice. Habermas (1971, p.4) writes that we must "counter the influence of scientism in philosophy and other spheres of thought. Scientism means . . . that we no longer understand science as *but* one form of possible knowledge, but rather identify knowledge with science".

In care in the community a true companionship of ideas is absolutely necessary if the patients' range of difficulties and personal complexity are to be flexibly and sensitively responded to. It is not just quality of service we have in mind, but also the mental well-being of clinical staff, knowing as we do that the mental health of mental health workers is put at risk not just by the disturbance of the patient, but by the lack of attention paid to the physical, intellectual, and psychological environment they are required to work in.

The Thatcherite political project of the 1980s was to change the culture and organization of the welfare state, and to disrupt what had became known as the "dependency culture". It was successful to the extent that it was able to mobilize understandable resentment towards, and disappointment with, low standards of services, and, more insidiously, the primitive fear that the stranger was taking more than their fair share. What eventuated is a dramatic re-organization of health, social care, and education driven by three primary stances. First, services driven by "evidence based practice" and by regulated objectives; second, the mobilization of "consumer" power; and third, the concept of the care in the community. None of these stances is inherently good or bad, but rather their promise or disappointment depends upon the degree to which reality and thoughtful engagement—as opposed to bureaucratic injunction—can be brought to bear upon the range of expectations and tasks with which services are presented.

It is no longer possible to imagine the reinstatement of "old" Labour or "old" welfare. Too much has changed and for too long. The changes relate to both policy and to how clinicians and users think about themselves and their relatedness to others in the caring system. Leys (2001) makes the point clearly:

> In 1975 elected local government still enjoyed tax-raising powers, was landlord to about a quarter of the population, ran schools and social services and public health and a large proportion of long term residential and nursing care . . . By 2000 its tax-raising power had effectively been removed as had its responsibility for housing, the operations of schools and nearly all residential and nursing care . . . [p. 39]

And where the NHS is concerned:

> The hospital service is stripped of its role as a provider of care and "reconfigured" as an increasingly industrialised provider of treatments . . . the boundaries between it and commercial medicine is increasingly breached. [ibid., p. 212]

Failed dependency and self-sufficiency

A middle manager, explaining why he and his team would benefit from a consultation, described how he felt his staff conveyed a sense of trust in him while at the same time he felt that they were not contained by this experience. In his perception they seemed "restless" and "anxiously alert", as if expecting a disaster. To his knowledge this team had had no disaster, but did have to manage a tremendous amount of disturbance. He felt that they were not in a good state of mind and could quite work out why.

The manager worked in a community setting for a Mental Health Trust and knew that the "health" of his staff and organization depended to a large extent on the degree to which he and the team could process what came at them from across their boundary; that is to say, the disturbance of the patients, the expectations and needs of the community and those who care for them, as well as the ambition and anxiety of senior management. The manager thought of himself as a door that should open both ways, so that he could convey what management had in mind to his team and likewise convey to management the lived experience and concerns of his staff. However, the door could only open in one direction and he was therefore more and more filled up with staff anxieties without knowing where to discharge it, while at the same time having to process a steady flow of management material.

The manager concluded the session with a powerful association, which provided the consultation with a place to start. He said that in thinking about the team, what came to mind was the word "orphan". An orphan, we came to think, who is made more desperate by the knowledge of how important a parental relationship is for future development, but does not know where such a relationship can be found. What this intelligent manager was conveying was the persecuting experience of working in a setting that was committed to the panoply of contemporary NHS policy initiatives—Agenda for Change, Improving Working Lives, and so on—that engaged in partnerships, in user involvement and empowerment, and yet that seemed to find less and less capacity to manage the psychological requirements of a service that claimed to "put the patient first". The persecuting nature of this system is that rather than provide the psychological environment necessary to deliver the service, what is required of the staff is psychological self-sufficiency. Tim Dartington makes the point succinctly:

> There has been a shift in dependency within systems as they have developed a culture of psychological self-sufficiency. . . . In the weakening or destruction of an external resource—welfare state, the permanency of corporate life—the experience of the employee is perhaps still of failed dependency of institutions to contain the inherent anxiety in their work. [2003 p. 11]

By and large, well-intentioned and motivated people are attracted to welfare work whether as clinicians, as teachers, or as a member of one of the essential administrative professions that support the clinical task. However, it is also true that the impact of the work is such that organizational and personal defences are constructed to manage the discrepancy between the wish to help and cure on the one hand, and the modesty of what is achievable on the other. In these circumstances, of appropriate therapeutic real-ism or pessimism, it is understandable that hope is invested in new policies. Thus, it is a complex and difficult process to extract what is best from new policy and practice guidance while at the same time retaining a sober and critical stance towards the rhetorical claims that accompany the initiation of each new policy. There is a danger that the hope invested in "new" policy generates a "wild", uncritical, and zealous quality in which fidelity to the new over-whelms the value of accumulated experience, and the systematic evaluation of what has worked, what has not, and why.

One of the architects of the modern welfare state, Richard Titmus, wrote as follows regarding the objectives of policy:

> The real challenge resides in the question: what particular infra-structure of universalistic services are needed in order to provide a framework of values and opportunities based within and around which can be developed socially acceptable selective services aiming to discriminate positively, with the minimum risk of stigma, in favour of those whose needs are greatest? [1976, p. 157]

The gap between aspiration and realization has inevitably been a constant feature of social policy. However, the gap becomes wider in those circumstances where the teacher or the clinician lose, or give up, their ability to practice and take responsibility for the development of their "trade" within the changed context. Without a professional voice predicated on what they have come to know in negotiation with the voice of the user, predicated on what they need or experience, and the voice of the community predicated on the articulation of what they are willing to support, there is little chance of creating the dialogue between these different contributions necessary for the alleviation of mental distress. This dialogue requires distinct voices and not, as discussed in Chapter Two, colo-nized minds.

Without such a linked-up dialogue between these three protag-onists the chances of discovering how to provide positive services "with the minimum risk of stigma, in favour of those whose needs are greatest" (Titmus, 1976, p. 157) is unlikely to be realized. We use the term protagonist in order to leave room for the tension, even conflict, that accompanies such dialogue, dependent as it is on real *differences* among them of role and experience. "Partnership" is a meaningless aspiration if the complex relationships among different participants upon which it depends are not interrogated and developed by participants themselves. Mental health services, as with all welfare services, cannot simply be instrumentally determined. No amount of targets, governance, or evidence based practice can disguise the fact that upon the presence or absence of a capacity to secure, and be nourished by relationships, depends the individual's sense of themselves and their relatedness to the social environment of which they are a member. Whatever the modality of treatment, the capacity for relationship is, in one way or another, what informs the mental health intervention, because symptoms of mental distress manifest themselves in absent, distorted, or damaged social relationships, which are the basis of psychological nourishment and mental health. Thus, a service system that dilutes or edits the centrality of relationships does so on the basis of a reductionism not just of complexity, but of psychic reality.

> What destroys the ecosystem of psychoanalysis is the health industry mentality that regards mental illness and human suffering as an enemy village to be taken out with surgical strikes as quickly and as cleanly as possible. It is ultimately the awareness that human life is marketed and controlled by these companies that destroys the psychoanalytic frame of mind. [Bollas & Sundelson, 1995, p. 101]

Here, Bollas and Sundelson are commenting on the "managed care" system in the USA, where insurance companies have come to dominate and define what is clinically acceptable and delivered. Their argument is straightforward: that there is an incompatibility between the search for profit, which is the primary task of such companies, and the search for appropriate clinical interventions.

This is a point also made by Marquand (1999): "The attempt to force these relationships into a market mould undermines the service ethic, degrades the institutions that embody it and robs the notion of common citizenship of part of its meaning" (p. 254).

Throughout this book we have argued that, in the context of mental health, the professional mind has become corralled into a disciplined state such that it has difficulty in preserving what it knows and its sense of clinical purpose. It is not our intention to critique the nature and organization of managed care or the new NHS social care organizations as such, but rather to point out that underpinning these organizational forms are particular ideas, expectations, and attitudes towards those that provide and use services. Meaningful "best practice" cannot be contingent upon management protocols and clear objectives; it is a product of these being deployed in a manner that is congruent with the ideas, needs, and experience of clinicians on the one hand, and the ideas, needs, and experiences of patients on the other. The discipline imposed by managed care, and the "achievable goals" of outcome-led practice, tend to rob the clinician of the ownership of their own ideas. This is not an argument for "anything goes" in the clinical domain, but a reminder that there is considerable contest about the nature and meaning of mental distress and what can be reasonably be expected from a successful intervention.

The loneliness of the community mental worker

A mental health worker, who had recently been the subject of a formal tribunal following the suicide of a patient, described how the patient had told him to tell no one that he was not taking his medication. In spite of the evidence that the patient was deteriorating, the worker felt in the grip of a conviction that he was bound by the confidentiality the patient had placed upon him. He could retain no sense of himself and the clinical role he occupied. He functioned as though mesmerized by a practice and policy climate that demanded the empowerment of the patient and their right to self-determination even in circumstances where this meant that his own clinical judgement and integrity were rendered superfluous. At no time in the description of events was there a consideration of the consequence of the patient's injunction. Seemingly, the clinician had long since given up the idea that a clinical intervention is predicated on the involvement of two people, and that any clinical progress depended upon his capacity to keep a professional mind able to distinguish the difference between a reasonable and a pathological request. It turned out that this patient was constantly tormenting his clinicians by making formal complaints and, in the process, recruiting advocates who would vociferously support him.

It was unsurprising that the tribunal found the mental health worker to be professionally negligent in as much as the "risk" protocol had not been followed. At no time did the tribunal concern itself with the more disturbing and systemic question of how a "good enough" employee becomes so tormented that he cannot think or ask for help. The team consultation that followed the tribunal was very painful. The "truce" between protocol and practice broke down in an atmosphere of recrimination and a "fight or flight" mentality in which management was experienced as vindictive, persecutory, and out of touch. Whatever judgements may have been appropriate with respect to "management", the more difficult question concerned the relatedness between the actions of the worker and the thinking of his colleagues. The prospect of his actions being a reflection of a shared problem in team thinking was very difficult for them to contemplate. It was difficult because the multi-disciplinarity of this team demanded a truce that supported the self-determination of the individual clinician at the expense of any interrogation of the different approaches to clinical work that were represented in the team. In the absence of this dialogue and interchange, the only place of safety for all the clinicians was a rigid adherence to risk and governance protocols. This clinician had, in effect, broken the rules paradoxically by becoming too involved with the patient and inadequately preoccupied with the system.

The difficulty the team seemed to have in thinking was predicated on the fact that all roles were rigid and not permeable to contact, let alone an intercourse, between one and another. This dynamic was most clearly illustrated by the promotion of the role user at the expense and demotion of the clinical role, leading to a context in which only one rather than two or more legitimate voices could be heard.

For this team the abdication from the professional state of mind was informed by two further perceptions. First, that management was experienced as more preoccupied with "star ratings" than with the clinical and emotional demands placed upon the staff; second, a systemic difficulty in knowing how to respond to a vociferous cohort of patients who described themselves as "survivors" of the psychiatric system had added to their sense of losing their capacity to assert their clinical worth. It became so much easier to become the patients' advocates rather than inhabit the more complex and conflictual role of clinician.

For mental health clinicians the work, if done well, disturbs the practitioner. Mental disturbance, like all threats in our society, is allocated to professionals and institutions that have as their task the removal of the threat from "conscious social concern". Out of sight, out of mind, was the policy that informed the long era of large psychiatric institutions, and now in the context of "Care in the Community" we must ask whether or not the patient is truly to be kept in sight, and in mind. If it is to be so, then by whom, and what must be done to secure the "sighting" from the impulse to "turn a blind eye" (Steiner, 1993)? It is not just individual clinicians who may have the impulse to turn a blind eye; institutions can also lose the patient, creating structures and relationships that purport to see but, in practice, turn away. As we explore in more depth in Chapter Seven, this is not a conscious process, it is a process engaged in by well-motivated workers who can develop an under-standable disposition to "forget" that which causes them unmanageable anxiety. But in our experience, disturbance in the staff and organization arising from the work is responded to with no more thoughtfulness or kindness than in the patient. It is a telling aspect of contemporary organizational practice that so many are sent home, or excuse themselves from work with stress, as if being at home will address what is stressful and anxiety-provoking about the task and the system in which anxiety is purportedly contained. Hirschhorn (1997) makes this point when writing about contemporary organizations:

> the enterprise asks its employees be more open, more vulnerable to one another. But in becoming more vulnerable, people compound their sense of risk. They are threatened from without and from within. . . . Thus the stage is set for a more primitive psychology. Individuals question their own competence and their ability to act autonomously. In consequence just when they need to build a more sophisticated psychological culture, they inadvertently create a more primitive one. [p. 27]

A sophisticated psychological setting is not an abstract idea but an essential prerequisite for all organizations, especially those whose task it is to contain and respond to mental disturbance. Earlier in this chapter reference was made to a contemporary NHS initiative called "Improving Working Lives", an important initiative aiming to support the employee to meet their needs so that they feel secure, involved, well treated, and more generally contained in a healthy workplace. However, what is so strikingly absent in this initiative is any reference to an idea of a management function capable of keeping in mind the degree to which a psychological environment is as necessary to well-being and development as is safety and opportunity. Angela Foster makes the point:

> The emphasis on management as monitoring the behaviour, to the detriment of management processing the feelings and facilitating thinking devalues the therapeutic skills that are central to the task and leaves staff at all levels of the organization feeling anxious. This renders the task of looking after patients more difficult and can lead to an emphasis on activity and "doing" to the detriment of reflection and the ability to stay with the client. [Foster, 1998 pp. 66–67]

Sites of tension in mental health work

The prevention of risk

The shift in mentality between a service concerned with prevention that works on the basis of the clinician doing the best they can—and setting high standards to achieve this—and a service where the failure to prevent can result in exposure, interrogation, and censure is very considerable. Social Service Departments used to consider themselves agencies of prevention, concerned with how to intervene in order to support an individual or family to mitigate the chances of reception into care of children, psychological deterioration and need for hospital admission, and so on. Not everything could be prevented, and at such times statutory authority had to be used. Certainly, there was always a tension between prevention and the use of authority, but it could be a creative tension that produced a plurality of ideas and practices. By contrast, being held "responsible" for the failure to prevent produces an anxiety that seeks reassurance in a command and control mentality in which fidelity to a sanctioned and boundaried set of practices may seem the most sensible way of preventing a risk *to oneself*.

Prevention. in its contemporary interpretation. means a practice driven by the anxiety that clinicians will be found culpable in not protecting the organization, the community, and the patient from risk. In this atmosphere it is hardly a surprise that clinicians play safe, avoid controversy, and favour compliance. Furthermore, the "manager-in-the-mind" is given too much authority at the expense of the professional responsibility for clinical judgement, which in turn diminishes. It is a process in which there is a search for reassurance from what is proven and sanctioned, and it is a process that can obscure both the unpredictable nature of mental distress and the *limits* of what is achievable in clinical work. The rhetoric of contemporary policy, with its directed, outcome-led, evidence based practice, is to imply that there are reliable and predictable outcomes in mental health work. The subtle implication is that when these are not achieved the failure is informed by professional failure or misconduct and not by the reality, and limits, of what *can* be resolved. Arguments of this kind may sound like professional paranoia as a response to being held accountable, but in the context of critical incident enquiries there is a strongly held belief that there is a systemic inequity in the protection provided for clinical staff, with those staff in the community settings being the most exposed and least protected. It is seemingly one thing to advocate a policy of multi-disciplinarity to inform clinical intervention, but quite another to ensure solidarity between professions when under fire.

When consulting to mental health organizations we are constantly struck by the absence of a management who can hold in mind that emotional experience in the organization is both data about its mental health and an indication of the experience of undertaking the clinical task. Armstrong (2004) writes:

> . . . emotional experience in organizations, at the level of the individual and the group, should be viewed as dependent rather than independent variables. This could be put another way, that one cannot fully understand the place of emotions in organisations without reference to the boundary conditions that define any particular organisation as a human construct . . . and what they have to say about the organisation as a system in context. [p. 13]

Partnerships

The success or failure of a comprehensive mental health service depends upon the quality of the multiple relationships that sustain it. These are relationships between purchasing Primary Care Trusts and the "provider" Health and Social Care Trusts, between statutory and independent providers, between one professional and another, between user and professional, between the community and the service delivery system. By any stretch of the imagination this is a complex matrix embodying as much difference as unity. The question is not whether partnerships, cross-boundary relationships, and multi-disciplinarity are desirable, but how we get them on the one hand, and tolerate not having them securely on the other. There is something very persecuting about being *told* to have relationships, as if making friends and partners was easy. The reality is that partnerships are difficult to establish, and harder to sustain. For example, it would be naïve in the extreme to think of marriage only in terms of love, because it involves so much more. In the first instance, partner choice is never simple and is always informed by both conscious and unconscious factors. Second, there is the expectation that the partner will become a fundamental part of the other's developing experience, and there is the hope and wish for creativity and intercourse. As Douglas Woodhouse and Paul Pengelly write, in the context of organizational collaborations:

> In marriage the attachment of each to the other, which has both positive and negative aspects, can provide a psychic container within which conflict and anxiety can be struggled with. This leads to modification of the individual defences in the service of the common task (i.e. the partnership). On the other hand partnership can also be one in which the maturational task is avoided or inhibited, in these circumstances each may confirm the others worst fears ... militating against emotional development, and collaborative engagement with the task. [Woodhouse & Pengelly, 1992, p. 5]

As with marriage, there is now considerable evidence that organizational partnerships can have recurring difficulties, which in turn have an impact of the quality of service provided. In the context of Care in the Community it is as if the period of reconnaissance or courtship has been bypassed. For the adolescent there is the need to explore and develop the capacity for partnerships, and it is often a fraught period; likewise organizations form partnerships only with difficulty and in the context of the need to come to terms with primitive anxieties and fears associated with what is desired and expected of these new relationships. Metaphorically, however, it may be better to go on an exploratory date than to have a premature engagement. For example, in many Community Mental Health Teams (CMHTs) administrative management is held in one place and clinical management in another that is related to core professional identities. This ambiguity of structure is an understandable response to the creation of multi-disciplinary teams, and the fear that they might corrode core professional identity without offering a secure alternative. The splitting of the administrative from the clinical management function creates a system in which there is an active conflict between two loyalties, one to the new team structure with emphasis on transparency, collaboration, co-working, and the inevitable blurring of professional boundaries, and another to the traditional core professional identity and practice. There is much at stake here, and however convincing the arguments for multi-disciplinarity, the continuing reality is that a powerful dynamic seeks to preserve and develop professional differentiation.

In our experience, there is evidence to suggest that some organizations may have formed partnerships before knowing themselves, or as a defence against getting to know themselves in the manner we explored in Chapter Two. Perhaps we need the capacity to tolerate the fact that, sometimes, respective organizational partners may not have found their own identities, let alone each other, and in this circumstance precocious partnerships are at best risky and at worst promiscuous.

The patient and the citizen

Just as the service user may have multiple roles at any point in time that cannot be joined up neatly, so a mental health system cannot be neatly joined up. We would argue that the tensions that arise in these circumstances do so because different parts of the community care system "carry" different projections; that is to say, they carry different sets of ideas and feelings about the user and about the mental health task. It is the "distribution" of ideas, tasks, and professional responses within the mental health and community system that are of interest. In spite of the general adoption of the term "community", the various stakeholders understand, experi- ence, and engage with the community and the experience of mental ill health differently. The core of trained professional mental health workers, far from being widely distributed in community agencies, remain concentrated within NHS Trusts, and so a fundamental question concerns the degree to which these professionals have become orientated towards and therefore *changed by their relation- ship* with community. Once more there is a mixed picture, and we see everywhere how the nurse and the social worker find them- selves much more exposed to the community than the psychiatrist and the psychologist. This, in turn, raises the possibility that differ- ent discourses of explanation concerning mental distress may be employed in the differing sites of mental health provision, on the one hand, or located in different professional groups on the other.

Thus, the environment may be such that the acute psychiatric (mentally ill) patient might be responded to in one place, for exam- ple the NHS Trust, while the disempowered citizen is thought about in another, e.g., the community setting. This propensity to split the patient from the citizen *within the system* is familiar. However, a process of splitting *between one system and another* might be a newer phenomenon with which we must now grapple.

The missing link: the "third position"

Care in the Community is fundamentally concerned with the production of a changed relationship between the patient and the professional. The two-person relationship between professional and client has given way to a triangular relationship between professionals, patients, and the commissioners, all of whom seek legitimacy by reference to one discourse of community or another. Which community depends very much on the location of the role occupied by these protagonists. As with the infant, so with social policy, the move from the dyadic relationship of provision into a more triangular configuration is undertaken neither smoothly nor without anxiety, confusion, and fear. Melanie Klein was "impressed at the ubiquity of the oedipal situation and its unique importance" (Britton, 1989, p. 83) and we have come to understand that oedipal themes are as crucial to organizational life as they are central to individual psychic development. If the child cannot come to tolerate the essential difference between his/her relationship to the parental couple and their relationship with each other, then he/she may become preoccupied with grievance or self-denigration. If, on the other hand, s/he can both acknowledge and tolerate the difference and exclusion, then an opportunity for experience and thinking occurs. Britton takes this thinking further by conceptualizing the experience of being able to tolerate the parental couple's sexual and excluding relationship:

> The closure of the oedipal triangle by the recognition of the link joining the parents provides a limiting boundary for the internal world. It creates what I call a "triangular space"—i.e. a space bounded by three persons of the oedipal situation and all their potential relationships. It includes therefore the possibility of being a participant in a relationship and observed by a third person as well as being an observer of a relationship between two people. [*ibid.*, p. 86]

It is this quality of observing, being observed, and observing oneself that creates the foundation for thinking that is so essential in organizational life, because it involves thinking about aspects of systemic experience that are complex and at times difficult, but are none the less rooted in reality. This process of linking involves being able to think of the parental couple as a couple and as two separate and different people. Britton once more:

> A third position then comes into existence from which object relationships can be observed. Given this we can also envisage *being* observed. This provides us with the capacity for seeing ourselves in interaction with others and for entertaining another point of view whilst retaining our own. [*ibid.*, p. 87]

Britton is describing the essential prerequisite for psychological *and social* development: the capacity to observe, and be observed, in interaction with others, and for engaging with another's point of view while keeping in contact with one's own. Community care, if it is to be more than rhetoric, has to establish precisely these capacities. A model for conceptualizing community care derived from these perspectives has been developed by Foster, Grespi, and Lousada at the Tavistock Clinic.

> In this theoretical triangle the corners represent mental illness, carers (both paid and unpaid) and the community. All three elements need to be kept in mind if care in the community is to become a reality. Only when this is done is it possible to find a third position, that is the position from which it is possible to think about the system as a whole and the different relationships within it in order to avoid getting stuck in a dyadic him/her and me or us and them mode. [Foster & Roberts, 1998, p. 67]

In the face of anxiety, threat of change, and the "intrusion" by the stranger, the developmental possibilities of the triangular experience are often felt as too risky and the attraction of the dyadic relationship—me and them—seems very attractive, but when this occurs in any system of care the result is always dysfunctional. When the three corners of the triangle are occupied by the community, mental illness, and carers in a relationship where the "third position" represented by observation, being observed, and interacting with other views can be maintained, then there is the opportunity for development. However, when conditions produce a system dominated by a dyadic relationship, then the developmental project is placed under considerable strain. For example, if the system is dominated by a relationship between the community and the carers, then it marginalizes the complexity of mental illness; when the systemic relationship is between mental illness and the carers, with the community split off, then the system becomes prone to institutionalization; and where the relationship is between the community and mental illness, with the carers split off, then the system becomes dominated by rationalization.

The "not" patient

The staff group in a residential unit, which offered tenancies to chronic patients discharged from psychiatric hospital, described a thirty-one-year-old resident (note the term) called Richard, about whom they were very worried. Richard was repeatedly asking the women staff if he could wear a nappy, a request he would usually make at night when only one member of staff would be on duty. The staff felt caught between two responses: first the unit's commitment to the notions of normalization, self-determination, and client empowerment, emphasizing, as they thought, the client's right to choose. Second, a much less available but none the less powerful intuitive knowledge that Richard's request contained not just a regressive wish, which was frightening enough, but also contained a communication about the nature of his mental state. They had responded to these requests with an attempt to divert Richard into a number of other activities, all of which failed. More recently Richard had begun to spend parts of the night leaning out of his window, shouting "Kill, kill", then phoning an ambulance and asking to be admitted to hospital. For some six weeks this was refused. He was finally admitted and discharged four days later, the hospital staff commenting that he was "quiet as a baby".

A social worker was assigned to Richard with a view to assessing him for alternative provision, but soon declared that Richard was not in a fit state of mind to undertake an assessment. An impasse had arrived, in which the staff, like Richard, were left without a container, a set of ideas for thinking that would provide them with the authority to explain or act. It was astonishing to discover, but not unfamiliar to the staff, that Richard arrived at the project without *any* medical notes and no discharge summary had been forthcoming concerning his future management after leaving hospital.

Neither the group of staff nor their management felt able to make an effective complaint. In the staff meeting the lack of medical notes seemed to reinforce the view that they were perceived as engaged in a different project to that pursued by the hospital. The lack of complaint seemed to suggest that, at least in part, they also thought this to be true. Richard's repeated yelling of "Kill, kill" resonated with something very basic in the staff's own state of mind. First, they were understandably concerned for their own physical, and implicitly their psychic, safety. Second, they seemed persecuted by the responsibility of keeping their residents alive on the one hand, and out of psychiatric hospital—associated with living death—on the other. It is not an exaggeration to say that one of the major criteria by which care in the community is judged is the extent to which it is able to contain suicide and murder and to prevent re-admission. This particular situation was compounded by feeling "stuck" with a patient whom they could neither discharge, nor for whom they could easily attract professional interest and support. This placed an overwhelming psychological burden upon the untrained and inadequately supported staff. It was to their enormous credit that they managed to survive at all. In view of this experience, it is possible to understand how one of the major defences within this team emerged as a reluctance to admit that they were involved in mental health work at all. They preferred, but were unable to sustain, a view that their work was educative, and concerned with the production of those skills necessary to take up the role of a citizen who had "survived" psychiatry. This was reinforced in their experience by the in-hospitability of mental health professionals, who in effect kept the "patient" in their minds, a person who bore little resemblance to the "tenant" who was resident in their community. The strength of the splitting between one discourse concerned with a psychiatric patient and another that was concerned with a citizen, produced a "part person" in each setting unavailable for integrative thought or action.

What this example draws attention to is a system that has difficulty in protecting a state of mind that can accommodate a third position. The hostel manager was invited to the Care Planning Approach (CPA) meeting, but the absence of the consultant in charge of Richard only served to reinforce the feeling that the manager of one system was unable to have a dialogue with the manager of the other.

Conclusion

This chapter tries to draw attention to the gap, or the broken link, between the rhetoric of policy change and the reality of working with mental disturbance. Our experience is that too often working in a community setting means an uncontained exposure to mental disturbance on the one hand, and the persecutory experience of failure to achieve change on the other, with the result that the individual employee, their organization, and the quality of their work is put at risk. Absenteeism and stress are evidence of a system that has difficulty in sustaining a belief in the function of emotion as a form of communication, whether manifested in the patient or the clinician. Bion (1967) wrote: "These attacks on the linking function of emotion lead to an over-prominence in the psychotic part of the personality of links which appear to be logical, almost mathematical, but never emotionally reasonable" (p. 109).

But perhaps the last word about the persecutory nature of rhetoric and instrumental policy logic should go to one on the great architects of the welfare state, Richard Titmus, who, when thinking about the "new" community strategy of the time, of which he was a great supporter, drew attention to the gap between aspiration and reality:

> The aspiration of reformers are transmuted, by the touch of a phrase into hard won reality. What some hope will one day exist is suddenly thought by many to exist already. All kind of unlovely weeds are changed by statutory magic and comforting appellation, into the most attractive flowers that bloom not just in spring, but all the year round. [Titmus, 1968, p. 111]

CHAPTER SIX

Surface tensions: emotion, conflict, and the social containment of dangerous knowledge

Introduction

The case study informing the argument of this chapter is child abuse, and especially child sexual abuse as it erupted into widespread social consciousness during the Cleveland "crisis" of 1987 (Butler-Sloss, 1988). However, this chapter is not an exercise in historical reflection. In line with our general argument, we are concerned to examine the dynamics surrounding the process through which this "dangerous knowledge" became assimilated into our society. In many respects a historical perspective on these events gives reason for optimism about the strength of our social containers. The prevalence of child sexual abuse has become an accepted fact in contemporary child welfare and adult mental health service delivery and policy.

However, this was not achieved without an acute struggle, some aspects of which we review in what follows. This struggle can be conceptualized in terms of an acute oscillation over whether "unthinkable" matters could be made thinkable or not, over whether the social capacity existed to allow more than fleeting emotional contact with the unwelcome experiences the crisis announced. Arguably, this was indeed possible, but socially as much as personally such achievements remain precarious and continually subject to dynamic influences and oscillations. Thus, in the next chapter we examine a second more recent episode in our social history of responses to child abuse, the Victoria Climbié Inquiry report, and suggest that we can find here evidence for a continuing battle with borderline states of mind, both in the practices that the Inquiry uncovered, and to a lesser extent in the discourses of the report itself.

This chapter is perhaps the most philosophically dense section of the present book. Via the case studies at its centre it also explores a fundamental question: how are our everyday dealings with matters like mental pain, child maltreatment, learning disability, and so on, made reasonably secure by a framework of knowledge and ideas? Definitions, theories and research into the origins and treatment of these phenomena are all highly contested. The current policy and scientific climate of the NHS and social care sectors relies heavily upon the generation of an "evidence base" to achieve the end of "securing" a framework of knowledge to inform clinical practice and service development. To some degree, the concept of evidence informing this venture is itself contested, but this debate remains largely marginal to the concerns of the policy makers as well as to the official and unofficial ideologues of contemporary health and welfare epistemology.

However, this chapter is concerned with a different kind of underpinning for our knowing relationship to the world, one that is presupposed by the kinds of debates mentioned above, but that also remains largely unexamined, partly by virtue of its status as presupposed. As we have stressed from the outset of this book, our individual and social capacities to enter into a full engagement with the distressing, disturbing, painful, and conflicted domains that are the "objects" of welfare, depend in their turn upon a capacity for sustained emotional contact with our own *experience* of these matters. In the face of disturbing experience in the social arena, we suggest that society's "agencies of concern" are as susceptible to the powerful and conflicting forces embedded within such experience as are individuals faced with acute or chronic anxiety in their own minds or in their personal environments. In either case, unless emotionally disruptive and threatening experiences can be tolerated they cannot be thought about and given the kind of symbolic shape that is a precondition for the more sophisticated processes of testing and examination through which we generate *knowledge*.

Psychoanalysis and the foundations of everyday knowledge

Broadly, our everyday dealings with our personal and social worlds depend upon a framework of confidence in our knowing (or epistemological) relationship to the world around us, and to ourselves. For the conduct of everyday life we need to believe that we are in possession of reliable ways to distinguish fact from fantasy, truth from lies, fiction from documentary, evidence from interpretation, knowledge from belief, possibility from probability, and so on. Knowing, or at least believing, that we know how to know is a precondition of a trusting rather than a suspicious relationship to reality. But from time to time our received social framework of confidence in these matters is profoundly shaken. Episodes of radical doubt are necessary for both social change and reflecting such change. But equally, these periods of disruption test our social capacity to assimilate and digest, in effect to integrate new experience.

Perhaps, as Ian Hacking (2000) has suggested, child sexual abuse is *the* paradigm case for exploring these questions, because sexual relations between adults and children are organized, or not, by the most fundamental psycho-social barrier—the incest taboo. But even this statement begins to open up the complexity of the wider field. Are sexual relations between parents and children, between siblings, between close cousins, and between adults and children not related through family membership, all prohibited through the agency of the same kind of psychic or psycho-social "law"? One may suspect not, but what are the differences and distinctions involved? Some psychoanalytic thinking would refer a wide range of superficially distinct prohibitions and transgressions to the operation or failure of a basic taboo or law—the Oedipus complex and the mechanisms of repression associated with it. If we want to investigate the wider field of social repression and de-repression, and the ambiguities of ontology and epistemology in this wider field, we might do better to work with a notion of "family resemblances" among different but related varieties of knowledge, representation, and defences or prohibitions against the representation and representability of dangerous knowledge. The value of investigating this terrain by examining "boundary cases" is that the specific character of what is at issue may be particularly clearly revealed as a particular phenomenon becomes the object of struggle for legitimation or de-legitimation. Writing in similar vein about the history of the concept of child abuse and the conundrums of construction and realism, Ian Hacking observed:

> It is not so often that we can experience a concept in rapid motion.
> . . . We shall see more than evolution in three decades of child
> abuse; we shall see mutations worth calling revolutions, conceptual
> displacements worth calling explosions. [1999, p. 132]

This chapter explores the role of emotional conflict in shaping what is available or not available to be known, and the reciprocal interplay of desire and the conditions for its social representation when conflict about what is, or can be, known surfaces in the public sphere. Thus, we are focusing on the nature of social and psychological processes that occur at the boundary of the private and public domains, at the boundary of different kinds of symbolic systems or sites of symbolic propagation, and therefore at the boundaries of the known or knowable, the thinkable and the unthinkable. The focus is on the emergence into public awareness and discourse of events and phenomena that may transpire to have been "there" all along but which were previously unknowable, denied, socially and linguistically unrepresented or unrepresentable; but also with the process by which such knowledge or awareness may recede and become once again unrepresented or unrepresentable. The concern is with phenomena that become the object of claims to legitimation as "real"; in which those seeking to establish their "reality" may succeed or fail to achieve the recognition they seek; with the seeking of such recognition, but where the claims made remain undecided or undecidable; or over the course of time all of these. The connection between linguistic representation and affect in the public sphere concerns our social capacity, and willingness, to know about painful and conflictual matters at the level of social discourse—or not.

One could say that the founding insights of psychoanalysis are about how we deal with unwelcome or seemingly dangerous knowledge. Ideas or representations, it might be said, can never be in themselves a source of trouble. It is the feelings, especially the anxieties, associated with them that give rise to the need to deny, disavow, repress, split, or deploy any of the other mechanisms of defence that psychoanalysis has described. As Laplanche and Pontalis summarize it:

> Psycho-analysis speaks of conflict when contradictory internal requirements are opposed to each other in the subject. The conflict may be manifest—between a wish and a moral imperative, for example or between two contradictory emotions—or it may be latent, in which event it is liable to be expressed in a distorted fashion in the manifest conflict, emerging especially in the formation of symptoms, behavioural troubles, character disturbances etc. [1988, p. 360]

When in the context of clinical work an individual's defences are relaxing, the emerging capacity for new self-knowledge may relate equally to experiences of historical events and truths, or psychic experiences and truths, or to complex and ambiguous interlacings of each. We suggest that the same conditions of ambiguity pertain in the social field when hitherto repressed or denied dimensions of psycho-social experience are becoming available for symbolization. In both cases, the emergent phenomena may be understood as being structured like dreams, and as standing in need of decoding (or interpretation) if they are to find a place within ordinary discourse. During those periods of disruption in which new phenomena seek symbolization and a discursive register via which they can be socially integrated, we see evidence indicating that "historical truths"—everyday social processes—may always be organized by unconscious desire, phantasy, and the primary process mode of thinking that characterizes the unconscious. Indeed, one part of the special interest of such unusual emergent phenomena is that they can reveal the symbolic and unconscious structure of the everyday, the epistemologically taken for granted. In this sense we propose that they function rather like natural experiments in the social or natural sciences, revealing aspects of the quotidian through the provision of special conditions that expose the unstable inner logic of the apparently stable and mundane.

The larger, and more tentative, claim is that a social epistemology embracing both a concept of the historically real *and* a simultaneous concept of the inherent ambiguity, representational multiplicity, and undecidability of the real, is capable of resolving some of the more obstinate tensions in social theory about the status of truth and truth claims. On this view, it is because social life and history are both real and determinate in certain respects, but also structured by symbolic ambiguity and indeterminacy of meaning, that disputes about the nature of truth and truth claims in this area arise in the first place. Indeed, we propose that only if we accept such a view can we hope to disentangle those phenomena that represent something beyond themselves from those that represent only anxiety or desire itself, or are efforts to hallucinate experience as a cover for there being nothing there. This holds out hope that we can evade familiar polarizations in social theory and practice between empiricist and reductive stances on the one hand, and idealist, radical constructivist or relativist ones on the other.

Containment: the emotional foundation of knowledge

The key anchor point in this way of seeing matters is emotion, and especially emotional conflict. Where social experiences or processes are imbued with emotional conflict, they require a social container if they are to become available for thought in society, as distinct from enactment, denial, repression, and so on. In this sense, social discourses function as a form of containment, constituting a set of conditions, a language, for representation of emotional experience. Psychoanalytically, the analogy here is with Wilfred Bion's (1967) concept of "thoughts in search of a thinker". Bion held that in human development the apparatus for thinking—the mind— follows rather than developmentally precedes the availability of thoughts to be thought. Difficulties arise for us as individuals to the extent that we have not developed a capacity to make certain kinds or intensities of thought thinkable. Emotional experiences can be there, and real but not knowable, or thinkable, because of the absence of a mental container robust enough to enable symbolization. Mostly, he suggests it is frightening, painful, or conflictual areas of experience that we may have trouble symbolizing; but also the failure to develop an apparatus for such thoughts renders them yet more terrifying.

The concern here is with a view of social theory not as a project of explanation, or even primarily interpretation, but of discovery or revelation (Lawrence, 2000). Following Bion's "theory of thinking" again, it suggests a variety of social theory framed by the question, "Which states of social being can be known, and which not, by virtue of the provision or lack of provision of an apparatus for thinking about them?" In its focus on liminal states of social being, that is, states of emergence towards representation or representability, there is a further analogy with the process, familiar to all of us, of waking with awareness (but not yet knowledge) of a dream that has been dreamt, and of rendering this experience knowable through the act of narrativizing to ourselves, or others, its process and contents.

Spaces for the unknown—the clinical and social management of child sexual abuse

In the following pages we first offer an account of a clinical experience in which aspects of knowledge of child abuse come to the surface for an adult in therapy. Their emergence into fuller awareness is attended by what can be described as epistemological uncertainty about aspects of historical truth. Therapy, it is suggested provides the conditions under which new or revised representations of historical events are developed. But these representations are not pure constructs. They are alternative accounts of realities that may never be independently checkable, although there is every reason to suppose that one set of representations more accurately captures the historical truth than does the other, partly because both cannot be historically accurate with respect to the same set of events. There is also good reason to suggest that it is the powerfully traumatic, conflicted nature of the emotional experiences in question that generates the epistemological confusions that afflicted the patient. Subsequently, we discuss aspects of the emergence into fuller social awareness of the whole phenomenon of child sexual abuse, and propose that the kind of crisis of knowledge that attended this process can equally be explained by reference to the potency of the emotional conflicts involved, but at a social level.

*Who did what to whom? Child abuse and the
indeterminacy of memory*

A man who reported that he had been quite severely and repeatedly physically assaulted by his father up until his early adoles-
cence came to a psychotherapy session one day and recounted a
memory in which at the age of about four, during a family visit to
some relatives, he had lost control of his bladder and bowels, causing his father to beat him. The therapist listened and made some
tentative observations about the painfulness of the experience and
the recollections. The patient returned next day and said that he
had gone away and felt able to think more clearly about the
memory, and it now seemed to him that events had been the other
way round—that his father had beaten him, perhaps because he
had been pestering to go home, and he had lost control of himself
as a result of the beating. Soon after, it began to emerge that in the
present this man suffered occasional near psychotic lapses, in which
he experienced catastrophic anxiety arising from a belief that he
had made some kind of a mistake, which he had not in fact made.
For example, he turned up on time at a supervisor's room for an
appointment, and not finding him in, collapsed into a state of anxiety believing that today was tomorrow and that the appointment
had therefore been the previous day, that the supervisor would be
furious and his career would be in ruins. He returned to "reality"
only when the supervisor phoned him in his room enquiring if he
was coming to the appointment.

However, rather characteristically, and hopefully, the patient
was able to regroup himself and bring these states of mind to therapy where he and the therapist could look at them together. As it
became possible to work with these states of mind more directly, a
whole area of very confused psychological functioning opened up
for exploration.

Writing in 1925, about trauma and memory, Pierre Janet says:

> *Memory*, like belief, like all psychological phenomena, is an action;
> essentially it *is the action of telling a story*. Almost always we are
> concerned here with a linguistic operation, quite independent of
> our attitude towards the happening . . . A situation has not been . . .
> fully assimilated, until we have achieved, not merely an outward
> reaction through our movements, but also an inward reaction

through the words we address to ourselves, through the organisation of the recital of the event to others and to ourselves, and
through the putting of this recital in its place as one of the chapters
in our personal history. [1925, pp. 662–663]

The patient's recitals in psychotherapy are of a special kind in a
special situation. The memory of the events brought to therapy by
the patient were not exactly "recovered". Rather, in the presence of
someone who he presumably experienced as sufficiently able to
hold his anxieties in mind, important uncertainties and confusions
about the veracity of his beliefs about the *ordering* of events became
open to re-examination; he was able to reconstruct and develop a
new narrative for this episode, in which he takes up a different
position in the constellation of events from the one inscribed in the
original; one in which he is in some sense less "to blame" for his
punishment and better able to see the connection between his past
experience and his contemporary tendency to believe that he brings
catastrophe down on himself..

What is recovered here, is something more like a spontaneous
capacity to see things differently. That something happened involving a beating by his father and his own loss of control is not in
doubt in the patient's mind, but who exactly did what to whom in
what order, is in doubt, and in his contemporary experience frequently remained so. The therapist believed that the patient's new
narrative almost certainly accorded better with events "as they
actually happened", although in the absence of corroborating evidence it is right to suspend absolute judgement about this. Via his
concept of *Nachtraglichkeit*, rather unsatisfactorily translated for us
as "deferred action" or *après coup*, Freud held that "the material
present in the form of memory-traces (is) subjected from time to
time to a *re-arrangement* in accordance with fresh circumstances—to
a *re-transcription*" (Freud, 1950a). Laplanche and Pontalis suggest in
their discussion of this concept that

It is not lived experience in general that undergoes a deferred revision but, specifically, whatever it has been impossible in the first
instance to incorporate fully into a meaningful context. The traumatic event is the epitome of such unassimilated experience."
(Laplanche & Pontalis, 1988, p. 112)

In the example above, the fresh circumstances to which Freud refers as providing the occasion for re-transcription might be the therapeutic context itself. Inside himself, this patient retained sufficient trust to enable him to make good use of a co-operative therapeutic alliance. His recall of abuse is available to him, and to us, but arguably has only been transformed into true *memory* by virtue of the presence of another mind able to help process and think about psychic experience in a new way. Yet how tenuous was this possibility became evident much later in the therapy when he told his therapist he had been afraid to let him know of his revised version of events in childhood, in case the therapist was angry because he had lied the previous day. Once again as Janet remarks:

> Strictly speaking, then, one who retains a fixed idea of a happening cannot be said to have a "memory" of the happening. It is only for convenience that we speak of it as a "traumatic memory". The subject is often incapable of making with regard to the event the recital which we speak of as a memory: and yet he remains confronted by a difficult situation in which he has not been able to play a satisfactory part . . . [1925, p. 663]

We arrive then, at an initial formulation that suggests why psychoanalysis can sometimes be so uneasily and ambiguously positioned with respect to child abuse. True memory, on the view advanced here, is *indeterminate* with respect to the question of the real event or what actually happened; *Nachtraglichkeit* or re-transcription is not about recovering a determinate or mimetic relationship between memory and historical events, but a meaningful and essentially creative one. And yet, where trauma has occurred by virtue of external impingement, or assault, events clearly are, or were, *determinate*. In some sense it happened this way, or that; it happened, or it didn't. Usually therapists are primarily concerned with meaning, but in cases involving trauma necessarily at times find themselves preoccupied with questions of historical accuracy. In the public domain, and especially the courts, where child abuse is concerned the focus or direction of concern may often be the reverse, and establishing the historical facts of the matter becomes the predominant concern.

Because there is little doubt that some version of the childhood events recounted by the patient involving an assault by his father did happen, and even less doubt with respect to the contemporary muddles he reported, we could characterize his state of mind as involving systematically distorted beliefs about causality and sequence, held (even if temporarily) with complete conviction. But the more general lesson we may draw from this episode, and from the theorizations of Janet, is that there is no form of memory that provides a privileged, certain, or mimetic relation to "the facts". The facts are often in principle and forever beyond recovery or even access, mediated or partly constituted as they are by imagination, hallucination, delusion—by the desire that all actors bring, but differentially, to the same event.

In which case, what status can we possibly assign to the effort to establish the facts, as we frequently must, and for the sake of psychic health, need to be able to? The man described is in possession of a fact that can be represented as something like "On a particular day, my father beat me and something terrible happened that may have been cause or consequence of his actions". But by itself what meaning does this have? We may notice that both accounts of his childhood events have a common narrative structure, or structure of meaning, which can be summarized as "Somebody did something to someone, which occasioned a catastrophic reaction". In the Kleinian psychoanalytic tradition, this relational configuration is seen as the basic, inalienable structure of meaningful experience, the elementary form of all unconscious phantasy. In this view, unconscious phantasy is the earliest form of mentation, and plays across the field of early experience, providing it with what we can later see as meaning. Early experience is frequently, and ordinarily, charged with powerful feelings, mostly of a bodily kind. "The bodily parts are suffused with active suffering" (Hinshelwood, 1994). But the structure of phantasy is *relational* and attributes both benign and malign intentionality to (some) other person(s) as the sources and objects of feeling states. However, attributions of causality, and perhaps causal sequence, are only gradually and precariously informed by "reality" and may reverse or fluctuate in the manner illustrated by the experiences of the patient described above (Hinshelwood, 1994; Isaacs, 2003).

This notion of a primitive but continually active process of psychic structuring of reality is captured at a more parochial level by the concept of "the drama triangle". Karpman (1968) described the triangle comprising the three positions "persecutor", "victim", and "rescuer", showing how, in the structure of myths and fairy-tales but also everyday social realities, these positions can be fixed or can be rapidly re-assigned. Indeed, we see this process in action in a graphic way in the illustration below at the level of social emergence of knowledge of child abuse during the so-called Cleveland affair.

From a psychological perspective then, we may propose that things happen, but that things always happen mediated by phantasy to a greater or lesser degree. Phantasy is structured and gives meaning to experience, but the relationship between meaning and historical truth understood in terms of causes, action sequences determining responsibility, and so on, is frequently inherently ambiguous exactly *because* historical events are always mediated by phantasy. When events or realities are charged with emotional tension or conflict between "good" and "bad", then ambiguity and reversal of meaning can become the agent of epistemological uncertainty, crisis, or confusion as the various conflicting (psychic or social) agencies battle it out for supremacy over what version of reality, if any, shall prevail.

As a final illustration of this, it is worth citing the work of W. R. D. Fairbairn on "the moral defence". According to Fairbairn (1943), the infant or child faced with psychic frustration and deprivation will prefer to identify with the "bad", that is, see himself as the source of badness rather than locate this in his parents or caretakers. He or she does this on the assumption that "it is better to be a sinner in a world ruled by God than to live in a world ruled by the Devil" (*ibid.*, pp. 66–67). Fairbairn was not a Kleinian and did not hold that the structure of unconscious phantasy was "given" at birth, but his account of the production of an internal world through various internalizing manoeuvres results in a picture of this world that is remarkably congruent with that of later Kleinian thinkers.

Who's been doing what to whom? The indeterminacy of the social

The kinds of social processes and events with which we are concerned in this chapter are well documented in Elaine

Showalter's (1997) *Hystories*, but her book does not engage very fully with the epistemological and ontological conundrums surrounding the ambiguous status of the processes described. They are typically highly affectively charged, and sites of considerable social conflict and contestation. The recent legitimation of the condition popularly known as ME as a medically recognized illness, following many years of scientific and public contestation, is a good example of the epistemological "career" of one of these phenomena. The appearance, contested status, and disappearance of "Satanic abuse" from public discourse, partly as a result of an "authoritative" enquiry that concluded it did not exist, is another (see Hacking, 1999, pp. 126–127).

As already proposed, ambiguity, indeterminacy of meaning, and the frequent undecidability of the nature of the "real event" are the stock in trade of the practising psychotherapist. However, the process by which a previously unrecognized, unnamed, or unknown social phenomenon that is a locus of psychic and/or social conflict achieves coherent *representation* in public discourse will also inevitably be accompanied by epistemological uncertainties that mirror their contested ontological status. But the presence or absence of social contestation turns on the question of emotional conflict. In the private domain, represented by the privacy of the consulting room, this may be more or less all that is at stake (as if that were not enough). In the public domain much more may be at stake—reputation, professional legitimation, legality, positioning within configurations of power, and structures of dominance/subordination and so on. All "representations" are "real", but a representation may make false or distorted claims about the status of what is denoted (as distinct from connoted) as represented. Equally what is "real" may have no representation, and so belong in the realm of what Christopher Bollas (1987) calls the "unthought known" or Bion "beta elements" (1962).

The "false memory" debates of recent years (Sandler & Fonagy, 1997) are among the most prominent moments of articulation between the consulting room and the domain of public affairs, extending to the courts. In Britain, their context was set by the Cleveland affair of 1987, when the mass diagnosis of child sexual abuse in Britain burst upon the social field, facing this society with a social crisis of epistemological undecidability. Whatever we now

think we know about child sexual abuse in general, or in any particular case, at the time, unless one was an active protagonist on one
side or another of the contest, the fact is that we did not know what
to think. We suggest we did not know what to think because:

(1)   there were no established epistemological categories with
      which to think about the claims being made. The claims were
      in various senses of the word "unbelievable", not so unlike
      (but in the end distinct from) being asked to believe that a
      group of Martians had been discovered living in Middles-
      borough;
(2)   the nature of our means of moving towards deciding on the
      "believability" of the claims was missing. What *kinds* of
      evidence would we need? We could not know, because we did
      not really *know* what kind of phenomena sexual abuse was. In
      the absence of concrete medically verifiable damage, how were
      we to even begin reaching decisions? Hence, the way in which
      so much came to depend upon the credibility or otherwise of
      the "anal dilation" examination;
(3)   *if* something "real" was in the process of being uncovered
      (which it undoubtedly was), then obviously the questions of
      knowledge involved were structured by extremely powerful
      emotional forces seeking both disclosure and repression.
      Under these circumstances, the representational conditions for
      knowing about the phenomena in question were subject to
      processes of distortion and displacement similar to those we
      encounter in the clinical psychoanalytic field, but at the level
      of the social.

However, as the crisis itself unfolded, there was little or no space
for such dispassionate philosophical analysis. Events were powerfully shaped by the structuring force of phantasy relationships, as
described by "the drama triangle":

> . . . what began as a triangle of "victim" children, "persecutor"
> parents and "rescuer" doctors and social services rapidly shifted
> into "victim" families, "persecutor" doctors and rescuer local MP
> and media, before swinging again into "persecutor" media and MP,
> "victim" doctors and social services and "rescuer" official inquiry
> report. [Hughes & Pengelly, 1997, p. 111]

The rapid reversals of perspective described here are analogous to those found in dream life. When dreams are "interpreted" via the subject's free associations in the context of clinical psychoanalysis they are taken (a) to contain or reveal multiple meanings but (b) these structures of meaning are taken to be organized around a determinate "event" or constellation of events. Such events may be located primarily in external reality or internal reality, but are either way in principle empirically specifiable—the wish to murder a colleague, the anxiety that he was having murderous thoughts during yesterday's meeting. Out of the epistemological chaos occasioned by the surfacing into the public sphere of phenomena like child sexual abuse, the task is to forge epistemological order—categories for thinking—capable of both distinguishing between, but also retaining the connections between, real events (internal or external) and our elaborations of these events in social phantasy.

The question becomes, what sociological tools do we have, and what do we need to develop, to satisfactorily approach such a terrain of analysis? As Hacking observes of the Cleveland affair, "The case illustrates how the concept of child abuse craves objectivity" (1999, p. 150). So, it is instructive to find that certain key passages of the Inquiry Report into the Cleveland affair (Butler-Sloss, 1988) are preoccupied with questions of epistemological clarification that echo some of the distinctions and differences outlined in the present paper. In the section of the report entitled "Listening to the Child" Justice Butler Sloss comments:

The concept of helping the child to tell [of sexual abuse] is recognised to have its uses in certain circumstances. When embarking on it for diagnostic purposes, it is important to remember at least three possible situations:

1.   The abuse has occurred and the child is speaking of it.

2.   The abuse has occurred and the child is unable to speak of it or is denying it.

3.   The abuse has not occurred, and the child cannot speak of it. It is clearly a difficult matter of judgement to know whether the child is not telling because of some sort of pressure, such as fear of the consequences, or because there is nothing to tell. At the end of a session, the professionals may not know which of those two situations is the true position. [Butler-Sloss, 1988, pp. 206–207]

The space of "undecidability", even if temporary, is key. In circumstances such as these, we require professional and social spaces in which the reality of undecidability, ambiguity and the emergent nature of knowledge of phenomena can be handled. As Butler Sloss indicates, this necessarily embraces the capacity not to know, to wait for meaning to emerge. The more the realm of conventional propositional and syllogistic logic asserts its claims, the further we will retreat from the possibility of knowledge:

> Dr Jones said: "A fundamental problem of the 'disclosure' approach is that it is inherent in the concept that there is *something* to disclose. The problem is highlighted by those professionals who consider that the child is either *disclosing* or *'in denial'*. The third, and crucial, alternative possibility, namely that the child has no sexual abuse to disclose, is not considered as a viable option . . . The premise that abuse has occurred, yet is hidden and shrouded from discovery, is inherent in the very term 'disclosure work'". [Butler-Sloss, 1988, p. 206]

Legal positivism, and indeed all manifestations of positivism in the social sphere, inherently incline towards an epistemology of excluded middles, of binary logical choice, of reasoned determination of truth and falsity according to the evidence available (Cooper, 1999). Perhaps we fail to appreciate how necessary such constructs of truth and meaning are for the conduct of any form of rational social life. Yet, simultaneously, because we are captured by the elegant simplicities they proffer, we forget how necessarily unstable must be their grasp on the nature of actual social realities. Our world is simply not made up according to the rules and precepts of positivist logic. The disruptive character of the unconsciously generated character of social reality will make itself known. At such moments, epistemological confusion will organize the public sphere, because different realms of logic, truth, and meaning are on a collision course.

We might say that the general questions thrown up equally by the Cleveland child sexual abuse affair, the public "career" of chronic fatigue syndrome or Gulf War Syndrome, or many other contested psycho-social phenomena such as the struggle over the definition and legitimation of institutional racism, are:

(1) Does the phenomenon "exist" at the level of empirically speci-
     fiable social relations, or is it the projection into the social
     sphere of conflicts and anxieties that subsist only or primarily
     at the level of phantasy?
(2) What are the criteria of decidability about existence or non-
     existence in the above sense?
(3) How far does decidability depend upon acceptance or rejection
     of particular varieties of knowledge, and conditions for estab-
     lishing knowledge claims, as legitimate?
(4) To what extent are conditions for establishing knowledge a
     question of contestation resulting from relations of power and
     social positioning rather than more abstract epistemological
     relationships analysable independently of relations of power
     or social position?

Social theory as revelation

A social theory that presupposes the active ubiquity in social life of
unconscious forces and thus an omnipresent interlacing of
conscious and unconscious logic in the production of social
phenomena has barely started to be developed. One or two sociological thinkers have articulated the character of such a theory, and
there are particular psychoanalytic clinicians whose theoretical
work lends positive illumination to such a concept of social
processes and formations. In the realm of knowledge about human
affairs (that is human understanding directed towards human
activity as distinct from towards the understanding of everything
not in itself human), it is assumed in this paper that the work of the
unconscious is omnipresent, and that this renders futile all attempts
to seek absolute closure in the empirical or theoretical study of
social life. This does not imply that relations between representations and the represented are arbitrary. There *is* knowledge, but
fragmentary, partial, "won from the formless void and infinite" as
Wilfred Bion (1967) put it. Waking consciousness and logic necessarily deals in separate representations, with bounded identities
that form the basis of the possibility of classical propositional logic
with its "law of the excluded middle". But,

> Of the essential stuff of the unconscious, the representation, we can say practically nothing, if we confine ourselves to our customary logic . . . The unconscious exists only as an indissociably representative/affective/intentional flux. [Castoriadis, 1987, p. 274]

And,

> Once we find ourselves within it, it is not so much the imaginary–representative magma of the unconscious that is the inexhaustible source of astonishment, but rather the schema of discreteness, the idea of identity, the relative effectiveness of the separation. [*ibid.*, p. 276]

In other words, for Castoriadis, the realm of bounded, conventionally logically ordered phenomena, susceptible to the kind of reasoning that ordinarily governs social life, is an inherently unstable, and in no sense privileged domain of being. A similar view, this time articulated by a clinical theorist, puts it thus:

> The unconscious is not "subconscious"; it is an aspect of the indivisible totality of consciousness. Similarly, meaning (including unconscious meaning) is *in* the language being used, not under or behind it. (Freud [1915] believed the term "subconscious" to be "Incorrect and misleading since the Unconscious does not lie "under" consciousness.) . . . Meaning is continuously in the process of becoming something new and in so doing, is continuously undoing itself (undercutting its own claims to certainty). (Ogden, 1999, pp. 215–218]

Ogden's work is original and relevant to the project of elaborating a psychoanalytically informed social theory of the kind adumbrated in this book. His interest lies in the way the clinical encounter creates a new third object, what he calls "the analytic third" out of the experiential and empirical field constituted by the dyad of patient and analyst. The unconscious is not over there "in the patient" or over here "in the analyst" but subject to a process of co-evolution in the space, or field, between them. Part of his originality lies in his articulation of fresh ways of accessing or tuning in to the contents of this field through attention to the reverie of the analyst. This suggests first, a view of the location of the point of contact between conscious and unconscious life that is liminal, and available at a more everyday level than traditionally supposed; and second, a view of this relationship as productive, generative, rather than only problematic or pathogenic. Sociologically, it suggests that if equipped with the right sensibilities, we might be able to read social processes for the evidence they contain of the interplay of unconscious and conscious forces. Borrowing from Lawrence's (2000) notion of a "politics of revelation" we think of the above in terms of the project of social theory being primarily revelatory rather than explanatory or interpretive, and of this book exemplifying something of this spirit of inquiry.

However, for such a project to be genuinely sociological, and escape the reductive and psychologizing tendencies implicit in much psychoanalytic sociology, it must take account of the structuring or delimiting action of social process on, as it were, what can be felt, as well as what can be known. Questions about what can be known are very much the terrain of discourse theory and constructionist accounts of social relations. An implication of the position taken in this book is that they tend to be intellectually impoverished to the extent that they eschew interest in the emotional roots of our knowing relationship to social and personal reality. Perri 6 (2002) has developed an interesting account of the social structuring of feeling, arguing that,

> Emotions, like any other human activity, are of course made possible by the biological substrate, and no doubt the extent of the menu is subject to biological limitations. However, the menu is given its effective structure by the elemental forms of institutional social organization which well up in different empirical forms in any society. [*ibid.*, p. 283]

Other perspectives take a more fluid view of the relationship between forms of psychic experience and social relations. Showalter, for example, suggests that "A constant cultural negotiation goes on, of course, over both the symptom pool as a whole and the legitimacy of its contents" (1997, p. 15).

This chapter has been concerned to re-assert the place of the emotionally "real" in this complex schema, not by assigning it a privileged position, but certainly a determinate one—what happens happens, and once known cannot be in any final sense un-known.

The conditions shaping representability in society are what are at issue, and these are in turn crucially shaped by the capacity or otherwise of the social container to bear knowledge of emotional pain and conflict. Oscillation in this capacity is what lies at the root of movement towards, and away from borderline states of mind in both society and individual.

CHAPTER SEVEN

Surface and depth in the Victoria Climbié Inquiry Report: exploring emotionally intelligent policy

"We have to conclude that [the social worker] lamentably failed to see what was crying out to be seen, namely, a grossly undernourished, limping child who could not conceivably be described by the most undiscerning of visitors—let alone by a trained social worker—as 'well and happy'. That description, contemporaneously recorded . . . was not just a travesty: it was empty of meaning."

(London Borough of Brent, 1985, pp. 292–293)

"During the final weeks of [his] life, the social worker made a number of home visits and found the downstairs of the house warm and clean. However, she did not see [the child] upstairs, who was starving in a cold and filthy room, as though he had cased to exist."

(Reder, Duncan, & Gray, 1993, p. 108)

Introduction

Victoria Climbié was an eight-year-old child who was systematically tortured and then murdered by her aunt and her aunt's partner in North London in the year 2000. This happened despite Victoria coming to the attention of four social services departments, two police child protection teams, and two hospitals in the months preceding her death.

In the wake of her death, the two short passages above seem to echo down the decades with a chilling and depressing familiarity. They refer, respectively, to the circumstances of the deaths of Jasmine Beckford in 1983 and Malcolm Page in 1979. Inevitably, noticing the elements of continuity in these three cases lead us to wonder how far we have really come in our efforts to protect our most vulnerable children? In this chapter we reflect particularly on questions of seeing and knowing in child protection work and in our social response to child abuse tragedy. The chapter takes the Victoria Climbié Inquiry Report (Laming, 2003) as its main point of departure.

In analysing aspects of the report's findings, but also the text of the report itself considered as a record of our social response to this tragedy, we think especially in terms of the psychic defence of "turning a blind eye". In a paper reflecting on Victoria Climbié's story and which is a valuable companion to this chapter, Margaret Rustin describes this psychic mechanism and its relevance to understanding the frequent apparent avoidance of contact with emotional and evidential realities described in the report:

> What is it that, at root, is being avoided? I think a significant component is the psychological impact of becoming aware of Victoria's dreadful life circumstances. Defences against such awareness are much to the fore in the story reported, and defences against recognising reality necessarily involve severe distortions in the mind's capacity to function. Of particular relevance are frequent examples of "turning a blind eye" (Steiner, 1987), that is failing to see what is before one's eyes because to do so would cause too much psychic disturbance—and of various forms of "attacks on linking" (Bion, 1959), the systematic disconnection between things which logically belong together, again a defence which is employed because to make the link would be a source of painful anxiety . . .
>
> Psychoanalysts have described this form of defensive organization in individuals in various ways, but one of the most useful conceptualisations has been by John Steiner. He named the protective structures created by the individual who is dominated by fear of reality (and this refers to both internal and external reality) as "psychic

retreats" (Steiner, 1993). Just as the individual can persuade himself unconsciously that reality can truly be avoided if he stays put within the narrow confines of his personal psychic retreat, so workers within the organizations described, and the organizations themselves as represented by their structures and practices, seem to have been convinced that they could escape having to think about their contact with Victoria and her aunt, Kouao. Thinking involves the attribution of meaning to our experience. Without a sense of meaning, it is difficult to imagine what personal responsibility for actions would amount to, and it is just this phenomenon which the report continually highlights. [Rustin, 2005, p. 12]

The document in question stands in a long line of similar public inquiry reports into the preventable deaths of children that have had a major, and many would argue disproportionate, impact on public policy-making in the field of child welfare and protection in Britain (Reder & Duncan, 2004). The analysis presented in this chapter suggests that the Climbié report also reflects a kind of breakdown of "linkage" between the emotional and evidential sources available to the Inquiry, and between the content and form of the report's narratives and conclusions. This leads us to proffer some thoughts about the concept of "emotionally intelligent" policy-making, which we believe are consistent with the general thrust of our wider theme of the great difficulty of maintaining contact with painful emotional realities as a part of the social task of generating effective welfare policy in our times.

Surface, depth and relationship in child protection practice and policy

David Howe (1996) has discussed the idea of "surface and depth" in social work practice with reference to a "second crisis" of modernity in which the collectivist project of social welfare begins to break down. In place of collectivism there is a resurgent emphasis on individual responsibility, but with the added dimension of a rejection of ideas of deep patterning or structuring of social and psychological processes. In turn, this trend finds expression in discourses of performance, behaviour, and professional competence, rather than explanation, interpretation, and understanding.

In many respects the intellectual culture of public inquiries into child deaths, including the Climbié Inquiry, can be understood as part of this pattern. Echoing Howe's analysis, the present chapter investigates "the breakdown of causal narratives as a way of explaining things" and the "lack of organisational interest in constructing client narratives" (Howe, 1996, p. 90) within the Inquiry report.

In his critical appraisal of the Department of Health research studies commissioned in the wake of the Cleveland affair discussed in the preceding chapter and published in 1995, Nigel Parton (1996) articulates similar shortcomings in the conceptualization of the relationship between working practices and the child protection policy process as the present paper does with respect to Lord Laming's report. Parton notes that in this major research programme there were no qualitative studies that attempted to explore how practitioners "made sense of the work and, crucially, how they made judgements about cases at the initial point of referral" (*ibid.*, p. 8). In the absence of research-based understanding of "the nature of child protection *work* and why it is constituted in the way it is" (*ibid.*), Parton is pessimistic about the possibility of research coming to grips with and influencing the nature of practice itself. In contrast to Parton's social constructionist stance, the present paper is more psychologically and socially realist in its assumptions about the kinds of experiences and processes that need to be investigated in pursuit of policy relevance, but they share a common preoccupation with the need for policy analysis that is rooted in real world analysis and enquiry. This preoccupation is another way of expressing our own conviction that the *nature of welfare work* is a proper and necessary point of departure for policy-making, if policy is in any way to respect the singularity of the activity it is designed to shape and lead.

Victoria Climbié died on 25 February 2000, when she was eight years old. The Inquiry report tells us that Victoria spent much of the last weeks of her life "living and sleeping in a bath in an unheated bathroom, bound hand and foot inside a bin bag, lying in her own urine and faeces. It is not surprising then that towards the end of her short life, Victoria was stooped like an old lady and could walk only with great difficulty" (Laming, 2003, p. 1). The post mortem examination found evidence of 128 separate injuries on her body, showing that she had been beaten with a range of sharp and blunt instruments, although the immediate cause of her death was hypothermia. Victoria had come to England from the Ivory Coast with her aunt Marie-Therese Kouao, after a period of five months during which they lived in France. Kouao told Victoria's parents that she wished to take a child back to France with her to arrange for her education, a practice that was not uncommon in the Ivory Coast. Between her arrival in England in April 1999 and her death in 2000, Victoria was known to a wide range of services including three housing services, four social services departments, and two police child protection teams. She was admitted to hospital twice. As the inquiry report notes, "Victoria was not hidden away . . . In his opening statement to the Inquiry, Neil Garnham QC listed no fewer than 12 key occasions when the relevant services had the opportunity to successfully intervene in the life of Victoria. . . . Not one of these required great skill or would have made heavy demands on time to take some form of action" (Laming, 2003, p. 3).

Marie Therese Kouao and her partner Carl Manning were convicted of Victoria's murder in January 2001. In September of that year phase one of the Victoria Climbié Inquiry, which took evidence from a wide range of witnesses, opened in London under the chairmanship of Lord Laming. Phase two of the Inquiry was established to consider the wider implications of the case for the organization of child protection services in England and Wales, and comprised the submission of written evidence and a series of five seminars. At the end of July 2002 the Inquiry was formally closed, and the report delivered to parliament in January 2003.

Victoria Climbié died in 2000, but at the time of writing she is still very much alive in our minds, in the public mind, and it seems she will remain so for some time to come. Public enquiries into the non-accidental deaths of children serve more functions than their official or explicit ones, and we might reflect on their significance as forms of public memorial. Whether or not we learn from professional experience through these exercises in the way we tell ourselves we are supposed to do, the conduct of a public enquiry obliges us to go on thinking about the child, about how and why he or she died and, as representatives charged with responsibility in the public sphere, about our part in their living and dying as well as our responsibilities in the lives and struggles of other people we work with. Looked at this way they are part of a process of public mourning.

Under any circumstances—whether they are private and individual or public and shared—such processes take a long time, and are nearly always attended by painful acts of self-examination. Did we do as much as we could? Did we do the right thing? Can we forgive ourselves, or believe we might be forgiven, if we feel we did not? Will we learn from this experience, which would be a form of proper remembering, or will we forget? If Victoria's death is to result in some real progress in our social capacity to organize what we call our child protection system, we are surely only now at the beginning. Mourning is necessary, and also extremely valuable if we can succeed in doing the work it demands of us—one part of which is to come to feel that we can in some way put right our sense of the things that went wrong in our relationship to the dead person while they were alive. But this work requires us to think about painful things. If we can manage it, then it is a kind of learning that leads to growth. Peter Reder and Sylvia Duncan have also alluded to this ritual dimension of the public inquiry process, but they also point out other overt and covert purposes it may serve: disciplining, reassurance, learning, as well as what they call "catharsis". However,

> All these purposes are legitimate but they may not be compatible if attempted simultaneously. Most especially, no one can learn when they are under threat of disciplinary measures, nor can they contribute to a learning process. When under censure, everyone becomes defensive and guarded. [Reder & Duncan, 2004, p. 108]

These authors are speaking about states of mind and we want to explore what states of mind the Inquiry Report embodies, evokes, and encourages—in the professions, in civil society, in the political sphere. Are they conducive to learning and reflection of a sort that will lead to better practice, or not? What are the appropriate states of mind in which to approach the task of making social policy in child protection? In particular, does the report help us, professionally and socially, with the very difficult but absolutely basic task of bearing to *know* about the terrible emotional realities of child torture and murder.

As intended, the inquiry report has been significant in reshaping child care and protection policy in the period since its publication. Yet, much of its contents focus in extraordinary detail on the failures of direct child protection practice that contributed to Victoria's death. If the policy-making process to which the report gives rise is to succeed in improving our direct practices with children at risk, then we must establish and understand the nature of the link between policy and policy change on the one hand, and the nature of child protection practice on the other. We do not think the report succeeds very well in doing this. It has many strengths by comparison with some previous reports of inquiries into child maltreatment and deaths and, as a former Director of a Social Services Department, and Chief Inspector of Social Services, Lord Laming and his team were better placed than many previous inquiry teams to address this link. But in the end they did not, and how and why this was so is our main theme. Central to our discussion is the role of relationships between professionals, children, and parents or carers in providing the link between surface and depth in this work, and the role of such relationships in linking the "extensive" concerns of the policy maker, which focus on structures (such as inter-agency working arrangements), procedures, and protocols (what should we communicate to whom about what) and conditions that support practice (who should get professional supervision or training); and in turn linking these with the "intensive" concerns of practitioners in their direct dealings with children and families, and with one another—what is it like to do child protection work, what personal and professional capacities do we need, and how does contact with abuse and abusers affect professionals?

The report provides us with an opportunity to tackle these questions, but only if we can extend and deepen the terms of debate and policy change it proposes. The Victoria Climbié Inquiry offered a great opportunity to transform our concept of how macro policies in child protection articulate with and sensitively inform the complex realities of actually doing child protection work. Our sense is that Lord Laming wanted to do this, but was unable for one reason or another to carry through the task. One explanation for this is fairly simple. The document itself is part of what we might think of as a *genre*—the public inquiry report—and we know that this necessarily represents a constraining framework. The author must do a job within certain more or less well established political conventions, if the report is to produce effects in the political or policy domain rather than be ignored or sidelined at the political level. A further aim of this chapter is to examine how we might test and challenge these orthodoxies.

To begin, we focus in more detail on two responses occasioned by the report. First, that through its meticulously reconstructed narratives of agencies' dealings with Victoria and with each other, the report describes the operation of a professional system that appears dismembered. Second, that the report itself is a dismembered document in certain significant respects. The events recounted in its pages constitute a story or network of stories with many missing dimensions, connections, lost threads, and silences. The stories presented are factually coherent, but also radically incomplete. At the same time, the storyteller—the author of the report— seems to begin by announcing a wish, perhaps a need, to approach the telling of this story in a particular way—with passion, urgency, and a sense of shock—but ends by doing something quite different.

In between, during the long narrative reconstructions of events from the standpoint of the different services and agencies involved, there are momentary glimpses of other stories, which might be recounted in different emotional and intellectual registers, stories that might have been told but that are not. We read the report more as practitioners than policy analysts, and our copies are full of marginal scribbles that say things like "What actually happened here?" "What happened in the experience, in the thoughts, feelings and responses of this doctor or social worker or police officer at this point?" Without this we find it impossible to understand how and why things went wrong, rather than just that they did go wrong because one thing or another was not done or followed through. While we cannot fill in the missing parts of this picture, nevertheless we can imagine in an intelligent way how they could be filled in. It is our conviction that we need to reclaim the importance of doing this if we are to create the link between surface and depth in the report and in child protection work.

Surface and depth in the Inquiry Report

On the basis of the report's meticulous narratives, it is as if Lord

Laming has presented the suffering and maltreated child at the district office and shown us some signs—but signs of what, we do not yet know. By implementing the report's recommendations we might, but equally might not, approach nearer to achieving better, safer, more consistent child protection practices in this country. In fact we might follow procedure to the letter in their implementation and yet make little impact on the real difficulties afflicting our system and practices, just as it is possible to implement procedures to the letter in a child protection case and still miss the vital clues as to what is happening. Lord Laming's justified complaint at so many junctures is that decisions made were *not* pursued, and that procedures were *not* followed. But the more searching inquiry concerns why they were not pursued and implemented. And it is in probing this that we surely encounter the limits of procedures, policy recommendations and, indeed, structures, as safeguards of practice and policy development. Structures, procedures, and protocols may be necessary, but they are not sufficient conditions of good practice. They are surface instruments, capable of guiding us and organizing us towards the relevant point of contact with the deeper, more complex, and ambiguous realities with which we need to engage in child protection work, but little more.

The report says , "I am convinced that the answer lies in doing relatively straightforward things well" (Laming, 2003, p. 13). In this we think it is right, in so far as not doing the straightforward things in child protection work can have disastrous consequences. These things must be done and done well. It is wrong in that beyond a certain point there is nothing straightforward about most child protection work. For, as the report also says,

> Staff doing this work need a combination of professional skills and personal qualities, not least of which are persistence and courage. Adults who deliberately exploit the vulnerability of children can behave in devious and menacing ways. They will often go to great lengths to hide their activities from those concerned for the well being of a child. [*ibid.*, p.3]

Nothing straightforward there, one might suppose, and here is the first of many missing links in the report. A significant factor in explaining why competent people may not manage to do the straightforward thing is that the very unstraightforward nature of the daily task may, under certain circumstances, easily derail them from doing the blindingly obvious. Here we are in the area of what Reder and Duncan (2004), in their analysis of public inquiries into child deaths, call the "human factor".

> There have been two fundamental failings of inquiries/reviews. Firstly, analysis of the problems and the nature of the recommendations are not at the most useful level, since they mainly focus on bureaucratic, instead of human factors. Secondly, inquiries/reviews must satisfy multiple agendas, all of which may be necessary yet can not be fulfilled through the same process. [Reder & Duncan, 2004, p. 102]

At a recent seminar we heard a senior manager in a social work agency express this rather more graphically. "Look", she said, "many of the adults we have to deal with in child abuse cases are complete bastards." No doubt she would temper her way of expressing herself in other contexts; and as we know there is always another story that is just as important to understand, about how people who are "bastards" to their own or others' children themselves came to be like they are. But her transposition into everyday language of what the child protection task means much of the time is worth staying with for a moment. It may mean waking up every day and wondering if today your duty will involve pursuing enquiries with people who will, in Lord Laming's more temperate language be "devious and menacing". Already, we can see that the perspectives presented in this report do not quite join up. We must pursue our own the inquiry much further, but to do this we need different capacities and instruments to guide us.

From anguish to anonymity

On receiving the report, we first read the Introduction, and then the recommendations, before turning to the body of the text. It was the disjunction between the introduction and the conclusion that provoked our earlier image of dismemberment. There is a kind of restrained passion informing the opening pages of the report. This is conveyed not just in Lord Laming's fury at the behaviour of some of the witnesses, or in how obviously moved and distressed he and the inquiry team found themselves to be at times. There is also a clear sense of political passion for change and betterment, rooted, it seemed, in the experience of raw emotional identification with Victoria's suffering, of shock at the dilapidated condition of some of our public services and their disengagement from the life of the communities they serve. There is a quality of emotional and intellectual turmoil about this piece of writing, as though the enormity and complexity of what has been exposed confronts him with the enormity and complexity of achieving a coherent analysis that might contribute to constructive change. Yet, by the end of the report, we are offered the same kind of terse, lifeless, abstract series of recommendations that has flowed from every other similar exercise.

In the space of a few paragraphs in the introduction, anguish, disbelief, judgement, and rational analysis tumble across one another. Given the emotional intensity and intellectual complexity informing this part of the report, it is hardly surprising that it sometimes does not seem to add up. But on balance we welcome this because we believe the truth is that the quality of experience conveyed here is close to what the reality of child protection work feels like. In our experience it is not possible to do effective child protection work, or supervise and mange it, unless there is a capacity to experience and engage with intense emotional pain, anger, disbelief, the desire to punish and retaliate, and the balancing impulse for compassion. This is why, once one is beneath the surface of the initial contact, the first referral or meeting with the child and her carers, it is never straightforward. When Lord Laming says that staff doing this work need "a combination of professional skills and personal qualities", we suggest this means the capacity to both endure intensity of emotional and intellectual pain and turmoil, and exercise measured thought, analysis, and judgement. The answer lies not in one or the other, but in both.

An experience of child protection work

To explore this further one of us (AC) recounts a fairly simple story from his own experience of child protection work. These events took place nearly twenty years ago, and we relate them not to hark back to a lost golden age of practice, but because while many procedural details would be different now, we suspect there is a core to this experience that remains valid today.

He was the duty social worker, and the headteacher at a local primary school phoned to say that Ahmed, a boy of seven, had arrived at school that morning with an unusual-looking bruise on his face. She and the school nurse thought that perhaps it had been caused by a belt or strap. When they talked to Ahmed he seemed frightened, but he had stuck to a story according to which he had been playing with his leather belt, slapping it against the stairs, and it had flown up into his face, causing the bruise.

He visited the school, and learned that the boy and his mother were living in local homeless families' hotel accommodation, and that Ahmed had only recently been enrolled. He talked to Ahmed, who told the same story as before, then asked about his mother, Mrs Callaghan, and any other family, and discovered that they had arrived in the area from Scotland. Ahmed's mother was divorced from his father, but had an uncle in the area whom she had hoped would be able to help with accommodation. He asked Ahmed to describe again how the bruise had been caused. Ahmed repeated his story, but when told it would be necessary to talk to his mother when she arrived home from work, Ahmed suddenly broke down in tears, saying "She has been hitting me", and explained that on this occasion he had been doing "something naughty" that had annoyed her very much.

The social worker took Ahmed back to the nearby office, and arranged for the headteacher to leave a message for Mrs Callaghan, asking her to come to the office once she returned. When she arrived at 5.30 p.m., she was very angry with the social worker, complaining rationally but forcefully about the fact that her son had been taken to a strange place, and not given anything to eat, and how frightened he must be as a result. The social worker felt guilty. It was very hard to focus any discussion on how the bruise had occurred, on her own present situation, or her relationship with her son. She constantly made him feel as though he was in the wrong, and would not respond to encouragement to talk about any stresses in her present life. After two discussions with her, lasting an hour and a half in total, the social worker felt at an *impasse*. He experienced Mrs Callaghan as very controlled, cold towards him, and hardened in her way of communicating. By now he was feeling very angry himself and thwarted by her. It was well into the evening, and he worried that Ahmed's mother would retaliate against her son, who might be at greater risk than before. As a result he wondered to myself about putting Ahmed in care on an emergency basis. By now the social worker was alone in the office, but had access to a senior colleague by phone.

He talked to that colleague, and it was possible to sort out the facts of the situation from the very strong feelings that had been aroused in him. Taking out an Emergency Protection Order would probably do more harm than good. The risks seemed acceptable. Mrs Callaghan, whatever her overt responses, had been given a clear and firm message about our concerns. Underneath, it was possible to speculate that she was very frightened herself. It was agreed that they return home, that Mrs Callaghan should keep an appointment the following day, and that there would need to be a Child Protection Conference. The worker left the office alone, feeling scared, and walked down the road to the tube station anxious that someone might leap out of an alleyway and attack him.

As an experience of doing child protection work, we suspect this is fairly ordinary. Nevertheless, the details, like many of our experiences as a practitioner are etched indelibly into the practitioner's memory. This is explicable in quite simple terms—it is a consequence of the emotional intensity and seriousness of the whole episode. The worker was often afraid when doing this kind of work; afraid of what he would discover about what was happening to children, afraid of facing parents or carers, afraid of what would happen if he did not find out what was happening, or if he backed away from facing the adults with my suspicions. As a front-line practitioner he was well supported in what he did, by his manager and supervisor, by other colleagues, by the department as a whole, and by the training he had received. This brings us to the main point of recounting this story—for surely one central purpose of the child protection system is that it works to support and enable *processes* of this kind, carried out by ordinary staff doing a difficult job. If it fails to do this, then it fails workers, who will then inevitably fail at their task of protecting children.

Untold stories

This brings us to the question of the untold stories which are the absent heart of the Climbié report. First, we are given a very limited emotional picture of Victoria's own experiences during the months she lived in this country. While it could be indulgent or masochistic to focus too exclusively on this aspect of things, we are not given an opportunity to *understand* Victoria's experiences from the inside, and thus make some deeper sense of how she presented herself to professionals and others. Without this perspective we cannot begin to learn anything about the subtle emotional complexities of relating to children who may be in terrible danger, but also profoundly frightened and conflicted about exposing this danger. These are the perspectives upon which Margaret Rustin (2005) concentrates in her paper. The question that must be borne in mind whenever we remove our attention from the suffering of the child is: do we do this in the service of helping the child or in the service of protecting ourselves from our own suffering? Good child protection work is always poised somewhere on this difficult boundary.

Second, we learn very little from the report of Marie Therese Kouao or Carl Manning's stories. Adequate child protection work entails being prepared to engage with the mind and behaviour of the abusers, and this is usually frightening and disturbing. The task is neither to demonize the abuser, nor to be captured by compassion for the damage they have often suffered in their lives, but to understand them and their relationship to the child clear-sightedly, so that we can evaluate the risks, and the nature of the usually complex bonds we find there. This is the work of good assessment, and it is difficult work. It is striking how thin is the quality of description in the report of the relationship between Victoria and her great-aunt. Certain important observations are repeated several times—of Victoria jumping to attention in her presence, of a lack of warmth between them, of Victoria sometimes seeming afraid. Enough to constitute clear signs of danger, but there must have been much more that could have been registered and reported—despite the fact that no proper assessment of the relationship was ever undertaken. The missing dimension is attention to what we would call detailed emotional observation.

When we look back at earlier inquiry reports such as Jasmine Beckford's, we find exactly the same questions hanging in the air.

The sentences immediately preceding the epigraph at the head of this paper read: "One last chance of saving Jasmine was presented when [the social worker] visited the Beckford home on 12 March 1984. We have described in detail in Chapter 10 what took place during the 45 minute visit on that day" (London Borough of Brent, 1985, p. 292). While there is indeed a detailed account of that visit, our attention should really be directed to what we know was *not* seen, not noticed, not taken in, and how this could be so.

There is an equally thin quality to the stories of professional's experience of their contacts with Victoria and Kouao. Just occasionally there is an exception that proves the rule. Here is an example, relating to the involvement of a senior social worker in Haringey. The report says:

> the third strategy meeting recommendation to seek some proof that the child was Kouao's, arose from a feeling she had when Kouao came into the office on 2 November that something was amiss in the interaction and bonding between Kouao and Victoria. [Laming, 2003, p. 179]

Later this worker is directly quoted.

> Part of me, with the feelings I got from the visit with mum, it must have been still something that was niggling at me and I suggested just to be on the safe side, just to be certain, just to make sure, that she was not returned to Manning's. [*ibid.*, p. 187]

The reason these short passages spring out is that they demonstrate, in the context of the report, a rare a quality of emotional aliveness to the situation facing the worker. Something troubling and perturbing is registered and is being thought about. This speaks to what it means to have, and make use of a professional relationship in child protection work. Through an emotionally alive relationship with the family, it is possible to access something the nature of *their relationships*. In registering a sense of disturbance, a practitioner registers signs of the potential risks, dangers, and disturbances in the family relationships. Such experiences are not sufficient grounds on which to act, of course, but they are necessary information that when ignored or reasoned away may be the first step on a path to tragedy.

Turning a blind eye

Evidence for what occurred at this level of experience for the many workers who came into contact with Victoria is just strikingly absent throughout most of the report. However, it is worth quoting one occasion when Lord Laming himself clearly commits to public record his own view about the matters we are trying to address. With reference to one of the social workers who had contact with Victoria he says that,

> Seeing, listening to and observing the child must be an essential element of an initial assessment for any social worker . . . [the worker in question] should have had such a conversation with Victoria on July 26th 1999, when she had clear case responsibility. She offered two explanations for her failure to do so. First, that she did not wish to "form a relationship" with Victoria. Second that she did not wish to compromise any future investigation. I reject these. The social worker's role in these circumstances is simply to listen without interruption and to record and evaluate what has been said. [Laming, 2003, p. 238]

There are many cumulative factors in recent years that tend to impede the requirement and the capacity of child protection staff to properly listen to children, and make appropriate relationships with them. Anxiety about compromising a proper forensic investigation is one of them. But considerations of these kinds may often intersect with, and unintentionally buttress, a deeper dynamic that is always in play in this kind of work. This is the continual and perfectly understandable wish on the part of workers to believe that what they are being presented with is not a case of child abuse. Because accepting that it is, or that it probably is, pitches them into immediate personal engagement with conflict, emotional pain, and the welter of difficult feelings and responses alluded to above. It is in fact only human not to want to be obliged to enter this territory.

So, time and again, the evidence of the inquiry report is that workers involved in Victoria's case *both saw and did not see what was in front of their own eyes.* We emphasize the "both" in this statement, because this is the best formulation we can find to explain how, as we read the report, it is as though the evidence for what was happening to Victoria stares at us from the pages (as it stared these workers in the face) while we also read how it was ignored, rejected by subsequent opinion, identified for action but not acted upon, and so forth. In ordinary language we call this "turning a blind eye". With one part of our mind we take in what is happening, but with another we repudiate what we have seen. This means we are unable to struggle consciously with the conflict, the dilemma, or with the anxiety arising from it; but neither do we make a complete psychological break with the unwelcome knowledge or suspicion of which we are aware, which would be to enter a state of true denial. Rather we disconnect, we break the relationship between different but actually related aspects of, or responses to, a single state of affairs while retaining some kind of consciousness of each. We do this, and it is a very ordinary defence, when we are deeply conflicted about what we are seeing, or about what we have come to know.

In *Beyond Blame*, Reder, Duncan, and Gray (1993) discuss a very similar process they identified at the heart of a number of the cases of child death that they analyse. They call this "the 'not exist' double bind", and their characterization of the process is more systemic than the one offered above, but refers to the same phenomenon. They say,

> At some time . . . the professionals realised that they had not seen the child and renewed their efforts to do so. The parents refused to allow them direct access to the child, yet the workers left the home satisfied that all was well and that the child was either safely asleep upstairs or staying with relatives" [*ibid.*, p. 107]

With respect to the case of Heidi Koseda they suggest,

> Her physical needs could not be tolerated or thought about, even though this led to her physical existence ceasing. If Heidi were to assert her physical existence, she could not be thought about or her existence acknowledged psychologically; so she was shut away, as though not existing physically; only then could her caretakers tolerate thinking about her; but then they would be in danger of having to give priority to her physical needs and existence; and so on. [*ibid.*, p. 110]

In other words, sometimes the child exists and sometimes the child doesn't exist—it is not one or the other but both.

This is the parents' relationship to the reality of the child with which child protection workers themselves *come into relationship* and which the authors analyse in terms of workers becoming caught in a double bind. It makes for no ordinary relationship, and it requires something considerably beyond ordinary, everyday psychological capacities to respond effectively under such circumstances—first and most importantly *to be capable of thinking about* and linking up apparently inconsistent elements of experience. Reder, Duncan, and Gray assign this kind of process a rather particular status in their broader analysis of the factors underlying serious child abuse and our responses to it. Although they are certainly describing extreme and tragic consequences, our own contention is that these are extreme instances of the central predicament of the whole child protection task. In any particular situation, but also at the level of our total social concern with the topic of child abuse, can we or can't we bear *to know what is happening, to think the unthinkable?*

What is "supervision" for?

We now trace the implications of this with respect to just one dimension of the report, and one of its recommendations. Recommendation 45 says:

> Directors of social services must ensure that the work of staff working directly with children is regularly supervised. This must include the supervisor reading, reviewing, and signing the case file at regular intervals. [Laming, 2003, p. 376]

In the main body of the report, we learn a good deal about what did not happen in supervisory sessions, and about supervisory sessions that did not happen at all. We learn much less about what did take place, or about what the inquiry team thinks should be the focus and content of professional supervision. Our conviction is that supervision in child protection work must always address the difficult psychological and emotional transactions that child protection work necessarily involves for staff—if they are doing their jobs properly. To continue with the theme outlined above, there is no shame in finding that one has "turned a blind eye"—it is often only human under the circumstances. But there is real danger in not coming to realize that this has happened. Very often we need help to realize such things. This is one central aspect of what supervision is for, or should be for. It is also the dimension of professional supervision that has been most eroded in the last two decades of child protection work.

Like most of the many similar recommendations in the report, Recommendation 45 is a good one—as far as it goes. We suggest it does not go far enough because it does not connect substantially and specifically with questions about the nature of the work being supervised, with the processes in which child protection staff are embroiled hour by hour. These processes, and the sensitive handling of them, are what may really make the difference between life and death. This recommendation, if implemented nationally, would be an example of the "extensive" concerns of social policy. It is the kind of recommendation that can meaningfully be placed on a semi-statutory footing. But it is also empty, and to make a difference to child protection practice on a national level, it needs to connect with developments that revitalize our relationship to the deep processes that lie at the heart of the work itself. In other words, with the kinds of things that routinely need to be thought about between workers and supervisors—what we term the intensive aspects of practice. These are not the kinds of things that can be prescribed, and so they are not usually seen as the province of social policy.

The task of policy—thinking the unthinkable

Herein lies the predicament with which the Victoria Climbié report faces us. We have argued that it reveals, as often through what it does not describe and evidence as through what it does, the absolute necessity to attend to the connection between the instruments that organize the surface of child protection work—structures of accountability, local policies concerning inter-agency communication, procedures to be followed in assessment and investigation, and so on, and the processes of deep engagement via relationships with children, parents, carers, and others involved with the child that the work entails. It reveals, if read in the right way, that we must attend to these connections, but also deep ambivalence about doing so.

Our broader hypothesis is that in both revealing and not revealing the stories of the terrible underlying pain and conflict of Victoria, of the professionals who tried but failed to engage with her, and even of those who murdered her when they were supposed to be caring for her, the report enacts the central difficulty that child abuse faces us with as professionals but also as a society. At the level of both the particular case and the general responsibility, we know that terrible things are happening, but the pain of knowing is often too great for us to be able to sustain our attention. Every day professionals succeed in the process of "going on knowing", sometimes fail in this, sometimes recover the capacity to know, but occasionally do not, with fatal consequences. Each public inquiry into a preventable child death is an opportunity for the agencies mandated by society to grapple with this profound dilemma more openly—and thereby assist the professional task. Yet each is also in some measure an act of social displacement, for we know that cases not so dissimilar to Victoria's are being reported to the authorities on a regular basis, and yet do not become the object of public attention or political hand-wringing.

In effect, then, this chapter is the basis of a call for a new kind of policy-making—a new way of thinking about what social policy in child welfare is, and what it is aiming for; one that is informed from start to finish by a concern to sustain connections between the fine grain of the transactions we ask staff and their managers to engage in, and the management and development of systems and structures.

In one sense Victoria Climbié stands for all children, for their vulnerability to abuse and the misuse of power by adults and sometimes by other children. If we can bear to stay connected to the feelings that such vulnerability and cruelty arouse in us, then we have some hope of better protecting children in future. If we cannot, then we fear that all the policies and procedures we can invent may not carry us much further than we are now.

"Emotionally intelligent policy"

The critique of the Victoria Climbié Inquiry report advanced in this chapter assumes, as does much of the analysis informing this book, that it would be in various ways "progressive" to have a culture of policy-making rooted in better integration of emotional, rational, and irrational factors. But how might we justify such a claim? We have argued that at the heart of the report lies a confusion, or elision, between a project concerning the pursuit of, in David Howe's (1996) words, "causal narratives as a way of explaining things", a project about adjudicating responsibility or blame, and an aspiration to prevent recurrences of such tragedies through change processes in both domains. Perhaps it is inevitable that both explanation and attribution of responsibility should play a part in a process of this kind, but it is important to register such overlap and slippage between categories and discourses. Public policy concerns change processes, but both the means and the ends of change processes can be construed in terms that are practical, ethical, or both of these. Because social policy concerns human interests, it may be impossible entirely to disentangle the ethical and practical dimensions of a policy process; whether we think in terms of the narrowest technical plan or the broadest of political objectives, their framing will always be value dependent. Despite this, it is always helpful to keep in mind a distinction between "practical reasoning" and ethical or "moral reasoning" when examining the nature of policy processes—never more so than in broaching questions about the place of emotional forces within such processes.

The core arguments in favour of better linkage between reason and emotion in policy-making, and in political life generally, may be of two kinds that reflect this distinction—"naturalistic" arguments that are intended to inform practical wisdom on the one hand, and ethical arguments concerning standards and norms of expected behaviour on the other. However, the tradition of psychoanalytic thinking informing our work also lends itself to the possibility of forging a link between these two varieties of argument.

The basis of a naturalistic case is well expressed by, for example, Sebastian Kraemer:

> Although there is a fiercely intellectual and rational tradition in politics, it is also a passion, a constant passion for its practitioners, and from time to time for the citizen too. We may like to think that we make entirely rational political choices, but this is far from the whole story. The emotions we bring to citizenship are just as

powerful as those we bring to intimate relationships: to love and sexual desire. [2000, pp. 115–116]

Simply enough, this line of thought proposes that because passion is the constant companion of reason, reason alone cannot be an effective basis for either political deliberation and action, or for the analysis of political processes. This position finds a powerful echo in the work of modern theorists who draw upon the findings of neuro-scientific research. One popular scientific exponent of this work sums up the case like this:

> In a sense we have two brains, two minds—and two different kinds of intelligence: rational and emotional. How we do in life is determined by both . . . it is *emotional* intelligence that matters . . . feelings are typically *indispensable* for rational decisions. [Goleman, 1996, p. 28]

So also, "there is intelligence *in* the emotions (and) intelligence can be brought *to* emotions" (*ibid.*, 1996, p. 40).

These notions suggest that we cannot easily divorce ends from means in emotionally intelligent thinking. The idea of emotional intelligence, and the increasing volume of research evidence upon which it is now based, tells us that *how* we think, *how* we make decisions and *how* we conduct our personal and social lives are inseparably bound up with *what* we think, decide, and do. This suggests two simple propositions.

First, that emotion can overwhelm or superimpose itself upon the faculty of reason. There is something we might call "emotional logic". The discussion, in the preceding chapter, of the logic informing initial attempts to come to terms with emerging evidence of child sexual abuse, exemplifies the power of such forces. As we saw, it is not that emotional forces contain *no* structure of thought, but that they are often organized by very archaic structures that consign actors to fixed positions—a structure of relatedness, but a very inflexible one that reminds us of the strictures of borderline states of mind. But second, that reason and cognition can become disassociated from emotion with equally problematic consequences. Emotional forces continue to be active in the process of deliberation or decision-making, but in an unacknowledged manner. Their logic impacts upon both processes and outcomes but this impact can only be discerned or recovered from a position external to the unfolding events.

The idea of emotionally intelligent policy-making may have a broad general appeal. But it is not a simple idea, and there are reasons why conscientious and well-meaning contributors to policy processes might be cautious of it. One of these reasons is fear of inaction, or paralysis. At one extreme, this might find expression in the familiar dismissive contempt of a therapeutic sensibility as "navel-gazing". Policy is about change, and change projects surely imply action. Interestingly as Daniel Goleman also notes,

> All emotions are, in essence, impulses to act . . . The very root of the word *emotion* is *motere*, the Latin verb "to move", plus the prefix "e" to connote "move away", suggesting that a tendency to act is implicit in every emotion. [*ibid.*, 1996, p. 6]

The duality of emotion in personal and social life is once again evident. In states of unfettered passion we are moved to act too quickly—impulsively, we say, without sufficient thought for the consequences. But if a person or their communications and way of relating to us are devoid of feeling, or an academic or political analysis of something is too dry and abstract, we say, "I was completely unmoved—there was something missing". In many different ways psychoanalysis has been concerned to elucidate the relationship between emotion and thought, precisely because people present to therapists with problems about action and inaction in their lives. We repeat patterns of relationship or behaviour in a seemingly helpless fashion; we experience ourselves as inhabited, and inhibited, by patterns of suffering upon which rational thought makes no impact. On the one hand it is the painful, frightening, or seemingly dangerous thoughts that lie embedded *in feeling* that are the problem; on the other hand, it is the difficulty of *thinking about* or being aware of the impact upon others of our emotionally charged actions, of those aspects of ourselves we mange by expulsion. However, we suggest that emotional intelligence is not about less—or more—action, but about action arising from a particular kind of thoughtfulness; thoughtfulness emanating *from* feeling, and about the feelings that habitually move us to act *without* thought for others.

A sceptic might ask about the relationship between political or social *values* and emotional intelligence. To say that policy processes, policy makers or politicians should be more rooted in feeling and emotion and less in rational, instrumental argumentation and analysis does not take us very far. When Enoch Powell foresaw rivers flowing with blood, or Mrs Thatcher conjured the disparaging metaphor of the "nanny state" they were each, no doubt, speaking with feeling as well as mobilizing what we term "popular feeling" in the service of political and policy ends. But we may or may not think that such emotionally charged evocations lead to "better policy", not because they are emotionally charged, but because we assent to or dissent from the political values they embody. So, is it a question of separating out value frameworks that conditions the aims and direction of policy, and reserving emotional intelligence for questions of "process"? Or does emotional intelligence imply particular kinds of policy doctrine, and disqualify others? This is an important question, but a large one.

Object relations psychoanalysis assumes that *relationship* is fundamental to what it is to be human—to be a psychological subject is necessarily to be a social subject. This way of thinking proposes that there is a kind of social and moral structure to experience from the very beginning (Rustin, 1991), in which we attribute benign or malign agency to others on the basis of phantasy and then gradually but always precariously, on the basis of a better empirical grasp of the reality of other people's separate existence and independence of psychological and ethical conduct. The capacity for more ethically attuned behaviour is understood as a developmental achievement. However, since it is impossible on this view of human nature to conceive of *being* human in abstraction from our condition of relatedness to other people, questions about how we relate one to another and how we "ought" to relate to one another are always directly implied by each other. Because our developmental achievements are precariousness, it is human to fail to respect the other for themselves, but it is rarely humane to do so.

In comparison to previous inquiries, the terms of reference and conduct of the Victoria Climbié Inquiry were unusual in a number of respects. One of these was the proceedings of Part 2 of the inquiry, in which specialists were convened for a series of day seminars to explore a range of selected themes in the functioning of the wider child protection system. This was notable in the sense that it constituted an exercise in something like "applied social science" at the heart of a statutory process. An opportunity was created for a process of disciplined and thoughtful reflection on complex and tragic events that could have resulted in a real engagement between the extensive and intensive concerns of policy and practice referred to above. However, the eventual connection between these deliberations and the recommendations of the report, as well as the "audit driven" implementation process that succeeded their publication, was not easy to discern. "Attacks on linking" (Bion, 1959) depend upon a process of splitting between the emotionally charged forces at work in our mental life and the cognitive and rational ones via which we communicate with and shape reality at a conscious social level. Our purpose in taking the Victoria Climbié Inquiry Report as an object of study has been to open up thinking about the meaning of emotional intelligence in the domain of public policy, in the belief that deeper, but also in the end safer, welfare practices might result.

CHAPTER EIGHT

The vanishing organization: organizational containment in a networked world

"There are worldwide networks that cut through geographical, political and cultural frontiers: art, science or technological discoveries and, increasingly the internet and communications in general. But there is also trafficking—in drugs, arms, currency, power, women, children, organs— and the malignant implementation of globalisation. It seems that before where there was a border, now there is a network. In its luminous aspect, it is a symbol-generating and containing fabric that modulates, diversifies and expands. In its ominous aspect, it spells dislocation, disintegration and degradation."

(Abadi, 2003, p. 223).

Introduction: welfare reconstruction and the organizational ego

I t is in the changed experience of everyday organizational life in the welfare state over the last decade that the metaphor of the "borderline" may have its most immediate and self-evident appeal. "Change is now the only form of stability" is a common way of encapsulating this transformation, one that impresses itself simultaneously at the psychological and the social level because of our everyday individual transactions with organizational forms, "in role" as both providers and consumers of health and welfare. Just as none of us can escape the impact of the "audit culture" as ordinary citizens (see Chapter Three), each of us in our dealings with schools, health services, local authorities, and so on is aware of having been reconstructed by the transformations discussed in this chapter. We acquire, and continually negotiate, an important part of our sense of social and personal identity through our relatedness to the organizations via which welfare is made real in our lives. Instability of core identity is a central feature of how we have characterized borderline states of mind, and as organizational formations and identities mutate, so must we; it is the social and psychic consequences of this state of affairs that we address below.

The traditional health and welfare organization was intended to function as the primary container for the complex, risky, and emotionally demanding exchange process between professionals and local populations that is the heart of welfare activity. Where it functioned well, it did just this. Patients and clients sought, and expected to find, a dependable relationship with these organizations, and the organization expected itself in its turn to provide this. In a real sense, the qualitative immediacy of local experience *formed* the culture of the organization, which therefore mediated between the abstractions of national policy and political economy, and the lived experience of people in communities. Even if the corporatist and statist aspects of welfare organization tended towards a "one size fits all" culture, local identifications and relationships could be strong, and strongly defended.

However, this capacity for "thickly textured" welfare relationships was associated with other qualities and functions that became objects of political contest in the period of post 1979 welfare reconstruction. First, local welfare organizations emerged as sites of political resistance to the neo-liberal reform project. The centrality of *relationships* between populations and their hospitals, day nurseries, and so on, and the emotional investments these carried for welfare workers and consumers alike, became a site of political struggle. The Conservative administration's assault on the institutions and practices of local government became one battleground in the neo-liberal reconstruction of social life. Second, as noted in earlier chapters, these same institutions were more often exposed as deeply fallible in the quality and ethics of the care they provided in certain key domains. The capacity of professionals and the institutions in which they worked to regulate and monitor their own standards of care was thus called into question in the political and public mind. Positive local institutional cultures, cultures of corruption, and cultures of political resistance to change could all be conveniently conflated by forces seeking to restructure the principles governing the organization of welfare. Third, as the new audit institutions went to work, huge differentials in the comparative efficiency and effectiveness of public sector organizations were revealed. Comparative performance ratings began to override all other criteria for the evaluation of quality of service.

The complexity and interdependence of the numerous institutions and professional disciplines comprising the welfare state had never been in doubt. But failures of multi-agency practice and multi-disciplinary working were at the heart of the some of the most notorious scandals that shook the faith in traditional institutions. The succession of public inquiries into child deaths, and the Cleveland affair of 1987 were only the most prominent of these (Stanley & Manthorpe, 2004). The policy ethos of "joined-up working", shorthand for a massive programme of reconfiguration in the way organizations and professional disciplines were to be required to relate, was one manifestation of the new welfare settlement. The New Labour government that came to power in 1997 was committed to improving quality in public services, and needs-led services in which the structures shaping professional activity would be holistically adapted to the complex needs of users, rather than vice versa, were central to this progressive aspiration (6, 1997). But the semi-marketized welfare state machine it inherited was arguably also the largest underfunded business enterprise in the world. The priority became to squeeze as much measurable and accountable public service output as possible from this enterprise. Clinical, social care, and educational "outputs", which appeared to depend upon efficient, focused, co-ordinated, networked multi-professional activity, were in tension with "inputs" perceived as rooted in traditional professionalism with its burdens of vested interests, rivalries, protectionism, and ineffectual mechanisms of self-regulation. We have already argued (see Chapter One) that adequately protected conditions for the delivery of welfare were the main sacrifice in this struggle. From the perspective of everyday professional experience in the welfare state, the outcome of this process is essentially twofold: the dispersal of the welfare "task" from its location inside bounded organizations towards a location within multi-agency and multi-professional project networks; and the re-siting of professional expertise away from a reliance upon the individual practitioner and his or her accumulation of experience and training, in the direction of the team, network, or project group and its "skill mix". It is the trend towards dissolution of the organizational "ego" as the mediating condition of a functioning welfare state that is the subject of this chapter.

The naked ego

Many of us now have direct experience of working in networked organizations in which hierarchies are not so much flat as complex, intersecting, and fluid. These are the new organizational conditions, the sociological history of which is discussed below. What follows is an account of one woman's managerial experience in a traditionally well-bounded but internally complex public sector organization, where the intersection and overlapping of tasks and responsibilities within the wider departmental, professional, and administrative structures, gives rise to an experience of continual uncertainty about the actual ownership of authority. In this account *any individual's authority must be continuously negotiated in relation to the current task.*

> I enter work on a particular day with a mounting sense of trepidation. By the end of the previous day I had discerned a familiar process gathering pace, a steady but invisible whirlwind of anxiety, rivalry, tension, forming among a knot of my close colleagues, but involving me. While I believe this state of mind to be located among within the management "system" of which I am a part, and not just in myself, I am also not wholly convinced it is not a "projection" of my own, the mobilization of my own competitive anxieties. I am the "lead" in an important decision-making process, where I know the views of the Chief Executive and support the stance he is adopting. Or do I? How do I know exactly? I feel I need to "know" for myself, because I allegedly "lead" this overall process of decision-making. To know I must have clearly separated

out my own view of organizational needs from any influence exerted on me by the CE's authority over me.

But why has he involved himself in this decision-making process? Does he not trust me to exercise effective authority and judgement? Is he keeping me under his watchful eye? I fantasize that a colleague, who is also a rival for my leadership functions, thinks I should challenge exactly this point. I am anxious that he perceives me as "weak". Am I? Or am I just a good, inclusive "team player" who exercises authority through consensus? The CE says we are taking these decisions through "teamwork", but how do I know when the CE's liking for "teamwork" is genuine, and when it's a cover story for the exercise of his ultimate authority? And do I use my support for the ethos of "team work", "collaboration", "discussion" as a way of evading disagreements and conflict?

As manager of a large sub-system within the organization, all of whom are anxiously awaiting the outcome of the resource decisions to be taken by the management grouping of which I am a part, I have certainly worked hard to keep everyone involved in this process of decision-making. But I seem to overlook the same people more than once—why I ask myself? By the time I complete these consultations with my network of about twenty colleagues, some of whom are peers, some senior and some junior, I feel emptied of all significance, all authority. I have become accountable to all of them, not they to me. My "authority" has been entirely dispersed into the intricate web of capillaries of power in the organizational nexus—or so it seems to me. I walk around in a fury telling myself (and everyone else in my head) that I am just a "gofer". My narcissism is threatened, injured. Or is it my genuine potency that is being subtly challenged? Have I given away authority through excess consultation, or have I demonstrated maturity, inclusiveness, and organizational sensitivity? Am I paranoid? Am I clear-sighted? Or have I capitulated and failed my followers? I have no idea. All I do know is—there seems to be nobody in overall control, no single, graspable, principle of organizational conduct to reassure me either externally in the organizational structure, or inside myself.

What can we learn from this story?

The psychological experience of operating as a manager in these circumstances is one of remorseless uncertainty, not only with respect to the status and meaning of relationships with others, but also within oneself. The need for perpetual negotiation of her authority and influence over matters requires the manager to constantly assess whether she is behaving too adaptively or too obdurately. The answer, if there is such a thing as a certain answer, is always context-dependent, and context shifts ceaselessly not least as a result of her own changing perceptions and constructions. Correlatively, the meaning of her own feelings is continually uncertain—is an experience of "weakness" or humiliation evidence of an inappropriate narcissistic eruption, or of a painful but helpful submission to the reality of interdependence within complex organizational systems? Adequate functioning in these circumstances requires the manager to patrol continuously the shifting internal boundary between fantasy and reality, and to accept feedback from others about how her actions are being interpreted, actions that are themselves grounded in her own interpretations of the meaning of her feelings and of the meaning of others' behaviours. This is about as much as she can do, without descending into madness. The organizational "script" is being continuously rewritten, via a process of continuous interactive negotiation. The organization produces and reproduces itself in an unceasing turmoil of change, but somehow remains stable, and well-bounded in its overall identity and patterning.

In *Reworking Authority: Leading and Following in the Post-modern Organization* (1997) Larry Hirschhorn writes:

> Building the post-modern organization is thus like walking across a trapeze. Facing greater market risks, the enterprise asks its employees to be more open, more vulnerable to one another. But in becoming more vulnerable, people compound their sense of risk. They are threatened from without and within. . . . Thus the stage is set for a more primitive psychology. Individuals question their own competence and their ability to act autonomously. In consequence just when they need to build a more sophisticated psychological culture, they inadvertently create a more primitive one. [1997, p. 27]

This more primitive psychology results from a nakedness in the individual organizational ego. Where once role, task, and authority in the context of a bounded system were the guarantors of the possibility of organizational sanity, the employee or manager now struts naked in the open-plan, hot-desking, office of inter-organizational vulnerability. Vulnerability is painful, shaming, and potentially maddening—as well as being endearing, democratic, and potentially empowering. We have all had this bad dream—of inhabiting or discovering ourselves undressing in a house without walls, or with walls made of glass. The thesis of "failed dependency" (Miller, 1993) with respect to traditional organizational forms helps to account for the sense of collective disorientation, disappointment and cynicism in the face of lost certainties of organizational hierarchy and job security.

> The problem is that institutions are the only way that society has found to . . . enable people to cope with primitive feelings like dependence, hate and rage. We have developed a pattern of projective receptacles. In the analysis of organizations we have a rational picture of a person in a a role in an institution. But implicitly we are describing a process through which we can get rid of bits of ourselves that we want to disown. Those are the bits that the person transmits into the "containers" of "role" and "organisation". So at present institutions are failing us either by becoming more humane and more like us, or they fail us by becoming more extreme and inhumane. [Miller, 1993, p. 26]

The trend towards more networked, interdependent or "joined-up" organizations seems to be driven by complex forces and motives. On the one hand, competitive advantage in a globalized market is enhanced by flexibility and adaptability of organizational forms, while on the other hand such organizational conditions are promoted as better serving the complex needs of those using welfare services. Here, the "marketization" of welfare, and the ethos of inter-agency working and "wrap-around" services appear to intersect. The positive aspirations at the heart of the new welfare project pose us a profound question: Are we socially mature enough to function *without* receptacles into which to dump our negativity and hatred? Denied the opportunity to "split" and project our rivalrous aspects into those with whom we "should" be collaborating, what happens to these dimensions of experience?

Thus, interdependence and failures of interdependence are the new watchwords. This is true of the intra-group dimension, and most importantly of the inter-group relationship. But as the requirement for interdependence grows, so also will defensive retrenchments against this demand. Customers and users of welfare services are no longer servile or passive recipients, but themselves expect to negotiate their own expertise in relation to that of the expert. This places new demands on the capacities of service providers for interdependent functioning—how much to concede, how much to hang on to (and who, by the way, is *right?*)—and these demands cause strain and stress, and above all take time. One response is to interpose some form of technology between provider and user, obviating negotiation while sustaining the illusion of "choice". Another is to instrumentalize relationships in the effort to eliminate the uncertainty that ensues in a culture of interdependence and negotiation.

Larry Hirschhorn asks: "What is the evidence that the wider culture values the feelings of interdependence and the behaviours associated with bringing these feelings about?" (1997, p. 88). This is one key question, but there are others. The very real social optimism and creative potential of the "new interdependence" is offset by the reduction in relationship time and psychic energy available for its fulfilment. This is a central factor in the decline of relationship-based practices in welfare, and the corrosion of commitment to depth engagements in the new organizational cultures. At the same time, there is a critical question about how, if this potential were to be released, we would manage at the level of psycho-social functioning. The experience recounted above, of the daily psychic pressures involved in working in a fluid, networked environment, is moderated and rendered creative by the continuing availability and strength of an overall institutional container, left over from previous organizational forms. This container allows the intrapsychic and interpersonal tension and uncertainty to be continually processed *through the medium of relationships*. Not perfectly, to be sure, but "well enough". More often, however, we think that the contemporary experience is one in which Hirschhorn's "primitive psychology" is unleashed both *within and between* organizations with the task of delivering health and welfare. Rivalry, survival anxiety, uncertainties about identity and role, and so on, predominate.

We now review more systematically some of the sociological trends that account for the emergence of this state of affairs, before moving on to ask what theoretical and experiential resources we might need to accommodate to these new conditions.

The new organizational order

As systems, organizations are less bounded than they were and the boundaries that exist are more permeable. This is true whether one thinks in terms of their capacity to control the exchange with their environments, their degree of interdependence within networks of commercial, governmental, and professional influence, their openness to information flow, and their need to engage in rapid information exchange, and so on. Partnership, collaboration, outsourcing, secondment, are all contemporary reflections of the trend towards "networked" organizational functioning. As Manuel Castells (2000) argues in his compelling analysis of modern socio-economic trends, the rise of the "network society" cannot be traced to a single unifying developmental trajectory in corporate functioning but the different strands

> all are different dimensions of a fundamental process: the process of disintegration of the organizational model of vertical, rational bureaucracies, characteristic of the large corporation under the conditions of standardized mass production and oligopolistic markets. [2000, p. 179]

The unit of economic organization, he argues,

> is the network, made up of a variety of subjects and organizations, relentlessly modified as networks adapt to supportive environments and market structures . . . It is a culture, indeed, but a culture of the ephemeral, a culture of each strategic decision, a patchwork of experiences and interests, rather than a charter of obligations and rights. [*ibid.*, p. 214]

Networks and networking may be fashionable terms and activities, but in Castells' view they *are* the new social structure.

In most western industrial societies, the boundary between public and private sector organizations is far less clearly defined than it was in the immediate post-war period, which witnessed the foundation or consolidation of liberal democratic welfare states in these societies. The demarcation of values and practices associated with these domains has weakened accordingly, and the great ideological oppositions that underpinned them (e.g., labour vs. capital) have also been significantly dissolved. Commercial values, practices, and management methods have penetrated the public sector in a major way and some argue that the welfare state project is now driven by an over-riding concern with "fitness for labour" rather than social justice or collective well-being (Hoggett, 2000). Political desire for flexibility and adaptability on the supply side of a capricious world market may largely account for the introduction of a national educational curriculum, less obviously for competency frameworks as the instrument of training for occupational groups such as social workers, but in both cases we see the subordination of "creative" pedagogic principles to rational instrumental ones. In the British NHS and social care sectors, the logic of "outcomes", "evidence based practice" and "best value" in the context of strategic partnerships and clinical networks prevails, and attests to a culture of commodification in human services undreamed of fifteen years ago (Esping-Anderson, 1990).

A number of these trends are gathered in a tendency towards "externality" in the methods framing occupational and professional training, and methods of assuring the quality (fitness for purpose) of the worker, his or her work, and the organization itself (cf. Chapter Three). Reliance upon traditions of craft or apprenticeship training with their associated institutions of self-regulation is increasingly eschewed in favour of "transparent" methodologies of skills development, assessment, deployment, and public scrutiny. There are many indices, some shallower and some deeper, of the impact of these changes upon the psychological orientation of individuals with respect to their work. One is the appearance of new cultures of *curriculum vitae*, emphasizing "key skills" and "key achievements" rather than a developmental history of accumulated expertise, and debts to mentors, supervisors, and teachers. Because organizations, including traditional sites of professional learning such as universities, are no longer assumed to produce workforce quality on the basis of an unbroken historical or developmental continuum of doing so (or at least having a reputation for doing so) the test of an individual's employability is no longer "Where did you work or train?" but "Can you evidence your fitness for the role we require of you?" The Power Point presentation and the observed task replace the personal interview.

In the course of a research project into European child protection practices, Hetherington, Cooper, Smith, and Wilford (1997) describe a young British social worker saying "How would we manage without the child protection procedures?" They contrast this state of mind both with the prevailing "relationship based" practice of child protection staff working in the era before the spate of Public Inquiries into child deaths that transformed the landscape of British childcare work, and with practice attitudes among continental groups in the research study that reflect a concern with relationships and social solidarity. But there is evidence that the more solidaristic welfare states of other European countries are moving the way of Britain and America towards individually-focused, procedure-based, and legalistic responses.

This connects to the ubiquity of risk awareness and risk management in the life of modern organizations and in the consciousness of workers and managers alike. Anthony Giddens (1990), one of the two great sociologists of risk in modern society (Ulrich Beck (1992) is the other), observes that we have moved from a social preoccupation with scarcity, and hence justice and redistribution, in the direction of deep concern about survival. A crisis in trust has been linked with the pressures of living in a risk society (O'Neill, 2002). If the power and vagaries of nature once dominated our awareness, now it is "manufactured uncertainty", the threats *we* have created for ourselves and our natural environment. This preoccupation extends right to the heart of the systems we have for trying to insure ourselves against social and personal risks and dangers. These proliferate, but so do their weaknesses and failings, and thus so do efforts to insure against failure to prevent failure. Collapsing pension funds, endowment mortgages that will not deliver, "failures" in the child protection system, dangerous personality disordered people who are "untreatable", "failing" schools and hospitals, unregulated alternative medical practitioners, family doctors who are serial killers—all these phenomena now gather under the single umbrella of actual or potential failure in our risk prevention strategies. In consequence there is almost no area of life, and especially no area of organizational life, that is not profoundly shaped by methodologies and responsibilities associated with risk prevention.

The dominant model of risk analysis in all spheres of social life is actuarial (Power, 1994), raising profound and difficult questions both about whether such methodologies can ever deliver what they promise in many domains, but also about the broader human significance of trends towards the quantification of all human processes of living. Habermas's (1987) general thesis concerning the invasion of the "life world" by the rational instrumental concerns of the "system" is sociologically pertinent here, while a few commentators have discussed the "audit explosion" phenomenon in terms of the social anxieties which it might be understood to be managing or defending against (Cummins 2002; Chapter Three, this book).

We hypothesize that there is a central tension emerging between complexity and control in all forms of life, with organizations and institutions functioning as important "hubs" that both generate increased complexity (through their networks of connectedness) while they simultaneously experience a dissolution of boundary, autonomy, and control (because of their subordination within networks). Governments and other agencies of national or global influence contribute to the complex, ephemeral, mutating character of socio-economic processes through increasing deregulation of many spheres of activity, while simultaneously attempting to claw back control through increased regulation of socio-economic actors and the outcomes of their work. As complexity in deregulated, networked environments threatens to escape central control mechanisms, so "risks" and risk management strategies proliferate. Organizational instability is experienced as continual ("change fatigue" ensues), and individual dependency needs cannot be met within organizations. New forms of privatized self-reliance and defences against anxiety evolve in the workforce. Castells has his own way of articulating this:

> Identity is becoming the main, and sometimes the only, source of meaning in an historical period characterized by widespread destructuring of organizations, delegitimation of institutions, fading away of major social movements, and ephemeral cultural expressions. People increasingly organize their meaning not around what they do, but on the basis of what they are, or believe they are ... *Our Societies are increasingly structured around a bipolar opposition between the Net and the self.* [2000, p. 3]

We are now becoming used to living "beyond the stable state". As Donald Schon observed in 1971, "The loss of the stable state means that our society and all of its institutions are in *continuing* processes of transformation. We cannot expect new stable states that will endure even for our lifetimes" (Schon, 1971). Our aim in this chapter is to think also about states of mind and relationship. We are accustomed to thinking about the "institution in the mind" (Armstrong, 1991) but what does it mean to live and work in a world of unstable institutions, and unstable organizational relationships? Must we embrace instability of mind to be capable of working *with* such conditions of life? Or can "containment" assume some new meaning and psychic location?

If there is any doubt about the degree to which organizational character and form is tending to be homogenized without reference to the particular nature of the work to be performed within organizational boundaries, thus throwing into question the capacity of organizations as containers to be adapted to their own contents (the "contained"), then we offer the following playful analogy for readers to contemplate.

The premiership club

Top class football is now big business, and organizations everywhere increasingly function like football clubs, and vice versa. There are no football *teams* any more, only squads, and players wear their squad number rather than one denoting their position within a team formation. The squad is a network, out of which functioning teams emerge, fluctuate, and evolve. "Squad rotation" is a fashionable term for this, comparable to the concept of the care team's "skill mix" as distinct from its "membership". Players move in and out of the squad on short term loan (like agency nurses and social workers), buttressing a defensive weakness here and a lack of strike power there. In truth, the entire international pool of professional players is a network, and clubs merely comparatively stable, geographically situated (although not always—witness Wimbledon FC's migration to Milton Keynes) "hubs" of activity. Players' and fans' identifications and loyalties with respect to one another must form and re-form rapidly. "Attachments" are surely weakened and "identity" (of club, player, supporter) is increasingly dislocated in time and space. Football passions remain as fervent as ever, and from the perspective of local populations as localized, but the objects of passion are fluctuating, unstable, and beyond even the fantasy of local control or influence. Sociologists of football in the 1980s suggested that part of the explanation of the "hooligan" phenomenon was the loss of grounds for belief in the fantasy that supporters could exert influence over their local team. Pitch invasions and other forms of disruption could be understood as frustrated efforts to re-assert a sense of control. In an era when local lads did make up the local team, and many people knew someone who was friends with the local Roy of the Rovers, this fantasy of influence had some grounding in social reality. Nowadays, we would think it deluded. And when a club such as Nottingham Forest, in the face of financial difficulties, recently re-launched itself on the basis of a local academy for home grown talent, they were hailed for their innovation. Likewise, from time to time we celebrate signs of revival, or survival, in some valued area of threatened professional activity. But a sober analysis suggests that there can be no simple return to the old ways. The struggle to sustain or recover forms of "depth" welfare must be conducted on new terrain. How possible, and how easy or difficult this will prove to be, is the ultimate question posed by this book. What is certain is that the contemporary situation does require us to face up to the fitness of our traditional modes of theory and practice with respect to organizations. It is to this that we now turn.

Psychoanalytic theory in a networked world

The orthodox psychoanalytic theory of organizational functioning and dysfunction is rooted in a series of central metaphors that are either increasingly challenging or increasingly irrelevant to their time, because the times have changed the nature of organizations. One dominant image in systems psychodynamic thinking is of the open but well-enough bounded organizational system, structured and ordered by the conceptual trinity of role, task and authority, transforming inputs into outputs. At root it owes much to that most deeply cathected and difficult to relinquish psychoanalytic image, the nurturant and protective relationship of mother and infant (Miller & Rice, 1967).

According to this image, faced with the inchoate and primitive terrors of infantile emotional life, the mother is either herself sufficiently emotionally available to experience something of these terrors, and drawing on her adult capacity for thoughtful endurance and suffering, to facilitate their transformation into states more tolerable for the infant—or she is not. Likewise, organizational processes are subject to distortion, disruption, and dysfunction in response to the anxieties and conflicts evoked by the primary task. In turn, the organization may succeed in providing forms of relationship and thoughtfulness for employees exposed to these anxieties, thus enabling the work to proceed effectively and efficiently—or it may not.

In both infant and organization the presence of these conditions for the transformation of experience is understood as the precondition for growth, healthy adaptation to the environment, mastery of developmental challenges, and depth of moral, emotional, interpersonal, and social engagement. The preponderance of attention within this schema to disturbance or "toxicity", and the task of managing it, is somewhat counterbalanced by recent ideas about the importance of emotional "aliveness", in both parental and leadership roles, for the development of creative capacities, whether in childhood or organizations (Armstrong, 2002). This perspective reminds us that understanding the pain or conflict that accompanies work does not in itself deliver us into a creative or "animating" relationship to the task. Efforts to rescue psychoanalytic organizational theory from an excessive preoccupation with the defensive management of anxiety, by, for example, reframing conflicts and anxieties as necessary tensions situated at the heart of the "idiom" that constitutes the unique character of the organization (Hutten, Bazalgette, & Armstrong, 1994) are valuable. But they are not by themselves an adequate language for the predicaments and conundrums of organizational forms as they are now present in our lives.

As organizational life is now configured and experienced, there is frequently no longer a *structure* of "parenting" either for organizations, or for those working within them, that can perform the kind of psychic work assumed to be necessary by traditional theory. At the broadest level, the founding conditions of the British welfare state entailed a kind of national "family consensus" as to its desirability, represented in government by each family member being securely housed within a defined ministry, governed by a single minister. Today, with cross-cutting ministerial agendas and pooled budgets overseen by cabinet style (networked) local government structures, there is no longer a nuclear family organization presiding over our affairs.

Essentially, the same points apply to another hallowed set of conceptual foundations for organizational thinking—the basic assumptions underlying work group behaviour. Bion's model of a work group and its various modalities of defensive distraction from "task" presupposes an image of the group as both bounded, and more or less functional depending on its capacity to manage its conscious and unconscious need for leadership. The brilliant and extremely funny opening sections of Bion's (1961) *Experiences in Groups* concern the struggle of groups to manage when the group leader refuses to be the group leader. Evolution in the direction of an autonomous "work group" is achieved once members relinquish the fantasy that they can rid themselves of responsibility for knowledge, hope, and thought on to the leader (BaD), a pairing of group members (BaP), or displace the impediments to their struggle on to some external group (BaF). All this privileges intra-group relationships as the key to "autonomy" and successful execution of the primary task. But the new preconditions of organizational life, in which the site of autonomy is persistently decentred, cast a long shadow of doubt over the contemporary relevance of these presuppositions. It is consistent with our argument that later thinkers came up with further basic assumptions—of "oneness" and "meness" (Lawrence, Bain, & Gould, 1996; Turquet, 1974) in an effort to adapt to emergent organizational and cultural conditions.

If this old theoretical order may be dying, is something new struggling to be born? It does seem possible that we stand on the threshold of a genuine paradigm shift that will help make sense of the new experiential order through the articulation of new principles for understanding the production and reproduction of social life, psychic states, and organizational forms—a revised logic of living systems. This is Sonia Abadi discussing the shift from a language of frontiers to a language of networks in her keynote address to the 2003 Congress of the International Psychoanalytic Association:

Little by little the idea arises of a potential being, virtually incommensurable. Thus in clinical practice models appear that speak of crises and ruptures, of undoing knots that had traumatic origins, of dissolving splits, re-establishing the continuity of existence. It is no longer a matter of making the concept of the border flexible but of entering the paradigm of the network—the true epistemological turning point that has materialised in recent years. And it has been precisely in Freudian theory where this paradigm has been implicit from the beginning, in harmony or discordant with the paradigm of the frontier. [Abadi, 2003, p. 226]

The new sciences of complexity foreground the self-organizing properties of systems, which is to say their capacity for the generation of qualitatively new properties once a certain level of dynamic complexity has been attained, their nature as "structured processes" (Watson, 2002). Possibly "strange attractors", the underlying pattern of inherently unpredictable ordering in such systems will transpire to be their site of "containment" but we have no experiential analogue for such an idea. Perhaps Hutten, Bazalgette and Armstrong's (1994) notion of "X generated management" approaches this thought, with its emphasis on the uniqueness of each organization's "idiom" or central tension that generates the particular character of work and hence management required within the organization

Conclusion: rethinking organizational containment

Because we hold a capacity for relationship to be the precondition for human psychic and social health, and because containment (in the very particular sense it has in psychoanalytic thinking) is a precondition for the growth and sustenance of relatedness (as well as itself being a particular form of relationship), the profound impediments that modern organizational forms pose for "containing practices" constitute a considerable threat to our capacity for social and psychological cohesion. We stress that this is an open, rather than a dystopian conclusion. The shift towards a culture of fluidity, flexibility, and negotiated interdependences in social life contains new possibilities for new forms of depth engagements, but in the absence of a *function* to do the work of containment these are as likely to be risky, volatile, enervating, destructive, and unpredictable as they are to promote solidarity, creativity, purpose, and growth rooted in a sense of security. The big question facing psychoanalytic theory and practice is "How can this function, congruent with the new conditions, be elaborated and made real?'

The concept of borderline states of mind may be helpful in this task. In Chapter Two we presented a vignette from a group relations training event in which fluid and emergent groupings of members at first failed to define any sense of their purpose, and hence seemed unable to name themselves and so posit an identity. We hypothesized that they consequently experienced themselves as "caught in the headlights" of an oppressive management system, unable to grow and negotiate their relatedness to other groups, or to management itself. As we hope to have made clear, organizational identity has traditionally been understood to depend upon a capacity to establish and maintain secure organizational boundaries. But organizational boundaries—in terms of time, space, task and location of authority—are what are thrown into question in the new order. The focus of organizational life, for all staff and not just management, is now *at the boundary* rather than *within the boundary*. This resonates with Larry Hirschhorn's notion of the increasing exposure to vulnerability as central to modern organizational experience. Equally, for the person afflicted by borderline anxieties, it is the threat of loss of self by engulfment in the "other" oscillating with the threat of isolation as a result of withdrawal from relationship with the other, that is the central predicament. The task of containment now also resides "at the boundary", in enabling people to manage the threats and opportunities of their relationships, which are conducted and continually negotiated *across* boundaries. It is the preservation of a secure enough sense of identity, free enough of the threat posed by relationship to the "other", that is the required focus of containing practices. Without this, fulfilment of the organizational task is threatened by the eruption of the "primitive psychology" that the demands of interdependence bring with them.

CHAPTER NINE

Conclusion: complex dependencies and the dilemmas of modern welfare

The limits of perfectability

At first sight, there are really only two ways to think about the meaning and purpose of social welfare; from the point of view of those who are afflicted, suffering, dispossessed, excluded, or incapacitated; or from the point of view of the planners, policy makers, politicians, professionals, and carers with responsibility for providing a response. Our point of view in this book is neither exactly one nor the other, nor both, but an attempt to articulate a vision of welfare that returns us to an idea of common humanity without denying the divisions and differences among us. The idea that there must be a third term to the relation between helper and helped—a concept or commitment, embodied in an institution or a politics, which transcends the apparently simple relation between giving and receiving care—is central to our understanding. The meaning of welfare, as distinct from just nurture, solace, charity, understanding, or concern, is found in the social organization of such impulses and practices. The existence of a welfare state gives expression to the fact that some superordinate principle that endures beyond individual acts of care, or even many lifetimes and generations of devotion to its provision, is a necessary part of the landscape of modern human society. Yet this recognition, this requirement, that we establish and maintain a commitment to a universal in matters of welfare, is not a certainty; it is everywhere now vulnerable to interrogation, doubt, and revision.

A main source of inspiration in our thinking in this book has been the theory and practice of psychoanalytic psychotherapy in social and public service contexts. A uniquely radical aspect of psychoanalytic practice is the requirement that for a lengthy period the practitioner submits to being a patient. To have suffered the knowledge and discovery of one's own afflictions in the presence of another is the central qualification for practice. As a result, the capacity to share in suffering that has been partially transcended in oneself becomes the precondition of helping another person to face it. Perhaps the most important discovery anyone makes in this way is of the limits to possible change or amelioration. Psychoanalysis is instruction in the imperfectability of man and woman. Because British psychoanalysis has always engaged directly with the problem of human destructiveness and the precarious character of mental health, maturity, adulthood, and social concern, it is often accused of pessimism by its more sanguine siblings and cousins. Yet a readiness to engage with the unceasing recurrence of destructiveness in human relationships is not, or should not be, a counsel of resignation or complacency, but of hope. The meaning of social welfare cannot be adequately grasped without a clear-sighted and painful recognition of the limits to possible change and betterment, and of organized welfare as the outcome of social and political struggle.

Mental pain and conflict are ubiquitous in human experience, and our various ways of banishing it from awareness give rise to corresponding limits to our ability to imagine life differently, and to realize our imaginings. One aim of this book has been to show that the project of social welfare is currently afflicted by particular imaginative restrictions, and that these are traceable to anxieties, fears, and imagined catastrophes of a specifically contemporary kind. We have tried to evoke our experience of an increasingly constricting culture of welfare, one that is dominated by a consumerist idea of its own goals as "need-satisfying" rather than relationship enhancing. But we have also tried to understand these phenomena, rather than simply bemoan or critique them. For the difficulties we identify in the contemporary welfare project arise partly in a context of genuine efforts to achieve progress. The aspiration to place the "user" at the centre of the *social* organization of welfare, rather than just at the heart of the individual clinical transaction must surely be applauded. However, our most pessimistic thought about this aim would be to ask whether we are actually developed enough as social beings to achieve the degree of complex co-operation required for its realization. When Larry Hirschhorn (1997) evokes the idea of "a more primitive psychology" of the modern workplace, we think of the rivalry, competition, status, survival anxiety, and so on that seem to haunt the experiences of so many welfare organizations in both their internal and external relationships. To this thought, it is not enough to respond that "it was ever thus". The demands for interdependence and collaboration across unfamiliar boundaries, set against a backcloth of uncertainty about where and how identities are formed and located, expose us all to new forms of anxiety. It is these anxieties that produce what we have termed borderline states of mind as characteristic responses.

Authority without authoritarianism

Thus, one of the great unanswered questions of our times is how to recover a basis for *authority* in social affairs without resort to authoritarianism. In the context of the present book, this means rediscovering how the project of welfare might be grounded in a decisively held view of human nature. Some trends in postmodernism have cast suspicion on the very idea of human nature, seeing it as one more legitimate target of the deconstructive effort, and its defence as evidence of the exercise of ideologically motivated interests directed at preserving one or another form of "domination". It is one of the ironies of twentieth century thought that psychoanalysis, which helped give birth to the postmodern sensibility by revealing the plasticity and instability of human nature, should now be called upon to reassert the limiting conditions of this nature in the face of postmodernism's radical excesses.

The socio-political world that embraced and valorized "differences", the world that gave birth to "identity politics" and welfare programmes organized around needs and aspirations articulated by new self-authorizing social groupings, largely also dismantled respect for vertical or hierarchical relations of power and authority. On this basis, traditional politics (including traditional forms of welfare state) had suppressed differences and controlled possibilities and destinies; now the project became that of liberation from the delimiting and oppressing forces of corporatist welfare and vested ideological interests and apparatuses. At least as much as the fiscal problems of Western nation states, this delegitimation of the means by which people's identities and cultural particularities were governed has led to the flattening of our social structures, the withdrawal of government from whole domains of civil life, and the burgeoning of "difference" as a principle criterion of legitimacy. On the one hand, we have argued in Chapter Four that the discourse of difference may in fact obscure rather than disclose the dynamics and sources of oppression that *use* real or imagined differences as objects upon which to project hatred. If that is so, then we are denying ourselves a basis upon which to unite in the struggle against human destructiveness. On the other hand, the right, and the capacity, to define a social or political identity, to exercise autonomy and seek fulfilment and recognition—these are quintessentially creative acts in which the uniqueness of experience that is the mark of creativity is central to the act of self-definition. But they stand in absolute tension with the "universal" principles of authority and hierarchy that were the binding, limiting forces of social life of an earlier age. To establish new sources of authority in social affairs that respond to these conditions, embracing both our need for genuine *relatedness* (which will incorporate dependency without this being all that relatedness consists in), and our need for separateness (or difference), we will need to negotiate the complex territory of true interdependence.

Thinking about dependency

A woman who manages a small organization in the independent sector dedicated to supporting carers spent several years in psychotherapy before she was finally able to allow herself a full and direct experience of her own dependence on the therapist. On this day she arrived very anxious about the hostile mood of her team in the wake of a decision she had taken; she was also due to deliver a speech that evening, in which she would need to refer to the state of the organization's work in the particular area relating to this decision. She dissolved into tears, sobbing deeply, feeling she could not possibly get through the day. The therapist did not say a great deal, relying on a sense that the woman's capacity to break down and feel so helpless was a sign that she felt more able to use him as an emotional rather than an intellectual resource. Simply to be there, and bear the distress with her, was the function that might allow her to muster her own internal strengths. This happened, and she was able to begin discriminating between those colleagues who she believed supported her actions, and those who were angry and threatened by what she had done; one of her colleagues had attacked her badly during a meeting the previous day, but much to her surprise had approached her in a quite normal and even-tempered manner immediately afterwards. She was able to see that her own capacity to tolerate the woman's rage had enabled this. All of this made her feel stronger, more grounded, as though there was help available to her in the outside world, and thus more able to face the anxieties of the coming day.

This woman's staff team work with people who provide informal care for very dependent disabled relatives, including children. Until now, she had functioned as a very conscientious, industrious, competent leader and manager, although she was often anxious about her professional worth. But she had little access in herself to her own conflicts about dependency on others, and thus few resources with which to think about the emotional contradictions to which her staff were often subjected in their work by the carers they tried to help. People who endure enforced states of dependency may often reject the care proffered to them, just because it serves to remind them forcibly of their need for it. Those who provide it may feel unable to confront such unreasonable and self-defeating (although understandable) behaviour, and allow themselves to be tyrannized or enslaved by the dependent person, who in turn experiences themselves as imprisoned by their own limitations. These patterns may or may not be widespread in any one context, but where they occur they give rise to disproportionate strain on all concerned.

The woman came to her next psychotherapy session and passed half an hour talking as though the events and feelings of the previous one had hardly occurred. The therapist felt as though something meaningful and important that they had been through together was being dismissed or diminished, in effect rejected. When he found a way to speak about this to her, the woman acknowledged that she had found it frightening that one session could make such a difference to her ability to feel she could cope; she was frightened of the discovery of her need for someone else to play a part in making emotional progress. This sequence was typical of her pattern of relating in the therapy at this time—a good and meaningful encounter would be immediately succeeded by one in which she stripped everything of meaning, to the extent where she often asked "What is the point in relationships, what are they *for*?" But as time went on, her capacity to stay in touch with her conflicts and anxieties about dependency increased.

Deep and shallow welfare

When we conceive of welfare only as the provision of services, albeit "modern and dependable" ones, we align ourselves with a shallow rather than a deep conception of welfare. Those aspects of welfare we used to call the "personal social services" always did, and despite reconfigurations and redistribution of roles, still do depend for their successful implementation on the quality of relationships through which they are offered. But the flight from meaning towards proficiency, competence, and other instrumental conceptions of well-being can occur at the level of the social just as much as that of the individual and interpersonal. The prospect of deeply engaged welfare provision frightens us at a social and political level, just as it frightened the woman to encounter her own dependent self; the fear is that once we allow real contact with a deprived, dependent, helpless population, any services offered to them will become rapidly enslaved to their needs for all time, draining resources from other important projects, and depleting our autonomy and flexibility as a society and an economy.

There is nothing new in this observation; the element of social fantasy that informs periodic moral panics and retributive policies directed against welfare scroungers and malingerers, has always had roots in anxieties of this kind. But it is hard to learn from experience. The paradox of the moment at which the woman described above is able to collapse into a dependent state, is that it is the start of her liberation from actual dependency on psychotherapy—she goes away not just "feeling better" but more able to cope autonomously by drawing on her own internal resources. It is not dependency that is the problem, but fear and hatred of dependency, which destroys the link to the source of support that may be the ground of our well-being—our welfare. This is a central conundrum that, at the level of social organization and self-awareness, this book is devoted to illuminating.

Dependence and interdependence—a national conundrum

We believe that a range of macro-political developments in the late modern world now conspire to make it very much harder to think and act rationally with respect to questions of this kind. A constellation of social anxieties is shaping social policy in ways that encourage and support our wish to settle for a shallow conception, and practice, of welfare. For a number of years, the idea of "globalization" was little more than an obscure concept within academic sociology; then suddenly, with the accession to power of the new Labour government in 1997, it became both a register within popular understanding of Britain's now diminished place in the world scheme of things, and a justification for an entire socio-economic programme. What is known in the economic jargon as "supply side measures" refers to the national need to have a suitably trained and experienced supply of labour and skills to meet the demands of the economic producers, who in turn function in response to the dictates of the market. As a nation of "suppliers" we must be in a permanent state of readiness to respond to unpredictable and uncontrollable fluctuations in the external economic environment, which may require us to alter economic course, re-train ourselves, in short to adapt. While we may continue to "produce" as well, our producers also believe themselves to be vulnerable to the negative impact of competition in remote and capricious corners of the globe, and so they too must subscribe to the necessity of permanent adaptability. Globalization, on this view, has not positioned us in a potentially constructive relation of greater interdependence with other nations, but at their mercy. We are a dependent nation, and the state of dependence is to be feared.

This state of mind, and perhaps also its denial, was well captured by Hugo Young in a short newspaper commentary the day after new Labour's 1999 budget.

> There was a silence at the centre of Gordon Brown's third Budget. The world was never mentioned. Yet the world economy—what will happen there, how Britain can win there—is the heart of the matter. It is the unspoken force with which the Chancellor is grappling . . . What was once a grand day of national reckoning, almost above party, has become an occasion of numerous micro-measures. Instead of the division of the national cake . . . we have the readying of the nation to fight for survival in a global economy whose all pervading influence, for all its absence in this speech, cannot be resisted. [Young, 1999, p. 1]

An important consequence of this collective state of mind, and of the policies and prescriptions that flow from it, is the positive encouragement to abandon hope for deep and enduring engagement with work. Ideas of vocation that imply an extended and deeply felt commitment to a developing personal project, or more simply of "loving one's work", are rendered dangerous—dangerous for the individual who is warned that she or he will inevitably suffer painful loss, and dangerous for governments who believe they need a cheerfully adaptable workforce ready to down tools, retrain, and pick up a different set with equal investment to the changed task. The political philosophy of "lifelong learning" might be construed as an expression of social commitment to the provision of opportunities for continual and renewed useful curiosity; but its inspiration is in reality other, more concerned with placing the labour force on a permanent war-footing, ready to confront deprivation, transition, and relocation. Paradoxically, however, at the time of writing we are not at war (unless one counts the occupation of Iraq as war) or threatened by the imminent prospect of it. As Richard Sennett remarks in *The Corrosion of Character*, "What's peculiar about uncertainty today is that it exists without any looming historical disaster; instead it is woven into the everyday practices of a vigorous capitalism. Instability is meant to be normal ..." (1998, p. 31).

In all of this, it is strong attachments that are discouraged.

This thesis is not intended to deny the reality of the impact of globalization. Rapid and bewildering technological change, organizational instability and uncertainty, cultural diversity, rapidity of information flow and decision-making, the ambiguities of a "flexible" world in which "all that is solid melts into air" (Berman, 1983) are part of everyday experience. Nor is it meant to evoke nostalgia for a lost, cherished age of stability and continuity. Rather we have a series of questions. To what extent do these changes entail any fundamental alteration in the nature of the human problems to which organized welfare is a response? Have people's experiences of illness, bereavement, trauma, mental disturbance, disability, domestic violence, child abuse been transformed in the same way that our experiences of shopping, travelling, schooling, or leisure have altered? The answer must be in part that they have, but also that they have not. The idea that our struggles with dependence and interdependence can be somehow eliminated is what we must resist, even if the contexts in which they are encountered are indeed subject to reframing and renegotiation.

In the period of quite acute emotional turbulence that succeeded the events in therapy described above, the woman dreamed she was on a beach; she approached the shoreline and peeked round one of the rocks that obscured her view of the sea. There she saw foaming, turbulent, frothing water. She withdrew, unable to look at it for more than a moment, and then walked back up the beach. Some weeks later she described her experience of the previous day, starting with a session of psychotherapy that she said was difficult but satisfying, followed by news that she had not been short-listed for a job and some hours of despair and dejection about this; none the less, she helped her flatmate with a task, then with trepidation phoned the organization to ask for feedback on the interview; this reassured her since the reasons offered made genuine sense and she no longer felt the rejection as such a personal matter. Then she had a satisfying phone call with a friend. Although unremarkable from one point of view, the therapist felt that he was hearing for the first time about someone who could endure complex and shifting changes of emotional state, and experience them as a continuous process in which the toleration of despair and anxiety was a condition of thinking, and acting, to surmount it. Hope and hopelessness could all be contained within her and were felt to be *linked*. This stood in contrast to a previous pattern in which the therapist often felt he was either required to keep hope alive, or to point out that the woman's hopeful communications disguised her fear of her underlying despair. In the past she had often commented that she knew she avoided the mess and uncertainty of "getting her hands dirty with the business of living".

The capacity to do meaningful health service or social care work presupposes being able to tolerate extreme states of feeling and thought and, to borrow a contemporary idiom, stay joined up with these extremes. It is difficult work, often directed at helping others negotiate difficulties and choices they feel they cannot bear. Yet there is a pervasive encouragement to believe that, in all spheres, work can be made easier. Richard Sennett (1998) describes returning to visit a bakery in Boston twenty-five years after he had first studied the working practices there. Computerization of bakery production means that workers now no longer know how to bake. When things go wrong with the machines,

> The workers can fool with the screen to correct somewhat for these defects; what they can't do is fix the machines, or more important, actually bake bread by manual control . . . Program-dependent labourers, they can have no hands-on knowledge. The work is no longer legible to them, in the sense of understanding what they are doing. [Sennett, 1998, p. 68]

Indeed these workers, freed from the constraints of bakery as a craft that must be learned through experience, do not think of themselves as bakers. The work is no longer "difficult" says Sennett, having been largely reduced to a matter of punching buttons to operate user-friendly computer screens. But,

> In all forms of work, from sculpting to serving meals, people identify with tasks which challenge them, tasks which are difficult. . . . When things are made easy for us, as in the labor I've described, we become weak; our engagement with work becomes superficial, since we lack understanding of what we are doing. [*ibid.*, pp. 72–74]

Consequently, the project of examining welfare from what some might posit as a traditional and redundant perspective (psycho-analysis) is, in our view, an attempt to articulate enduring charac-teristics of a social and human project of fundamental significance. It is about the search for what Joel Kovel called "the trans-histori-cal" dimensions of welfare, a set of core processes, requirements, dilemmas, and contradictions which remain identifiably the same despite their constant mutation as a result of historical, political, and social ideologies and circumstances. Or, as Kovel says, some-thing which is "across history and through it, entering history and shaped by history yet preserving some element that is beyond history and transcendent" (1981, p. 34). An exploration of the nature of welfare *work* is one portal through which these enduring phenomena can be entered and understood.

Between despair and cure—growth

In our experience, when health and social work teams and organi-zations ask for external training or consultancy, their relationship with complex and painful dependency is often the problem with which they are wrestling. After a few sessions of staff group facili-tation, two continuing care teams working with children and fami-lies in one Social Services Department both expressed the fear that they did not know whether, in the end, their work made any difference to the children and parents. They described becom-ing involved with the first child, then the second, third and so on, until they were called upon to intervene further in relation to the babies of the children who had now become young adults. Looking back over a decade of work, and case files several vol-umes thick, it seemed that maybe nothing had really changed. The impact of this upon professional staff was profoundly depressing, and seemed to throw into question their own valuation of them-selves. The offer of consultative support to these teams had come via the senior management of the department who were concerned about the level of emotional strain on most, if not all, operational staff, but when the consultant himself started work, it became clear that the team members believed they had been singled out for attention by management because they were failing or performing badly in some way. This idea, that "you only get attention if you've done something wrong", seemed to reflect the way families themselves experienced the presence of social workers in their lives—as a consequence of failure or inadequacy. In turn, this belief renders the "helping relationship" one dominated by fear of criticism or allegations of failure, and this extends to the helping relation that might pertain between managers and front-line staff.

In another local authority, a research programme evaluated the work of a specialist team established to resolve the circumstances of a large number of children in care without permanent placements (Cooper & Webb, 1999). The research concluded that a proportion of the cases were likely never to be satisfactorily resolved in the terms normally required by "permanency planning" principles. Often these cases involved older children who, apart from histories of abuse, had experienced many changes and disruptions of placement, and now combined impossible demands with behaviour that attacked the resilience of even the best carers. When this conclusion was fed back to the team themselves, they seemed to experience immense relief; one worker spoke of her working experience being properly recognized. The capacity to face the fact of the obstinacy or recalcitrance to our efforts at transformation *by* "the object of our work", can release us from the continuing sense of failure which arises if we persist in believing that we *ought* somehow to be capable of doing better. In a broad sense, all these teams were struggling with the problem of dependency, with the unwelcome knowledge that some children and parents just do go on requiring our services over very long periods of time, and even across generations. The idealist in all of us objects to this recognition, and rightly. For certainly more could be done, but whatever this more might turn out to be, it will only be discovered if we are capable of accepting rather than denying the depressing facts with which we are, at given time, now confronted. Thus there is a terrible irony in the current fashion for promoting British health and welfare services as dependable. For it is far from clear whether we actually want people to depend upon them, and where they do, whether we believe and communicate to them that this is acceptable, rather than evidence of someone's failure—theirs, ours, or some undefined other's.

Between the extremes of failure and success, the fear of absolute dependence and the illusion of complete independence, there does indeed lie a third way. It seeks development and growth as its goal, not cure; it embraces interdependence and acknowledges degrees of relative dependence as facts of psychological and social life; and it understands that work is a relationship neither of total estrangement nor harmonious merger. The woman described above who managed a small voluntary organization was partly afflicted by difficulty in occupying this intermediate area. She experienced the organization's problems and her staff's varying degrees of competence as all her own responsibility. Thus, the anxiety of leading the organization became an intolerable burden. While her staff did, in fact, just get on with their work and the organization largely flourished, she frequently could not experience her staff as properly *separate* from but also *related* to her, so that she was unable clearly to identify ways in which *she* could help *them* develop or mature as professionals.

The italicized words merely emphasize the centrality of the idea of relationship to that of welfare work, of transformative endeavour aimed at realizing potential. Behind this difficulty lay deeper problems about accepting the frustrations entailed by the obstinate reality of other people with separate powers and different ideas. This was again illustrated in a dream she reported. It began with her sitting opposite a man and woman, to whom she was explaining her ideas for a training course connected to her work. The man said something about how one could think about these ideas in a different way. Having set out feeling confident about her own proposals, she now felt they were bad and that she had exposed her incompetence. In the second part of the dream, she was lying on a mat opposite the woman, and they were mirroring each other's movements and gestures. Thus, the dream seemed to show how, faced with the fact of someone with a separate mind and different ideas, everything turns bad, and she replaces this with a scene in which the other person is exactly like her, and vice versa. The possibility of negotiation between two different people, or creative productivity through dialogue and reciprocity, simply collapses.

Such reciprocity and dialogue between separate people, including people in non-symmetrical relations of power and dependence, is the foundation of the possibility of transformative work, indeed *all work* including the work of welfare. Separateness is not necessarily the same thing as estrangement, but there can be no such thing as work under *any* social conditions unless the object upon which we act materially or psychically or politically is experienced as separate from ourselves and thus capable of potentially resisting and thwarting our efforts. The work of individual personal development is equally all about this—negotiating the thresholds of anxiety and facing the reality testing that growth and a capacity for social belonging require.

Borderline welfare

We have suggested that welfare is not best understood as the province of any single intellectual discourse—of politics, economics, culture, psychology or social theory and action. We have tried to show that it requires the application of a complex sensibility owing something to each of these. In this book we have used our own particular psychoanalytic sensibility, which is a clinical one, and we have aimed to show this at work, rather than telling about it. Our stance accepts the validity of an interplay of perspectives, while privileging none, and thus it is written firmly in the tradition of the "late modern". However, we eschew the relativistic extremes that can be associated with the "postmodern". Suffering, deprivation, insult, madness, corruption, and illness exist—as personal affliction, as inner world experience, as social injustice. They are social facts. The absence of a grand narrative to interpret or explain any or all of these social facts renders the task of their empirical study more difficult and methodologically uncertain, but not impossible; and the conditions of contemporary welfare can also be made better or worse.

This book has discussed some of the forces shaping the development of modern welfare. They are simultaneously located deep in the inner worlds of individuals and across the field of the globalized markets within which traditional nation states are now struggling to maintain themselves. The welfare policy process remains, more or less, the province of traditional government. But traditional government is also fighting for its life. Beset from within by voter apathy and the failure of conventional representative democracy to cope with the complexity of modern civil society, and from without by the economic logic driving the development of supranational markets, governments believe they cannot any longer afford (in several senses) to support and promote the conditions that informed the original welfare contract. Nation states, like welfare organizations and multi-disciplinary teams, find themselves locked into systems of interdependence that attenuate their sense of control over individual destiny, even if they have the potential to promote survival and creative collaboration.

Our thesis in this book has been that contemporary social policy is organized by profound anxieties arising in the face of the experience of such complexity. An adequate response to the impact of globalization and to the multiple interdependencies it brings with it will demand new forms of political sensibility. If these cannot be found then political culture will resort to constricting or fragmenting solutions. The distinctive term we have given to this constriction of response in the field of social policy and action is "borderline welfare". We have attempted to show that the borderline response is not grounded in a failure of intellectual or political acumen. We think it is rooted in a breakdown between the capacity for *emotional* toleration of the experience of extreme complexity and anxiety, and the capacity for creative thinking and action that can flow from holding on to and reflecting upon complex emotional experience.

Throughout this book we have argued that psychoanalysis is peculiarly well placed to elucidate the forms of feeling and behaviour that flow from the local and global conditions of existence we have been outlining. In most of its incarnations psychoanalysis has assumed that the problem of simultaneous individuation and relationship with respect to others is the first and most basic continuing struggle of human existence. Our effort in using psychoanalysis has been to show that, although we are employing a term from clinical psychopathology, borderline functioning is not the preserve of a diagnostically labelled few. The psychoanalytic perspective argues for a continuity of experience between "normal" and "abnormal" states of mind, and faced with the anxieties of negotiating complex emotional experience and relationships, any individual, group, or organization can be observed to retreat from full engagement with their own emotional experience. Most crucially, this will include a retreat from the forms of thought which attend complexity, and which might help to master it. The strategy of retreat—into what might be thought of as an emotional and cognitive bunker—is usually not absolute, for this would constitute a psychosis. It is, as we have repeatedly aimed to describe, a tendency to adopt a narrowed, constricted, and limiting world of experience that avoids emotional need, and hence, fulfilling relationships. It is a solution that entails great cost. The possibilities of intimacy and creativity are sacrificed; and, we have been suggesting, at the level of the social, there is a sacrifice of the commitment to full-blooded welfare.

We have chosen not to end this book with a set of prescriptions or recommendations for change. In this sense we wish to remain faithful to the spirit in which psychoanalytic psychotherapy is conducted. Change, if it arises, does so because of a process of liberation from delimiting conditions of thought rooted in fear of emotional engagement. It is experienced as a process of radical risk-taking, but the risks are met because a sufficient degree of confidence in the capacity to negotiate external realities differently has become established. Like a single act of interpretation in therapy, this book can only be a contribution to a long and difficult struggle. All we can hope for is that it is well timed, thoughtful, and speaks well enough to the states of mind with which it seeks to engage.

Methodological reflections: clinical sensibility and the study of the social

"Curiosity has itself to be under scrutiny while being exercised; we must not be directed towards understanding other problems by inhibiting observation of our own curiosity."

(Bion, 1976)

Introduction

I n the introduction to this book we noted that the methodology informing its argument and analysis is not primarily about the deployment of psychoanalytic concepts and theories in relation to welfare and society, but about the application of a clinical sensibility to the study of these phenomena. Our primary intention was that the book should be an exercise in such an application, rather than a theoretical or methodological defence of its possibility. Nevertheless, we think that a justification of our method deserves some attention. There is an inevitable, and perhaps necessary element of *ex post facto* theorization in this. We did not sit down and establish methodological ground rules before we began research and to write. Instead, drawing upon our own established intellectual, social scientific, and clinical resources we went to work, examining and refining what emerged as we went.

The essence of our thinking about methodology needs to be broached via questions about *how* theories and concepts of both individuals and social life are generated. For us, psychoanalysis is first and foremost a way of *knowing* and *relating* to people in the world, not a theory *about* the world. Psychoanalytic theories and concepts are produced in and through practice, via processes of hypothesizing and testing in relation to clinical realities. If the generation of theory about extra-clinical realities departs too far from this simple set of precepts, it will cease to be psychoanalytic, even if psychoanalytic concepts are deployed as part of the theory produced. Theorization is simply a form of systematic thinking. But it must be recognizable as thinking *about* something. It is a relational activity, and so the object of thought must, as it were, make its own impression upon the mind of the theorist and his or her theoretical products. Otherwise, we have departed the realm of thought for the realm of fantasy. Unfortunately, today much theoretical work in the social and cultural sciences has too much of just this fantastic quality, in which the intellectual activity of theorists seems to take itself as its own object.

Society as "an intelligible field of study'

However, there is a very real and difficult problem in insisting that theory or conceptualization must originate in and through direct experience or evidence of some kind. These problems are similar to those encountered by traditional "empiricists" when confronted with apparently legitimate knowledge or truth claims about matters which are, in fact, or in principle, outside the scope of experience. We do not propose here to review the history of philosophical debate about these matters; instead we will note some continuities and discontinuities between our own position and that of some others who have tried to ground the study of social phenomena in psychoanalytically informed experience, namely Miller and Khaleelee (1993), and Dartington (2001). These authors are associated with the work of OPUS (an Organization for Promoting Understanding in Society), and in the second part of this piece we draw upon our own experience of working with the OPUS method of "Listening Posts". Miller and Khaleelee (1993) engage implicitly with the question about the limits to experience, in their discussion of the idea of "society as an intelligible field of study". The Listening Post methodology derives significantly from the method of Group Relations training, discussed in Chapter One, which makes use of a combination of large group (50–70) and small group (8–12) experiences within the boundary of a temporary learning institution. Reflecting on the limits and potential of this form of work for the study of society, Miller and Khaleelee note that,

> Splitting and projection manifestly occur in the "conference-sized" large group . . . but the projection in these cases is into identifiable sub-groups. Even though the large group at times feels boundless and even though the boundaries of the sub-groups may in some instances be blurred . . . there is in every case a nucleus of perceived sub-group members who are known to the individual by direct contact and many more who are known by sight . . . At least potentially, therefore, projections in groups up to this size are discussable, examinable, negotiable and even capable of resolution. [1993, p. 268]

Beyond this, and for cogent reasons if one is tied to an experientially based practice, these authors appear at something of a loss in this paper to know how to conceptualize the study of larger social processes. However, in another contribution where the basis of the Listening Post method is adumbrated, Miller (1993) proposes: "The Conference itself is a microcosm of society" (p. 275). The justification for this proposition is that:

> I have a picture of "society" in my head. It is not at all a coherent picture. It is made up of the meanings I give to and feelings I have about all sorts of groupings which I believe to exist out there . . . If we create a setting which refrains from providing the security of a temporary structure, and especially if in that setting people are defined as citizens of the wider society, then they will import into it their internal pictures of society and impose them on that setting. They need to do that to hold onto their identities, to feel sane. [ibid., pp. 275–77]

This reasoning is similar to that which informs the theory of "focus groups" in contemporary parlance.

Our own thinking about these matters is different in certain respects, although not, we believe, at all incompatible with the thoughts outlined above. The basis of Miller and his colleagues' theoretical reflections seem to be constrained by a set of assumptions according to which analysis of social processes must refer back to defensive processes enacted by individuals. Perhaps this derives in part from the authors' dependence on certain formulations of Bion's about group processes that also appear excessively individualistic:

> Bion insisted that the behaviour observed in groups was not a product of groups as such but of the fact that "the human being is a group animal" ... The individual's very belief in independent existence of "a group" was evidence of regression; and at one point Bion defined a group as "an aggregate of individuals all in the same state of regression". We carry our groupishness with us all the time. (Miller & Khaleelee, 1993, p. 244]

By contrast, as we hope to have made clear at numerous points in the course of this book, we regard social and group phenomena as having discrete, independent existence; existence that is dependent upon but not thereby entirely reducible to the properties, behaviour, or states of mind of the individuals comprising it or contributing to its formation. It is the "state of the system" considered as a social entity that we take to be an intelligible object of study. Notwithstanding the above citations from his work, perhaps this is closer to how most people actually interpret Bion's (1961) concepts of "basic assumption" states and behaviour in groups. Below, we offer our own commentary upon the way in which the Listening Post methodology enables the study of unconscious processes in society. The method seems to us to be extremely valuable—in fact the only systematic psychoanalytic method known to us for attempting the *experiential* study of social processes (as distinct from group processes). But, there are many ways of conceptualizing what is actually happening in these events, and we do not want to be constrained to think only in terms of basic assumption or any other theory. Nevertheless, there can be no method without appropriate constraints, and the ones we have tried to operate with are discussed in some detail below.

Most traditions of social theory are concerned either to explain social phenomena as the product of implicit or explicit causal processes, or to interpret social life in terms of the systems of meaning and belief that pattern social behaviour and institutions. Social constructivist traditions tend to view symbolic and linguistic systems as autonomous or quasi-autonomous formations shaping and producing the social world via the activity of social actors, who are themselves products of the discourses they reproduce. While some species of social theory reserve a place for emotional life and the unconscious in their explanatory schemata, hardly any have shown interest in developing or using empirical methodologies for *studying or researching* social life as a (partial) *product* of these dimensions of human relationship and experience. It is ethnography, and the traditions of theorizing rooted in classical anthropology, that most nearly approximate an empirical psychoanalytic methodology, both in their preferred method of study (naturalistic observation) and in some of their main objects of study (mythological structures). As one commentator has observed, every unconscious phantasy is the potential basis of a complete metaphysic.

The project of making explicit the implicit methodological principles of the present book has several aspects: defining what we mean by clinical sensibility in its application to society; articulating our social scientific theoretical and methodological reference points in order to locate the present work within a tradition; reviewing established methods of clinically informed psychoanalytic social research, such as these are; and synthesizing the aforementioned into a preliminary statement of the elements of a methodology for clinically grounded psychoanalytic social inquiry.

The psychodynamics of theory

As a proper starting point, then, we are sympathetic to the way Ian Craib (1987) ponders his relationship to theory as a social scientist and psychoanalytic practitioner in his paper "The psychodynamics of theory". He writes:

> Looking back on my life as a student and then as a lecturer, it now seems that theory provided me with a way of living that I did not

have to own and an arena for some fairly basic desires and feelings to be acted out, but not recognized . . . Whenever I read theory now, part of me is listening for the unspoken desires—omnipotence, envy—and defences—denial, rationalization, splitting, projection—that I suspect are there, and which I know were and to some extent are there for me. At the same time, I still think theory is important and I still find pleasure there. [Craib, 1987]

Craib wants to defend theory, believing it ". . . is a way to freedom. It is not all-powerful but can give us some control over the things that happen to us, whether a happening is outside or inside", but wants to criticize "the sort of theory that loses contact with the world—that becomes 'unreal'". This knowing ambivalence about theory is reflected in his five "rules" for theorizing:

1.   Avoid wishful thinking
2.   Avoid monistic assumptions and explanations
3.   Try to argue intelligibly.
4.   Avoid logical hatchet work
5.   Maintain a respect for the available evidence

These five rules are not commandments. There are occasions when they ought to be broken (Craib, 1987, pp. 34–35).

Craib's paper is a kind of manifesto for imaginative realism in the practice of producing theory. There is a tendency in the human sciences to see theory as somehow above and beyond the product of a mind or minds, as occupying a transcendental realm of its own, independent of (literally not dependent upon) the nature of the mind and the mind's capacity for thinking. Ironically, at the same time much of this theoretical work is directed at supposedly elucidating the functioning of mind or patterns of thinking in society. However, writing as a successful and respected theorist, Ian Craib turns his psychoanalytic understanding of the workings of his own theory-producing mind towards the nature of the *activity* of theorizing. Better or worse theory and theorizing is, in his view, a matter of "distinguishing between a theory which sublimates unconscious processes in the attempt to understand the world, and theory which simply acts out those processes". Theory can be a vehicle for defensive and destructive purposes on the one hand, or creative and transforming ones directed at illuminating the nature of the world and our relation to it, on the other. As his final statement says, "The important point is that it is possible to think openly, without being a failure and without being destroyed".

Applied clinical sensibility

Ian Craib's rules of theorizing capture much of the spirit, and the letter, of what we mean by applied clinical sensibility. The elements of our account of this concept follow.

We assume the social world is partly shaped and structured by unconscious processes and forces, and that a clinical sensibility is required in order to notice, name, and give conceptual shape to their presence. While some social theory allows theoretical space for the unconscious, there is very little empirical social research that makes use of psychoanalytic methods for coming to know the world. The unconscious at work in the social world can only be apprehended through approaches to knowledge based on clinical and observational methods drawn from psychoanalytic practice.

Knowledge of this kind can only be acquired via a degree of direct emotional contact with the object of study. This is largely because emotional experience, and the meanings and beliefs that emotional experiences carry within themselves, is the central object of study. Registering experiences of the social, attending to their complex attributes, then describing these as a step to conceptualization, are the core skills involved. The principal task is one of *discovery* though the registration of experience and the identification of patterns in experience. A psychoanalytic approach to the study of social life is close to the variety of anthropological study known as ethnography, and has much to learn from this.

If clinical psychoanalytic practice directs attention towards psychic reality then applied clinical sensibility directs attention to psycho-social reality.

When we reflect on the philosophical basis of our method of applied clinical sensibility we arrive at the following formulations:

- the unconscious, especially in the form of unsymbolised or unrepresented emotional forces, shapes and structures the social world;

- knowledge of social life must be grounded in direct emotional, as well as cognitive experience of social processes;
- there are "surface" phenomena and "depth" phenomena in social life, although depth can be lateral as well as vertical, and what is surface at one point in time or space may be depth at another;
- the social world can only be fully known through methods capable of accessing these deeper, structuring layers of reality and their relationship to appearances and surfaces;
- applied clinical sensibility legitimately involves the discriminating use of emotional sensibilities and the analysis of countertransference-type experiences arising from direct contact with social situations;
- it is consistent to see meanings, causes, and reasons as compatible types of agent in shaping psychic and social life.

Meaning and truth are always multiple, but they are not indeterminate or relative

The unconscious shapes and structures the social world.
Our methodology assumes that the social world is partly constituted by unconscious processes, including unconscious phantasy (Isaacs, 2003). While emotional forces play a much greater part in shaping the development of social life than is usually allowed for in social theory and research, much of the affective dimension of social life is fairly easily accessible via conventional qualitative approaches to research and social observation. Less available are the unconscious dimensions of affective life, which always entail specific ideas or beliefs about the nature of relationships. It is this arena, or theatre, of social process that requires a clinical sensibility if it is to be apprehended and made available for conscious theoretical reflection.

Knowledge of social life must be grounded in direct emotional experience.
In this methodology, the task of generating knowledge or understanding of the social world is grounded in direct experience, and direct observation, of social processes and social relationships. Nothing can be known and no adequate theory developed unless the knower has been in some way directly impacted by the object of knowledge. The observational stance with which we are

concerned involves particular attention to the emotional qualities of social experience. This is because we assume that all social processes, including social action and behaviour, are knowingly or unknowingly grounded in emotionally charged responses to the world, often at unconscious levels. An understanding of the social world that omits this dimension can only be partial. We are concerned to develop a way of knowing social life that incorporates this dimension as a matter of course.

There are surface phenomena and depth phenomena in social life.
The formulations above imply the following theoretical commitments: that unconscious processes structure and help to give particular determinate form to social life. This implies, crudely, a distinction between surface appearances and structures on the one hand and deep, or comparatively inaccessible structures and processes on the other. Depth can be recovered through connecting up related elements of a situation that have been sundered through splitting, projection, or disavowal, as much as through repression. However, for depth phenomena to be accessible at all, there must be evidence of them at an empirical level, or in a manner that can be registered via experience. Thus, we are in agreement with Ogden's (1999) formulation that:

> The unconscious is not "subconscious"; it is an aspect of the indi-visible totality of consciousness. Similarly, meaning (including unconscious meaning) is *in* the language being used, not under or behind it. (Freud [1915] believed the term "subconscious" to be "Incorrect and misleading since the Unconscious does not lie 'under' consciousness".) [*ibid.*, pp. 215–218]

However, our own focus on the concept of emotional experience is closely tied to clinical technique concerning the use of counter-transference experience in connecting up symbolized (surface) and unsymbolized (depth) aspects of phenomena. Steiner (1980) offers a compelling account of the decoding of conscious clinical material in relation to the analyst's registration of countertransference expe-rience in the "here-and-now" of the analytic session. The psycho-analytic project of apprehending the structuring activity of unconscious forces in individuals, groups, or social systems is what makes it scientific in its aspirations. Science is concerned with the explanation and interpretation of patterns and regularities in the world, but this does not imply a world in which causes and effects are the only structuring principles, as we discuss below. These principles are consistent with those of the "critical realist" school of thinking in the philosophy of science, whose relevance to psychoanalytic research and theory has been well argued by Rustin (1991). (For an overview of critical realist theory, see Archer, Bhaskar, Collier, Lawson, and Norrie, 1998.)

The social world can only be fully investigated through methods capable of accessing the kind of phenomena that lie "beyond surfaces".
The preceding suppositions imply the need for particular ways of coming to know about comparatively inaccessible or unsymbolized phenomena. Our ways of knowing the social world must be adapted to the nature of that world, to the variety of structuring principles at work in producing it. In more formal language, our idea of clinical sensibility is tied to certain ontological assumptions (about the way the social world is made up) which in turn imply certain epistemological commitments (about how, given the way the world is made up, knowledge of its nature can be acquired).

Applied clinical sensibility legitimately involves the discriminating use of emotional sensibility and the counter-transference.
The particular capacities that a psychoanalytic researcher brings to social research are adapted from his or her training in psychoanalytic ways of knowing and working. These are theoretically laden ways of working, but the theories have been evolved through clinical and observational practice, as well as formal research programmes, and are necessarily "discovered" again by each practitioner through clinical training and practice. Bion wrote that:

> It is important recognize that there is a world in which it is impossible to see what a psycho-analyst can see, although it may be possible for some of those who come for analysis to realize that we see certain things which the rest of the world doesn't see. We are investigating the unknown . . . We may be dealing with things which are so slight as to be virtually imperceptible, but which are so real that they could destroy us almost without our being aware of it. *That* is

the kind of area into which we have to penetrate. [Bion, 1976, pp. 319–320]

There is nothing especially mystifying in this stance, although much ink has been spilled in claiming there to be. The same point about training and education being a prerequisite for practice could be made of the physicist, biologist, painter, or farmer. Clinical sensibility depends upon a range of specific craft skills honed through practice and supervision, in the same way as specialists in other fields develop their own techniques and applied epistemologies (Rustin, 2001). What psychoanalytic research in the social field lacks so far are many examples of systematic research programmes through which the specific skills of applying a clinical sensibility are refined and codified in the direction of an established methodology. However, it is not a completely barren landscape, and below we review some of the work that has been done.

In his paper *Evidence* (1976) from which the quotation above is taken, Bion is drawing attention to an important point. Psychoanalysis relies upon gaining access to a particular realm of data, i.e., unconscious experience or process, and it has a human "technology" for doing this. It is important to be neither too modest about this capacity, nor too grand. In the realm of psychoanalytic social theorizing we are at the very beginning of a process of discovery, but it is perfectly legitimate, until some conclusive arguments are made against it, to think we can adapt the key skills of clinical and observational practice—the careful registration of emotional experience, the conceptualization and theorization of unconscious processes in the social field, the use of our counter-transference skill—to the task of understanding the social world.

However, it may be important to distinguish between the application of a psychoanalytic sensibility to the social field, and its application to "cultural objects" such as literature, drama, painting, or film. Cultural objects do not think and feel, answer back, react, or mutate in response to spoken interpretations. It seems legitimate, if perhaps limited, to say that in analysing "texts" there is nothing outside the text. Indeed, there is a variety of psychoanalytic work directed at cultural objects, from which we would disassociate our methodology, which functions as though cultural objects really were a living person. Equally, it does not seem legitimate to extend the precept that there is nothing outside the text, to objects of study that are not texts, but living systems of one kind or another.

It is consistent to see meanings, causes and reasons as compatible types of agent in shaping psychic and social life.
Social experience and patterns of social life (institutional, cultural, political, etc.) are produced and reproduced by social actors functioning in the context of more or less stable systems of relationship. These systems can be understood as rule-governed at both conscious and unconscious levels, and/or as constituted by systems of shared meanings at both conscious and unconscious levels, and/or as ordered by law-like processes of cause and effect some of which may be transparent and some opaque. Meanings can, and invariably do, function as both causes and reasons in human relationships and in the patterning of social life. The capacity to generate and experience meaning is what differentiates human beings from other animals and from the inanimate world. But meaningfulness depends for its existence upon investing symbolic activity with emotional responsiveness. So there can be forms of activity that make use of accepted symbolic markers and rules, but that are nevertheless divested of meaning, and there are clinically and socially observable states of mind in which this is the case. Once more, these principles are consistent with the view of social science and social processes developed by the critical realist school. (Bhaskar, 1979)

Meaning and truth are always multiple, but they are not indeterminate or relative.
The point of the above statement is to reiterate our methodological and ontological realism. Unconscious processes and structures produce real effects in individuals, in groups, and in social formations. There are psychoanalytic theorists who privilege meanings over causes in their view of how the psyche is made up—the hermeneuticists—and who tend towards a view of knowledge as produced through "sense-making" activity, but also see this activity as unconstrained by any truth criteria, as distinct from criteria of meaningfulness. While we also hold that meaningfulness is a condition of knowledge or thought, we further hold that meaningful thoughts and systems of thought have referents, that is to say, objects in relation to which meaning is being made.

There are always multiple meanings or systems of meaning with respect to any particular object, whether internal or external to the psyche, but this is not the same as holding that *any* set of meanings are as good as any other. To hold this is, once again, to say that fantasy and thought are indistinguishable. There are *many* meanings that are symbolically representative of a particular experience, but not *any*. Neither truth or meaning are a matter of correspondence, but neither are they fully relative or indeterminate. This kind of realist position has been lucidly argued by various psychoanalytic thinkers, but Marcia Cavell's (1998) paper is a particularly good instance. She writes:

> As distinct from fantasising, thinking allows for self-reflection and for appraising one's thoughts as true or false, realistic or unrealistic, and so on. We think with thoughts, about things, and we cannot think about these things unless we recognise our thoughts about them as thoughts. Someone gripped by a fantasy has for the moment put aside the possibility that what he thinks might be false, or a case of wishful thinking, or just a partial view of things. He has put aside questions of evidence and reasons. [*ibid.*, p. 464]

and

> Of course to investigate the truth of any belief or sentence we must first know its meaning, which is constructed by us. Meaning is constructed: so are theories. Furthermore, the meaning of a belief or sentence is constrained by its place in a network of other sentences in the language, or beliefs in the person's mind. But truth is not constructed. [*ibid.*, p. 451]

Appplied clinical sensibility in the social field—The OPUS methodology. In what follows we offer a conceptual commentary on the process of attempting to study unconscious factors in social phenomena through establishing what could be thought of as temporary laboratories for this purpose. For many, as with other varieties of clinical or experiential activity, participating in these events carries its own sense of immediate conviction. Part of the difficulty of articulating the methodological underpinnings of psychoanalytic practice of any kind is in remaining faithful to this experience, while proffering an intelligible account of the forces and generative structures that might render the experience rationally intelligible.

The "Listening Post" is a method developed by the organization OPUS for exploring the relationship between society and the individual through attention to, and interpretation of, the social experience of groups of citizens. Social experience is taken to involve and be shaped by unconscious processes that emerge in the course of the Listening Post itself. Dartington (2001) outlines the Listening Post method like this:

> The Listening Post is a free-floating discussion, drawing on the experience that participants have of the society they relate to at a certain time. The discussion is not structured therefore and allows for associative links to be made. There is a convenor who introduces the event, and then participates like others, and closes the event. As in the Group Relations tradition, there is a strict keeping of the time boundary. [p. 95]

And he asks:

> In what sense may a smallish group of people, not randomly selected but recruited through existing networks, be thought to be a microcosm of the large group that is society? What is the citizen role that participants are invited to take, and what is society, as understood in this context?

> It is sufficient now to acknowledge that the proposition that a small group may act in ways that in microcosm offer insights into the working of a much larger group does not fit easily with the rational politics of representation and differentiation. Nevertheless, it is a familiar experience in group relations work to explore ways that the individual takes up a certain role, like it or not, as part of the unconscious dynamics of the group. In an OPUS listening post this may mean that individuals are expressing more than their individual understanding as they take up an inner city perspective say, or an immigrant or establishment position. [*ibid.*, p. 97]

We will give some illustrative examples of processes in Listening Posts in a moment, but first it is worth delving a little further into the methodological assumptions informing these events, which can be thought of as a variety of experientially based psychoanalytic social research.

A Listening Post establishes what we may think of as a temporary social field, analogous to the psychoanalytic session in the freedom and encouragement it offers to freely associate. The objects that participants are invited to explore are psycho-social—their emotionally and attitudinally laden experiences of current social life.

The work of the group is situated on a number of boundaries—between social and individual experience, between conscious and unconscious apprehension of the dynamics of social life, between attention to what is outside the group and what is unfolding within it, and so on. However, it is the *emergent* preoccupations of the group that are the central object of interest and learning.

Typically, a productive Listening Post experience will centre around the emergence of a conscious preoccupation with an external social theme that is then linked, perhaps through the interpretive insight of the convenor, with enactments in the group or with apparently unrelated material from another phase of the group's reflections. This process is like a decoding of surface and depth in the group's preoccupations. One could theorize this as a process in which the group's engagement with its own experience, allied to interpretive skill, creates an apparatus for thinking previously unthinkable thoughts about social reality (cf. Chapter Six, this book).

The raw material of the group's work is current emotional experiences of society; these experiences are inherently about forms of relatedness in society, and something of the tension, ambivalence, conflict, and anxiety associated with these comes alive in the process of group engagement with others. But these anxieties and tensions become more fully knowable when it is possible to name them, to symbolize them in the heat of a lived emotional engagement in which group members' relatedness to others is exposed as a part of the matrix of their production.

Two examples may help to illuminate the working of these processes. In the first, the group had been preoccupied with the meaning of events and interpretations of events surrounding the Bill Clinton/Monica Lewinsky scandal and the role of Linda Tripp in their exposure. Discussion centred around the collapse of the boundary between private life and public roles, and a sense of the intrusive prurience of the media. Participants spoke variously of fascination, repulsion, or indifference at being made public witnesses to the sexual peccadilloes of the most powerful leader in the world. Some considered the revelations rendered him unfit for office, others thought them irrelevant to the performance of his public duties, while a few held that his failure to protect himself from exposure was the real failing. However, when the plenary group reassembled at the end of the day and reported on (publi-cized) the reflections in small groups, one small group interlocutor was at pains to anonymize his feedback on the grounds that a group member had left early, and was thus not present to hear how his contributions were reported. The convenor eventually inter-preted that perhaps we were all in close touch with a sense of vulnerability about our private lives being fair game for public reporting and misreporting should the wrong circumstances befall us. This chimed with the experience of the interlocutor, who was now able to identify that he had felt inhabited by an anxiety to protect the not especially controversial contributions of the absent member, who had expressed no wish for anonymity.

This example shows how a preoccupation in the group, although thoroughly explored through debate and conscious disagreement, may nevertheless have its source *as a preoccupation* in deeper and less readily articulated anxieties. Until the anxiety is enacted, and the enactment noticed and given a symbolic form so that the group can think about it, its potency remains invisible. In the example cited, we may hypothesize that in the group or social unconscious there is an unarticulated disturbance with respect to familiar assumptions about our intrapsychic and social settlements concerning transgres-sions, thoughts about (desire for and fear of) transgression, the trust-worthiness of those to whom we confide our transgressions, and the likelihood of repercussions should our misdemeanours leak into the wrong hands. "There may be a Linda Tripp in the room" might be one formulation of the collective anxiety; "Someone is going to expose someone publicly, for exposing what should have been kept private" could be another. Unexamined, such fantasies shape subtle alterations in both private and public behaviour, and blind us to the possibility of seeing that this is happening.

In the second example, the relationship between surface and depth in the groups' behaviour took a more accessible and perhaps more multi-layered symbolic form. Group discussion had focused on "the changing relationship of the individual to society, a do-it-yourself social contract where we use networking to invent our own institutions. Our relationships allowed us to connect without being attached" (Dartington, 2001, p. 107). Participants evoked their sense of bewilderment and apprehension in the face of rapidly shifting organizational environments, in which the relationship of leaders and managers to the work, and to those depending upon services, seemed increasingly tenuous. Later, one small discussion group became interested in gypsies, stimulated by the experience of a participant who had a gypsy encampment at the end of her road. She described how, when a member of the gypsy community dies, his caravan is burned and the group moves on. She got to know this group of people a little, but now they had departed.

Later, the convenor suggested that the Listening Post's interest in the nomadic lifestyle of these people, their comparative lack of need for "stable and permanent attachments to property and territory, while retaining a strong attachment to the group" (Dartington, 2001, p. 107) mirrored the concern with everyone's sense of living in a transient, fluid, complex world in which traditional dependencies and attachments can no longer be taken for granted.

> As citizens do we need to be named and labelled or do we prefer a more fluid anonymity as we take account of a fragmented existence, as if our identity is made up of a portfolio of shares in the social economy, and we pursue our portfolio careers? We have not yet learned, or we are learning painfully and slowly, to "travel lightly". [Dartington, 2001, pp. 108–109]

Here, one can speculate that the story of the gypsy encampment and the burning of caravans operates in much the same way as does the day residue in forming the manifest symbolic content of a dream. Perhaps the individual group member herself "selects" (cf. Bion's (1962) concept of the "selected fact") this story for vocalization because its meanings resonate with the wider preoccupations of the group. But equally the story attracts interest to itself (is selected by them), simultaneously drawing the group both away from and towards a deeper engagement with its own emotional themes. The element of displacement of these emotional themes into a preoccupation with gypsy life requires interpretation if the ambivalences, anxieties, and conflicts in the group concerning states of reluctant internal and social homelessness are to be more fully known and assimilated.

Levels of thinking and interpretation

Contemporary psychoanalysis is increasingly concerned with understanding and working with people's most basic capacity to have a mind, and with how the roots of mental functioning lie in the transformation of primary emotional experience into forms that can be known through symbolic activity. Ann Alvarez (2001) writes about four levels of psychoanalytic interpretation, each roughly corresponding to a level of psychological development or psycho-pathology, and implicitly to the rows of Bion's grid. Freud, she says, taught us to think in terms of "why/because" interpretations, which relate to symptom formation and repression; Klein showed us how to think about "who/where" interpretations, related to processes of projection and the disownment of parts of the self into others; Bion, Winnicott, Joseph, and others have shown the need with certain patients, or at certain times, to "go more slowly, to make more purely descriptive, containing comments, and to respect paradoxes" (Alvarez, 2001, p. 5); and finally clinicians working with children with autism or severe developmental deficit have under-stood the need for a level of work that involves "waking the patient to mindfulness or at the very least, offering realizations to barely experienced preconceptions. Bion suggested that a preconception needed to meet with a realization in order to form a concept. Where realizations have failed, preconceptions may fade or even atrophy" (*ibid.*, p. 12).

It is Alvarez's third level that mostly interests us when thinking about the kind of social theorizing that Listening Posts generate, and, indeed, throughout this book. This is nothing to do with any assumption of pathology in these groups, or in society. Rather, it concerns the value of reaching for a particular form of emotionally based *understanding* of social life, on the assumption that the evidence for what is happening in society is coursing through us all the time in the form of more or less digested emotional experience, as we ourselves course through society—if only we can come to know about what *is* happening to us. In Alvarez's clinical language,

> I have had to learn that there are situations when it is better to avoid the whole question of *who* is having the experience. It is better with some patients to spend more time exploring the whatness of an experience. If the patient is very persecuted or desperate, or simply confused, it may be better to get an adjective or two attached to the noun, an adverb or two attached to the verb, and let it rest. [2001, pp. 8–9]

Conclusion

What are the implications for social theorizing of this way of conceptualizing the work of Listening Posts? The culture of inquiry that initially becomes established in a Listening Post has all the appearances of mature, rational, reflective, argumentative group discourse. It may even make use of some psychoanalytic concepts and a certain psychoanalytic sophistication. But a psychoanalytic sensibility applied to modern social life rejects the supposition that we have somehow progressed beyond the primitive, the irrational or the mythic. The savage mind and savage thoughts are never far below the surface. As Tim Dartington says (2001, p. 100), in one of his more direct passages when reviewing the content of Listening Posts in the last decade of the millennium, "the wish for violence was never far below the surface of civilised debate".

This is not to equate the primitive with the violent or aggressive only. In the simple illustrations provided above, it is loss, mourning, death, homelessness, witnessing the primal scene, and the fear of retribution that seem to organize the significant occurrences. Such preoccupations will tend to be necessarily anxiety and guilt laden, occasioning depression, mental pain, and the wish not to know as much as the wish to know or make reparation. This is the arena of the primitive, and likely primitive mental functioning. Much social theory (and of course passages of theorizing in the course of Listening Post discussion) can display qualities of logical and intellectual wizardry, but equally disconnection from any engagement with the realities of human social experience. The task of a psychoanalytic social scientific methodology is to generate ways of studying and theorizing social life that grasp the inherently affective, unconscious, and mythic structuring of all social phenomena, and, indeed, to forgo theorizing that does not root itself in these dimensions. The deep patterns or structures constantly make themselves known (but also not known) at the surface. Thus, the surface is not the realm of the superficial, but of the available "to be known", if only we have at our disposal the means to come to know.

REFERENCES

Abadi, S. (2003). Between the frontier and the network: notes for a metapsychology of freedom. *International Journal of Psyhoanalysis*, 84(2): 221–234.

Alvarez, A. (2001). Levels of analytic work and levels of pathology. Unpublished paper presented at the Tavistock Clinic, London

Archer, M., Bhaskar, B., Collier, A., Lawson T., & Norrie, A. (1998). *Critical Realism: Essential Readings*. London: Routledge.

Armstrong, D. (1991). *The Institution in the Mind*. London: Grubb Institute.

Armstrong, D. (2002). Making present: reflections on a neglected function of leadership and its contemporary relevance. *Organisational and Social Dynamics*, 2(1): 89–98.

Armstrong, D. (2004). Emotions in organisations: disturbance or intelligence? In C. Huffington, D. Armstrong, W. Halton, L. Hoyle, & J. Pooley (Eds.), *Working below the Surface: The Emotional Life of Contemporary Organizations*. London: Karnac.

Bateman, A. (1991). Borderline personality disorder. In: J. Holmes (Ed.), *Textbook of Psychotherapy in Psychiatric Practice* (pp. 334–357). London: Churchill Livingstone.

Baudrillard, J. (1988). *Selected Writings*. Stanford: Stanford University.

Beck, U. (1992). *Risk Society: Towards a New Modernity*. London: Sage.

Bell, D. (1997). Primitive mind of state, *Psychoanalytic Psychotherapy*, 10: 45–47.

Berman, M. (1983). *All That is Solid Melts into Air*. London: Verso.

Beveridge, W. (1942). *Report on Social Insurance and Allied Services*, Cmd 6404. London: HMSO.

Bhaskar, R. (1979). *The Possibility of Naturalism*. Brighton: Harvester.

Bion, W. R. (1959). Attacks on linking. *International Journal of Psycho-Analysis*, 40.

Bion, W. R. (1961). *Experiences in Groups*. London: Karnac.

Bion, W. R. (1962). *Learning From Experience*. London: Karnac.

Bion, W. R. (1967). *Second Thoughts*. London: Karnac.

Bion, W. R. (1976) Evidence. In: W. R. Bion, *Clinical Seminars and Other Works* (pp. 312–320) [reprinted London: Karnac, 1994].

Bion, W. R. (1984). *Transformations*. London: Karnac.

Bion, W. R. (1990). *Brazilian Lectures*. London: Karnac.

Bion, W. R. (1992). *Cogitations*. London: Karnac.

Bion, W. R. (1993). *Second Thoughts*. London: Karnac.

Bochel, C., & Bochel, H. M. (2003). *The UK Social Policy Process*. Houndmills: Palgrave MacMillan

Bollas, C. (1987). *The Shadow of the Object: Psychoanalysis of the Unthought Known*. London: Free Association Books.

Bollas, C., & Sundelson, D. (1995). *The New Informants*. London: Karnac.

Briggs, S. (1996). *Growth and Risk in Infancy*. London: Jessica Kingsley.

Britton, R. (1989). *The Oedipus Complex Today*. London: Karnac.

Britton, R. (1998). *Belief and Imagination*. London: Routledge.

Butler-Sloss, E. (1988). *Report of the Inquiry into Child Abuse in Cleveland 1987*. London: HMSO.

Castells, M. (2000). *The Information Age. Vol 1: The Rise of the Network Society*. Oxford: Blackwell.

Castoriadis, C. (1987). *The Imaginary Institution of Society*. Cambridge: Polity Press.

Cavell, M. (1998). Triangulation, one's own mind and objectivity. *International Journal of Psycho-Analysis*, 79: 449–467.

Chasseguet-Smirgel, J. (1985). *Creativity and Perversion*. London: Free Association Books.

Cohen, P. (1993). Home rules: Some reflections on racism and nationalism in everyday life. London: University of East London.

Cooper, A. (1999). With justice in mind: complexity, child welfare and the law. In: M. King (Ed.), *Moral Agendas for Children's Welfare*. London: Routledge.

Cooper, A., & Webb, L. (1999). Out of the maze: permanency planning in a post-modern world. *Journal of Social Work Practice, 13*(2) 119–134.

Craib, I. (1987). The psychodynamics of theory. *Free Associations, 10*: 32–56.

Cummins, A.-M. (2002). "The road to hell is paved with good intentions": quality assurance as a social defence against anxiety. *Organisational and Social Dynamics, 2*(1): 99–119.

Damasio, A. (2000). *The Feeling of What Happens.* London: Vintage.

Dartington, T. (2001). The preoccupations of the citizen—reflections from the OPUS Listening Posts. *Organisational and Social Dynamics, 1*(1): 94–112.

Dartington, T. (2003). Skirmishes in the war between human nature and organisational change. Unpublished paper.

Emanuel, L. (2002). Deprivation × 3: the contribution of organisational dynamics to the "triple deprivation" of looked-after children. *Journal of Child Psychotherapy, 28*(2): 163–179.

Esping-Anderson, G. (1990). *The Three Worlds of Welfare Capitalism.* Cambridge: Polity Press.

Evans, J. (2003). Vigilance and vigilantes: thinking psychoanalytically about anti-paedophile action. *Theoretical Criminology, 7*(2): 163–189.

Fairbairn, W. R. D. (1943). The repression and return of bad objects. In: *Psychoanalytic Studies of the Personality* (pp. 51–89). London: Routledge.

Foster, A. (1998). Psychotic processes and community care. In: A. Foster & V. Roberts (Eds.), *Chaos and Containment: Managing Mental Health in the Community* (p. 61–70). London: Routledge.

Foucault, M. (1977). *Discipline and Punish.* Harmondsworth: Penguin.

Freud, S. (1923b). The ego and the id. *S.E., 19.* London: Hogarth.

Freud, S. (1927c). The future of an illusion. *S.E., 21.* London: Hogarth.

Freud, S (1930a). Civilisation and its discontents. *S.E., 21*: London: Hogarth Press.

Freud, S. (1950a). Extracts from the Fliess papers. *S.E., 1.* London: Hogarth.

Froggett, L. (2002). *Love, Hate and Welfare.* Bristol: Policy Press.

Geras, N. (1998). *The Contract of Mutual Indifference Political philosophy after the Holocaust.* London: Verso.

Giddens, A., (1990). *The Consequences of Modernity.* Cambridge: Polity.

Giddens, A. (1994). *Beyond Left and Right.* Cambridge: Polity.

Goleman, D. (1996). *Emotional Intelligence.* London: Bloomsbury.

Habermas, J. (1987). *The Theory of Communicative Action, Vol. 2: The Critique of Functionalist Reason.* Cambridge: Polity.

228   REFERENCES

Habermas, J. (1971). *Knowledge and Human Interests*. London: Heinemann.

Hacking, I. (1999). *The Social Construction of What?* London: Harvard University Press.

Harvey, D. (1990). *The Condition of Postmodernity*. Oxford: Blackwell.

Healy, K. (1998). Clinical audit and conflict. In: R. Davenhill & M. Patrick (Eds.), *Rethinking Clinical Audit* (pp. 38–56). London: Routledge.

Hetherington, R., Cooper, A., Smith, P., & Wilford, G. (1997). *Protecting Children: Messages from Europe*. Lyme Regis: Russell House Press.

Hinshelwood, R. (1989) *A Dictionary of Kleinian Thought*. London: Free Association Books.

Hinshelwood, R. D. (1994). *Clinical Klein*. London: Free Association Books.

Hinshelwood, R. (2003). Group mentality and "having a mind". In: R. M. Lipgar & M. Pines (Eds.), *Building on Bion. Vol. 1, Roots*. London: Jessica Kingsley.

Hirschhorn, L. (1997). *Reworking Authority: Leading and Following in the Post-modern Age*. Cambridge: MIT Press.

Hoggett, P. (1992). *Partisans in an Uncertain World: The Psychoanalysis of Engagement*. London: Free Association Books.

Hoggett, P. (2000). *Emotional Life and the Politics of Welfare*. Houndmills: Routledge.

Howe, D. (1996). Surface and depth in social-work practice. In: N. Parton (Ed.), *Social Theory, Social Change and Social Work* (pp. 77–97). London: Routledge.

Hughes, G. (Ed.) (1998). *Imagining Welfare Futures*. London: Routledge.

Hughes, L., & Pengelly, P. (1997). *Staff Supervision in a Turbulent Environment*. London: Jessica Kingsley.

Hutten, J., Bazalgette, J., & Armstrong, D. (1994). What does management really mean? In: R. Casemore, G. Dyos, A. Eden, J. Kellner, J. McAuley, & S. Moss (Eds.), *What Makes Consultancy Work—Understanding the Dynamics*. London: South Bank University Press.

Hutton, W. (1996). *The State We're In*. London: Vintage.

Isaacs, S. (2003). The nature and function of phantasy. In: R. Steiner (Ed.), *Unconscious Phantasy* (pp. 145–198). London: Karnac.

Jacoby, R. (1977). *Social Amnesia*. Brighton: Harvester Press.

Jameson, F. (1991). Postmodernism: or the cultural logic of late capitalism. *New Left Review, 146*: 53–92.

Janet, P. (1925). *Psychological Healing*, Volume 1. London: Allen and Unwin.

Karpman, S. (1968). Fairy tales and script drama analysis. *Transactional Analysis Bulletin*, 7 26: pp. 39–44.

Klein, M. (1946). Notes on some schizoid mechanisms. In: *The Writings of Melanie Klein*, vol 3, *Envy and Gratitude and Other Works* (pp. 1–24). Reprinted London: Hogarth, 1975.

Kovel, J. (1981). *The Age of Desire*. New York: Pantheon.

Kraemer, S. (2000). Politics in the nursery. In: W. Wheeler (Ed.), *The Political Subject* (pp. 114–120). London: Lawrence & Wishart.

Laming, H. (2003). *The Victoria Climbié Inquiry: Report of an Inquiry by Lord Laming*. London: The Stationery Office.

Laplanche, J., & Pontalis, J. B. (1988). *The Language of Psychoanalysis*. London: Karnac.

Lawrence, W. G. (2000). The politics of salvation and revelation in the practice of organisational consultancy. In: *Tongued with Fire: Groups in Experience* (pp. 165–179). London: Karnac.

Lawrence, W. G., Bain, A., & Gould, L. (1996). The fifth basic assumption. *Free Associations*, 37: 28–55.

Leys, C. (2001). *Market-Driven Politics: Neo liberal Democracy and the Public Interest*. London: Verso.

London Borough of Brent (1985). *A Child in Trust; Report of the Panel of Inquiry into the Circumstances Surrounding the Death of Jasmine Beckford*. London: London Borough of Brent.

Lousada, E. (2001). Private communication.

Lyotard, J.-F. (1984). *The Postmodern Condition*. Manchester: Manchester University Press.

Marquand, D. (1999). *The Progressive Dilemma*. London: Orion.

Marx, K., & Engels, F. (1970). *The German Ideology, Part One*. London: Lawrence & Wishart.

Meltzer, D. (1986). *Studies in Extended Metapsychology*. Strathclyde, Perthshire: Clunie Press.

Meltzer, D. (1994). Sincerity. In: A. Hahn (Ed.), *Sincerity and Other Works: Collected Papers of Donald Meltzer*. London: Karnac.

Miller, E. (1993). *From Dependency to Autonomy*. London: Free Association.

Miller, E., & Khaleelee, O. (1993). Beyond the small group: society as an intelligible field of study. In: E. Miller (Ed.), *From Dependency to Autonomy* (pp. 243–272). London: Free Association.

Miller, E., & Rice, A. (1967). *Systems of Organisation: Task and Sentient Systems and their Boundary Control*. London: Tavistock.

Money-Kyrle, R. (1978). The aim of psychoanalysis. In: *The Collected*

Papers of Roger Money-Kyrle (pp. 442–449). Strath Tey, Perthshire: Clunie Press.

Ogden, T. H. (1999). *Reverie and Interpretation: Sensing Something Human.* London: Karnac.

O'Neill, O. (2002). *A Question of Trust: The BBC Reith Lectures 2002.* Cambridge: Cambridge University Press.

O'Shaughnessy, E. (1999). Relating to the superego. *International Journal of Psychoanalysis, 80*: 861–870.

Parton, N. (1996). Child protection, family support and social work: a critical appraisal of the Department of Health research studies in child protection. *Child and Family Social Work, 1*: 3–11.

Perry, B. (2002). Childhood experience and the expression of genetic potential: what childhood neglect tells us about nature and nurture. *Brain and Mind, 3*: 79–100.

Phillips, A. (2004). Necessary journeys: *Guardian Review*, pp. 4–6.

Philps, J. (2003). Applications of child psychotherapy to work with children in temporary foster care. Unpublished Professional Doctorate thesis. London: University of East London.

Power, M. (1994). *The Audit Explosion.* London: Demos.

Power, M. (1999). "The audit fxation": some issues for psychotherapy. In: R. Davenhill & M. Patrick (Eds.), *Rethinking Clinical Audit* (pp. 23–37). London: Routledge.

Preston, P. (2000). They're not great, or even very good. The *Guardian*, 25 November.

Reder, P., & Duncan, S. (2004). From Colwell to Climbié: Inquiring into fatal child abuse. In: N. Stanley & J. Manthorpe (Eds.), *The Age of the Inquiry* (pp. 92–115). London: Brunner–Routledge,.

Reder, P., Duncan, S., & Gray, M. (1993). *Beyond Blame: Child Abuse Tragedies Revisited.* London: Brunner–Routledge.

Rey, J. H. (1988). Schizoid phenomena in the borderline. In: E. Bott Spillius (Ed.), *Melanie Klein Today, Vol. 1: Mainly Theory* (pp. 203–229). London: Routledge.

Rey, J. H. (1994). *Universals of Psychoanalysis in the Treatment of Psychotic and Borderline States.* London: Free Association.

Rustin, M. E. (2005). Conceptual analysis of critical moments in Victoria Climbié's life. *Child and Family Social Work, 10*: 11–20.

Rustin, M. J. (1991). *The Good Society and the Inner World.* London: Verso.

Rustin, M. J. (2001). *Reason and Unreason: Psychoanalysis, Science and Politics.* London: Continuum.

Rustin, M. J. (2004). Rethinking audit and inspection. *Soundings, 26*: 86–107.

Salter, B. (1998). Virtual politics in the new NHS. *British Medical Journal*, 317: 1091.

Sandler, J., & Fonagy, P. (Eds.) (1997). *Recovered Memories of Abuse: True or False?* London: Karnac.

Sartre, J.-P. (1948). *The Anti-Semite and Jew*. New York: Schocken.

Scheff, T. (1997). *Emotions, the Social Bond, and Human Reality: Part/whole Analysis*. Cambridge: Cambridge University Press.

Schon, D. (1971), *Beyond the Stable State*. New York: Random House.

Schon, D. (1979). Generative metaphor: A perspective on problem setting in social policy. In: A. Ortony (Ed.), *Metaphor and Thought* (pp. 254–283). Cambridge: Cambridge University Press.

Sennett, R. (1998). *The Corrosion of Character: the Personal Consequences of Work in the New Capitalism*. New York: W. W. Norton.

Showalter, E. (1997). *Hystories: Hyasterical Epidemics and Modern Culture*. London: Picador.

6, P. (1997). *Holistic Government*. London: Demos.

6, P. (2002). What is there to feel? A neo-Durkheimian theory of the emotions, *European Journal of Psychotherapy, Counsellling & Health*, 5(3): 263–290.

Stanley, N., & Manthorpe, J. (Eds.) (2004). *The Age of the Inquiry*. London: Routledge.

Steiner, J. (1980). *Psychotic and Non-psychotic Part of the Personality in Borderline Patients*. London: Tavistock Paper no.8.

Steiner, J. (1993). *Psychic Retreats*. London: Routledge.

Titmus, R. M. (1968). *Commitment to Welfare*. London: Allen & Unwin.

Titmus, R. M. (1976). Welfare state and welfare society. In: N. Timms & Watson (Eds.), *Talking About Welfare*. London: Routledge and Kegan Paul.

Toynbee, P. (2004). Why isn't New Labour proud to be the nation's nanny? The *Guardian*. 17 November.

Turquet, P. M. (1974). Leadership: the individual and the group. In: G. S. Gibbard, J. J. Hasrtman, & R. D. Mann (Eds.), *Analysis of Groups* pp. 349–386. San Francisco: Jossey-Bass.

Waddell, M. (1998). *Inside Lives*. London: Duckworth.

Waters, M. (1994). *Modern Sociological Theory*. London: Sage.

Watson, S. (2002). Complexity and the transhuman. *Organisational and Social Dynamics*, 2(2): 245–263.

Wideman, J. E. (1995). *Fatherland*. London: Picador.

Williams, R. (1993). *Drama from Ibsen to Brecht*. London: Hogarth.

Winnicott, D. W. (1965). Ego distortion in terms of true and false self. In: *The Maturational Process and the Facilitating Environment* (pp. 140–152). London: Hogarth.

Wright Mills, C. (1959), *The Sociological Imagination*. London: Oxford University Press.

Woodhouse, D., & Pengelly, P. (1992). *Anxiety and the Dynamics of Collaboration*. Aberdeen: Aberdeen University Press.

Young, H. (1999). We're all right, Gordon, but what about the world? The *Guardian*, 10 March, pp. 1–2.

Zizek, S. (1989). *The Sublime Object of Ideology*. London: Verso.

INDEX